THE EVERYTHING

HEALTH GUIDE TO

DEPRESSION

Dear Reader,

If you've been told that depression is "all in your head" and that you should just "snap out of it," you know how frustrating that can be—and it's physically impossible as well! It makes about as much sense as telling someone to snap out of diabetes. Depression is a common medical condition that can take a variety of forms. In mild cases, it's annoying; at its most severe, it can become life threatening.

If you or someone you know is struggling with depression, this book can provide you with the information you'll need to understand this troublesome disorder and make informed decisions about your health care. You'll learn about the different kinds of depression, how to recognize depression's symptoms, and what to do about them.

Everyone gets down, at times. Loss is part of life. However, when your mood stays down and nothing seems to help, depression may have moved in on you. Depression isn't picky about choosing its victims. Everyone has the potential for developing a depressive disorder—children, adolescents, adults, even seniors. It's my hope that this guide will help you cope and find the resources you need to get your life, or the life of a loved one, back on track.

Sincerely,

Karen K. Brees

THE

EVERYTHING®
Series

THE EVERYTHING® HEALTH GUIDES are a part of the bestselling Everything® series and cover important health topics like anxiety, postpartum care, and thyroid disease. Packed with the most recent, up-to-date data, THE EVERYTHING® HEALTH GUIDES help you get the right diagnosis, choose the best doctor, and find the treatment options that work for you. With this one comprehensive resource, you and your family members have all the information you need right at your fingertips.

 Alerts: Urgent warnings

 Essentials: Quick, handy tips

 Facts: Important snippets of information

 Questions: Answers to common problems

When you're done reading, you can finally say you know EVERYTHING®!

DIRECTOR OF INNOVATION Paula Munier

EDITORIAL DIRECTOR Laura M. Daly

EXECUTIVE EDITOR, SERIES BOOKS Brielle K. Matson

ASSOCIATE COPY CHIEF Sheila Zwiebel

ACQUISITIONS EDITOR Kerry Smith

DEVELOPMENT EDITOR Katie McDonough

PRODUCTION EDITOR Casey Ebert

Visit the entire Everything® series at *www.everything.com*

THE

EVERYTHING®

HEALTH GUIDE TO

DEPRESSION

Reassuring advice to help you
feel like yourself again

Karen K. Brees, Ph.D.

Technical Review by Linda L. Simmons, Psy.D.

Aadamsmedia

Avon, Massachusetts

To all the dedicated and compassionate mental health care professionals who truly make a difference in all our lives.

• • •

An Everything® Series Book.
Everything® and everything.com® are registered trademarks of F+W Publications, Inc.

Published by Adams Media, an F+W Publications Company
57 Littlefield Street, Avon, MA 02322 U.S.A.
www.adamsmedia.com

ISBN 10: 1-59869-407-3
ISBN 13: 978-1-59869-407-9

Printed in Canada.

J I H G F E D C B A

Library of Congress Cataloging-in-Publication Data
is available from the publisher.

This publication is designed to provide accurate and authoritative information with regard to the subject matter covered. It is sold with the understanding that the publisher is not engaged in rendering legal, accounting, or other professional advice. If legal advice or other expert assistance is required, the services of a competent professional person should be sought.
　　—From a *Declaration of Principles* jointly adopted by a Committee of the American Bar Association and a Committee of Publishers and Associations

Many of the designations used by manufacturers and sellers to distinguish their products are claimed as trademarks. Where those designations appear in this book and Adams Media was aware of a trademark claim, the designations have been printed with initial capital letters.

The Everything® Health Guide to Depression is intended as a reference volume only, not as a medical manual. In light of the complex, individual, and specific nature of health problems, this book is not intended to replace professional medical advice. The ideas, procedures, and suggestions in this book are intended to supplement, not replace, the advice of a trained medical professional. Consult your physician before adopting the suggestions in this book, as well as about any condition that may require diagnosis or medical attention. The author and publisher disclaim any liability arising directly or indirectly from the use of this book.

This book is available at quantity discounts for bulk purchases.
For information, please call 1-800-289-0963.

All the examples and dialogues used in this book are fictional and have been created by the author to illustrate medical situations.

Contents

Acknowledgments

I'd like to thank Andrea Hurst, who asked me, "Are you interested?" She's the best darn literary agent a girl could ask for. Thanks to Kerry Smith, Acquisitions Editor at Adams Media, for her patience and good advice. In addition, John W. Brees, D.V.M., for his keen insight into some complex topics; Park Brees, Personal Fitness Trainer, for his contributions to the chapter on exercise; Mary Benson, for sharing her vast knowledge and many resources with me; and Shawn Briley, L.M.S.W., for her professional contributions. And finally, Christie Gorsline, Linda Corder, and Bobbi Schaefer for their encouragement.

Introduction

IF YOU OR A LOVED ONE is suffering from depression, you know what a challenge life with this condition can be. Some days your depression probably feels insurmountable; other days you may feel okay, but still something's not quite right. In short, depression can become a controlling force in your life. But it doesn't have to be. There's never a *good* time to suffer from depression, but you're battling it at the best time in history to do so.

Researchers are making significant inroads into understanding the causes of depression. This is the first step toward a cure. It may seem that a cure is a long ways off, but life—and science—move quickly these days; today's commonplace items were yesterday's wild dreams. Where science is concerned, it's a good idea to keep current. Any day that one item you've been hoping for may come along.

Also, the medical community and society at large are more tolerant and accepting of the idea of depression as a legitimate condition than ever before. Dismissive reactions and harsh stigmas are fading away. People are more eager to seek help for depression, as well as to offer it to those in need. There are countless books out there on the subject, and new medications and therapies are emerging every day.

Depression is not all in your mind. You know that, because you feel lousy all over, and now science agrees with you. Depression involves both your brain and your body. It's called the mind/body connection. Treating depression, then, becomes a holistic endeavor. Today there are antidepressant medications that work quite effectively to manage many kinds of depression, and psychotherapy, called talk therapy, can help you find the root causes of your depression. Together, antidepressants and psychotherapy, combined with positive lifestyle changes, work well to keep depression under control and manage its symptoms.

If terms such as "psychotherapy" are still a bit foreign—and frightening—to you, don't worry. This book will give you an introduction to depression, the various ways to deal with it, and all the details in between. You'll read about choosing the right therapist for your needs, the benefits and risks of alternative therapies, the necessity of exercise, and the importance of a good diet. And you probably have questions about how you'll cope on a daily basis. What about work? Will your job be in jeopardy if you can't keep up your former level of productivity? What about your relationships? Will they survive such a test? These are honest questions that deserve compassionate and realistic answers. In this guide, you'll find those answers. Remember, knowledge is power.

Acknowledging that you need help is the first step toward getting that help, and just picking up this book is a step in the direction of a better life. There's no time like the present to make a change for the better!

CHAPTER 1

A Broad Look at Depression

YOU CAN'T PUT YOUR FINGER ON IT. You can't tell somebody where it hurts. All you know for sure is that something's not right. Perhaps you're feeling sluggish, with some vague aches and pains, or you're grouchy and irritable. It seems that at times it's almost impossible to work up any enthusiasm about anything. Other times, little things you usually brush off are really getting to you. What you're experiencing could be depression. In this chapter, you'll learn what depression is and get some background on this common and frustrating condition.

A Working Definition of Depression

Want the concise version? The U.S. National Library of Medicine and the National Institutes of Health (NIH) define depression as a treatable medical illness. That's pretty vague, but it contains three essential components. In reverse order, here's what each one means:

- **Illness:** Depression is an illness with specific, characteristic symptoms that produce changes in the way you feel about yourself, your world, and your life. To qualify as depression, these symptoms must be ongoing for at least two weeks.
- **Medical:** Depression is real. It's not a figment of your imagination. It exists and it hurts. It affects your body, your mind, and your emotions.

- **Treatable:** There is no cure for depression, but it can be treated. It can be managed with lifestyle changes, medications, psychotherapy, or a combination of these.

Psychologists refer to this condition as clinical depression—a psychiatric disorder characterized by certain symptoms, including an inability to concentrate, sleeping too little or too much, loss of appetite or eating more than usual, anhedonia, irritability, lack of energy, feelings of extreme sadness, guilt, helplessness, hopelessness, and sometimes, thoughts of death.

 ## Question

What is anhedonia?
Anhedonia is a term used in psychology. It refers to an inability to experience pleasure from events or activities that should be pleasurable. These events can range from eating and drinking to pursuing hobbies and sports and socializing. This includes sex!

You'll sometimes hear clinical depression called unipolar disorder. This is to distinguish it from bipolar disorder. *Uni-* and *bi-* are Latin prefixes, meaning one and two. In unipolar disorder, moods are consistently low. In bipolar disorder, two moods—extreme elation and extreme sadness—are involved, usually with periods of normal feelings in between. Depression can take many guises, and you'll learn about each of them in Chapter 4.

Creating a useful, comprehensive, working definition of depression is challenging. The essentials, however, are that depression is a treatable medical illness with symptoms that impact your physical, emotional, and mental well being. Since symptoms can worsen over time, depression should be treated.

What Are the Causes?

Excellent question. Unfortunately, there's no simple answer for it. There are many kinds of depressive disorders, some more serious than others. It seems that depression has a wide variety of ways to enter your life:

- Some kinds of depression seem to run in families, so you may have a genetic predisposition to depression.
- Trauma and stressful life events can cause depression. The trauma doesn't have to have involved you personally to affect you. Stressful life events that can lead to depression include divorce, financial setbacks, chronic illness, loss of a job, and so forth.
- Hormones can cause depression. This means either a rise in hormone levels or a drop in them. Testosterone in men and progesterone and estrogen in women may be the culprits.
- Some medications can trigger depression or cause depressive symptoms. This includes prescription medications, as well as recreational drugs and alcohol. Also, drug interactions may have dangerous side effects, including depression.
- Certain other medical conditions can cause depression. Among them are heart disease, cancer, and HIV/AIDS.
- The weather can cause depression. The dark days of winter may lead to seasonal affective disorder (SAD), also known as The Alaska Effect.

Discovering what kind of depression you are dealing with may lead to understanding what caused it. Following the clues may lead you to the proper treatment.

Twins or triplets tend to run in certain families—it's a genetic trait. So is left-handedness and red-headedness. So, also, are certain forms of depression, including bipolar disorder. If you are beginning to wonder if you might be suffering from depression, it just makes good sense to take a look at your family tree and find out everything you can about the medical conditions that tend to appear more frequently than might be expected.

Did your father experience severe mood swings—so much so that you never knew quite what to expect from him when you were growing up? Was your mother constantly sad—to the point that you can't ever remember her being really happy? These are the kinds of things to look for as you take a trip down memory lane. Ask your aunts, uncles, cousins, or grandparents what they remember about other family members. Their responses may not come in medical terms, but they'll help you establish a connection to your past that will help guide your future.

You're in Good Company

When you're feeling all alone and struggling to cope, sometimes it helps to know that you're in good company. Depression has touched the lives of many prominent people, including many of our presidents. A recent Duke University study, published in January 2007, in the *Journal of Nervous and Mental Disease,* suggests that almost half of our presidents suffered from some form of mental illness, with 24 percent affected by depression. Anxiety disorders came in second— certainly understandable, given the responsibilities of the job!

Abraham Lincoln

Lincoln is perhaps the most well-known figure, among his presidential peers, to struggle with depression. Living in the nineteenth century meant that Lincoln did not have access to the medical resources enjoyed today. One thing he did share with modern-day sufferers, however, was the need to cope with his disorder. He had chosen a public life. This meant that his adversaries would be watching, should he falter.

Recent biographers, such as Joshua Wolf Shenk in *Lincoln's Melancholy: How Depression Challenged a President and Fueled His Greatness* (2005), have looked deeply into Lincoln's medical history and found that Lincoln tried an assortment of substances and strategies to treat his depression. He tried a pill (known as the blue mass) with mercury as its main component. On one occasion, he also tried cocaine.

Apart from that, Lincoln also cultivated his sense of humor and he wrote prolifically. His writing served as a means of working through his depression, and among his poems is one titled "The Suicide's Soliloquy."

 ## Fact

When Ann Rutledge, Lincoln's first love, died, his friends put up a suicide watch over him. Lincoln's depression became evident while he was in his twenties, became chronic in his thirties, and haunted him the rest of his life. Yet Lincoln became one of our greatest presidents.

In Lincoln's day, melancholia was seen as a personality type with attributes such as deep self-reflection. What helped Lincoln cope with his depression?

- He understood his illness for what it was—something he'd have to deal with every day for the rest of his life.
- He realized depression didn't have to define him.
- He had a support system in place—those friends who cared for him and accepted him, with all of his idiosyncrasies. Those were the friends who watched over him through his darkest times.
- He had a self-deprecating and well-documented sense of humor. He had learned to laugh at himself.
- He'd also learned that depression doesn't mean that everything else that's good in one's life vanishes. The good things just might be a little more difficult to call upon and might not stay accessible as long as you'd like.
- He journaled. He wrote and he wrote and he wrote.

- He made himself get up every morning and face the day, whatever it held. The effort that this must have taken, when he was feeling so low, was Herculean. When he experienced suicidal thoughts, he wrote them into poetry.
- He never gave up. In fact, Lincoln employed many of the same practices that are current, state-of-the-art approaches to treating depression today.

Thomas Eagleton

By the late twentieth century, you might guess that things would've only gotten better for those suffering from depression. Unfortunately, mental illness still carried a huge stigma. In 1972, vice presidential candidate Thomas Eagleton was dropped from the McGovern ticket when news of Eagleton's treatment for mental illness was revealed. The contrast between Lincoln and Eagleton is sharp and painful to study. Lincoln was not treated poorly for his mental illness. On the contrary, he was seen as intelligent, introspective, and complex. Eagleton was seen as a liability, and his disorder became the topic of gossip columnists and comedians. Was Eagleton the first one to be shunned because of his mental health condition? Of course not. The roots of this fear, for fear is what it is, go back a long way.

Society's Fear of Mental Illness

Where and when did the fear of mental illness originate? Simply stated, what the world doesn't understand, it fears, and for a very long time the world couldn't even begin to understand mental illness. For millennia, depression was a secret one kept. Of course, this just made matters worse. Those closest to the depressed person knew there was a problem, even if they were unaware of its nature. If one was fortunate, they didn't shun you or lock you away. They just dismissed the problem, if they could, with a knowing glance.

Sometimes people have an unreasonable but real fear that depression is contagious, in some way. They don't want to get too close and catch it. Then there's the very real worry that mental illness affects who one is at the core—that it's changed the person in some way. If you break an ankle, you've got a broken ankle. If you have a heart attack, it's definitely worse than the broken ankle, but it doesn't approach the incalculable fear of losing your mind. After all, your mind is who you are. It's where you live.

Moving Beyond the Stigma

How to solve this dilemma? The answer, of course, is education. The more you know about depression the more you can understand it, learn to cope with it, and seek solutions. But this isn't something you can do on your own. You need support. Luckily, society has finally begun to display an increased sense of urgency and responsibility regarding treatment of mental illness.

 Fact

> The Surgeon General's 1999 Report on Mental Health revealed that, with nearly one out of five people affected by some form of mental illness, the costs of diagnosis and treatment are escalating. In established market economies such as the United States, mental illness was the second leading cause of disability and premature mortality, and depression was the leading form of mental illness.

What's the current status? Some gains seem so small as to be nearly insignificant, while others are enormous. First, the terminology has changed. People no longer speak of the mentally ill; instead, it's people with mental illness. What's the difference? It's subtle, but it's important. Instead of equating the person and the disability (you are mental illness), we're now putting the person first and saying this person has a condition. There's a separation inherent in these few words, and it's a positive, healthy separation.

Essential

Terminology has changed across the board. For example, instead of deaf people, it's people with deafness; instead of blind people, it's people with blindness. People are no longer confined to wheelchairs; instead, wheelchairs assist them. Once you get the hang of it, it makes sense.

What else has changed? Information. Information about depression is now available around the world to everyone with access to a computer and the Internet. Typing depression into an Internet search engine produced 88,400,000 sites. Depression is a hot topic. People are seeking information and seeking help for themselves and for loved ones.

Is the stigma of mental illness still out there? Of course it is. But as researchers delve more deeply into genetics, and as our knowledge base builds, the stigma will fade. Cancer used to hold a stigma. People couldn't even refer to it by name. Superstitions still flavor our thinking. But new discoveries mean new advances in treatment and diagnosis, new drugs, and the hope of a cure. If you're suffering from depression, don't suffer alone and in silence. Force yourself to venture out to see and to be seen. Remember, what you see, you can begin to understand. What you understand, you can learn not to fear. What you don't fear, you can conquer. It's all about little steps, one at a time. Keep your balance, and if you stumble, pick yourself up, dust yourself off, and start all over again.

Taking the First Step

If you're feeling depressed and hopeless and are unsure of where to turn, what do you do? A needlepoint tapestry on the wall of a family therapist's office in Santa Cruz, California, bore the following piece of embroidered wisdom: "When you're down and out, lift up your head and shout...'I'm down and out!'" It's good advice. Being honest with yourself is the first step toward relieving the symptoms of depression and coming to terms with this disorder.

Acknowledging that there's a problem is not only the first step, but it's also the most difficult step. From infancy, you're taught to handle problems on your own. "Deal with it!" has become a not-so-gentle admonition from our culture. So, when you can't "deal with it," you tend to think that you're flawed. You should be able to cope. Depression is not just a routine problem, however. You need help to get better—and this does *not* make you weak or helpless or pathetic. It's just the way it is.

Remind yourself what a courageous move it is to admit you have a problem and need help. And also remember that getting this far is evidence that you still have some control over your situation. This means you're not powerless. Once you acknowledge this, take a deep, cleansing breath, and make an appointment with a physician or psychotherapist to have a chat. Such professionals have the training necessary to provide you with the tools you'll need to tackle depression.

There's no point in suffering in silence. In fact, there's no point in suffering at all. It's highly overrated as a health option. Even when your emotional gauge tells you there's nothing left, remember: There are always at least two gallons left in the tank. That's plenty to get you to the gas station. That's more than enough to get you to help. As long as you remain in the driver's seat, you still have some control.

CHAPTER 2

Understanding Depression

EXPERIENCE HAS BEEN CALLED life's best teacher, and life provides many experiences as you pass through it. Some of those are good and some not so pleasant. In the case of troubles, once you've been through something, you can usually recognize it, should it pass by your way again. It's getting through that all-important first time with anything that can be difficult. If you haven't had experience with depression, and even if you have, this chapter will give you some insight into what depression is and how to tell when it gets serious.

Feeling Depressed Versus Having Depression

It's true that everyone experiences feelings of depression from time to time. However, feeling depressed isn't the same as having depression. This is an important distinction.

Though feeling depressed can be a pretty unpleasant experience, it's actually a healthy response to certain events. For example, if you've ever experienced the loss of a loved one or the end of a romantic relationship, you probably felt sad, upset, or just generally down afterward. This is perfectly normal and, in fact, a healthy emotional response. The key is how you deal with the feelings of depression and how you express those emotions thereafter.

If you are mentally healthy, you will experience a down time and say, "Man, I'm having a bad day. I sure hope tomorrow gets better." You accept that circumstances may be out of your control or accept some responsibility for what's happening, if that's appropriate. In any case, you know that, come the dawn, you're going to give it another go and see what you can make out of the new day.

If you suffer from depression, on the other hand, you sink lower and lower with each negative experience. Your entire mood tends toward the negative rather than the positive. Every bad thing that happens to you only serves to reinforce your already gloomy outlook.

That feeling of being down in the dumps means that you're depressed. It's part of being human. Some days go better than others, and you may even enjoy feeling sorry for yourself, at times, when the world seems to be conspiring to get you down. In emotionally healthy people, this mood soon passes. Whether caused by hormones, as in premenstrual syndrome (PMS); a stressful situation, such as a romantic breakup; problems at work; an argument with a spouse or partner; or getting some bad news about your income taxes, those funks are transitory. You kiss and make up or you find another romantic partner. You resolve the problems at work or you find another job. You soldier on through the menstrual cycle and emerge on the other side your own sunny self. You can see the low points for what they are—isolated occurrences. It's when these moods last more than two weeks that being depressed can mean having depression.

How Do You Know?

There are many online questionnaires available to help you determine whether your symptoms indicate that you are suffering from depression. However, only a qualified mental health professional is able to make a diagnosis of depression. The following self-questionnaire is provided solely for informational purposes and is not intended to take the place of a professional medical diagnosis.

1. Have you been feeling down or blue for at least two weeks?
2. Are you having difficulty falling asleep or staying asleep?
3. Do you find yourself sleeping much more or much less than usual?
4. Are you eating significantly more or less than you usually do?

5. Do you find yourself having difficulty concentrating?
6. Do you feel helpless or that life just isn't worth the effort?
7. Do activities that used to give you pleasure now seem too much work?
8. Have you had thoughts of suicide?
9. Has your energy level decreased?
10. Have any of the symptoms you are experiencing interfered with the quality of your life?

If you've answered yes to any of these questions, have a talk with your primary health care provider. Depression may be the problem, but often other medical conditions have symptoms that mimic those of depression. Your doctor is in the best position to advise you.

Anger Turned Inward

When people have a conversation, it usually involves an exchange of information. When two people are talking to each other, it's called a dialogue. But when you're trying to have a conversation with someone who's suffering from depression, what transpires sounds more like a monologue than a dialogue, which can be frustrating for all involved. Here's how such a conversation, in which one of the individuals is suffering from depression, might sound.

Friend: "What's wrong with you?"
Person with Depression: "I don't know."
Friend: "That's not very helpful."
Person with Depression: "Okay.
Friend: "Are you angry with me?"
Person with Depression: "No."
Friend: "I don't understand you."
Person with Depression: "I don't understand me either. Just leave me alone."

The friend wants to help but doesn't know how. The person with depression doesn't have a whole lot to contribute, and so the conversation goes nowhere, until one of them has had enough and either gives up the effort and sits in uncomfortable silence or leaves.

If you've had this experience, or something similar, then you've had a glimpse of what Sigmund Freud meant when he referred to depression as "anger turned inward." In the snippet of conversation above, the uncommunicative person is angry—perhaps not at the other person involved in the conversation, but angry nonetheless.

The Anger Continuum

Mental health is measured on a continuum, and so is anger. You'll learn more about the role of anger in depression in Chapter 18, but for now, an overview should be helpful. At different times and under varying circumstances, you may find yourself angry, miffed, annoyed, irritated, and even downright furious. When your anger is a reaction to a specific event and is a logical response, it's normal.

Generally, you'll find socially acceptable ways of venting this anger, but when you can't let off steam, the stress continues to build. The stress has to go somewhere, so it turns inward on you, causing all manner of physical problems. You may suffer from stomach troubles, indigestion, heartburn, headaches, raised blood pressure, or a host of other symptoms that mask the true problem—you're angry.

You may have been taught from childhood that it's not nice to express anger. Unfortunately, if you internalized this message, you may reap a nasty harvest. Anger is negative energy, and it's destructive.

⌐ Essential

In classical Greek drama, as the play unfolds, the audience's emotions of fear and pity for the characters must be cleansed or purged, in order for balance to be restored. Aristotle called this deep cleansing catharsis. Today this word is used to refer to an experience that leaves us drained, but drained with the promise of renewal. You may have heard someone say, "I'm tired, but it's a good tired." That's catharsis.

Healthy Expression

Appropriately expressed anger is healthy. Repressed anger or inappropriately expressed anger is not. There are numerous ways to release this energy. Punching a bag, running, playing sports, singing, dancing, gardening—anything that lets you exhaust this negative energy and leaves you feeling cleansed works to keep your anger managed. This process is called catharsis.

Finding the Right Outlet

Children and adolescents need outlets for their energy. This is why depressed children often spend too much time alone, unengaged and disengaged. It's also why they can do well with play therapy. Play is serious business for children. It's a time of emotional, mental, and physical growth.

For teenagers, healthy activities that let them use their bodies full-out are essential to keeping a good balance and preventing the build-up of stress that can lead to depression. In this time of cost-cutting and budget tightening, the very activities that adolescents need—such as sports, drama, choir—are being axed from the school curriculum. It's a real case of penny-wise and pound-foolish. It's a false economy. The costs of not having these outlets are borne by the medical system and ultimately, the taxpayer.

Adults, and that includes the elderly, may be so caught up in the daily routines of everyday life that they don't take the time to recreate—to re-create themselves. If you neglect this important aspect of promoting mental and physical health, your body pays the price in a variety of ways. The human body was meant to move and be active. It's nature's way of letting go of worries, releasing negative energy, and replenishing your resources.

The Cycle of Depression

You may find that your depression is usually at its worst upon waking in the morning and tends to improve during the course of the day. Why? It has to do with the quality of your sleep. Sleep studies at the

Human Givens Institute, associated with MindFields College in the UK, have found that, if you're dealing with depression, you tend to dream more than people who are not depressed. All this dreaming takes up a considerable portion of sleeping time, stealing the time that otherwise would allow for deep, restorative sleep.

Normally, you'll move through different levels of sleep during the night. There are cycles of REM sleep (Rapid Eye Movement) when you dream and non-REM sleep when you don't dream. Non-REM sleep is broken into four different phases, with phases 3 and 4 being the deep levels of sleep. Those levels are the restorative, healing levels of sleep. When you're dreaming (in REM sleep) too much, because your mind is working through your problems, concerns, or troubles, your body doesn't spend adequate time in deep, restorative sleep. What happens then is that you wake up in the morning and still feel tired.

Worrying Makes It Worse

Worrying is not productive. Worriers are not pleasant to be around; they focus only on the problem, not on solutions. When you create a mental list of worries, and the list grows as the day goes on, your mind is forced to keep track of them. You can't stop worrying; you can't stop stressing. Depression won't let you. You're constantly inside yourself, brooding. And you start to dread going to bed, because you know your sleep will be restless at best, nonexistent at worst.

Dealing with Insomnia

Some nights you can't shut off your brain and go to sleep. Thought after thought pummels away at you. Sometimes you give up, get up, and read or watch a little TV until you try again to sleep. You may begin taking sleep medications or perhaps having a nightcap or two before you go to bed. But this doesn't fix the problem and may not even mask the symptoms for long.

When this happens occasionally, not to worry. When this becomes a predictable pattern, there are some simple things you can do on your own to help stop the negative thought flow. For example, before retiring for the night, write down everything that is currently causing you stress. The act of committing these thoughts to paper can relieve your brain. You've taken action.

The next day, look to see if there is a pattern to your worries. Do they center around your children? Your spouse? Your job? Your finances? Organizing your worries can be a productive exercise, allowing you to consider them with some objectivity. You're beginning to exert some control.

Once you've identified the categories, take a look at what you've listed under each. Put them in order from biggest worry to smallest worry or smallest to biggest—whatever seems more comfortable to you. You're identifying what is making you sleepless.

After each worry, consider what kind of action could be appropriate. For example, suppose you worry about your daughter's safety, as she lives on her own in an urban area. You realize you've been consciously or unconsciously looking for news stories that focus on the problems of young adults working in the inner cities. You worry about crime and about her becoming the victim of a break-in or a mugging. In your worst-case scenario, you picture her running for her life. You also worry she won't have enough money to cover all her expenses, or that she's not putting enough away for the future. You worry about her job security and what she'll do if she's laid off. What's most important here? First comes safety; after that, it appears job and finances are connected. Now what?

Acceptance Means Relief

The most difficult part of this process comes in realizing and accepting that you have no control over another individual. Your daughter is living her life, just as you are living yours. As a parent, you will always worry about your grown children. It comes with the birth certificate—a lifelong commitment of love. Take a deep, cleansing breath. Close your eyes and visualize a positive city scene. It may be a museum, art gallery, anything that evokes good images. Next, place your daughter in that scene. Then add the following caption to that picture: "I trust my daughter to live responsibly." Just as repeating negative thoughts can imprint them on your mind, so can repeating positive ones—and you have also associated a positive image with the positive thought.

How to convey your worries to her? The next time you chat or meet, discuss them as you would with any other adult. This can be tough, but keeping channels of communication open is the best antidote to worry. You may be surprised to learn that she worries about you, as well!

Another Example

Here's one more worry example. You are worried you'll be all alone one day, with no one to care about you or for you. Is this a reasonable worry? Possibly, but focusing too much on that scenario can create a self-fulfilling prophecy. What to do? Back to your list. This time, instead of concentrating on a possibility, you're going to look at solutions that will eliminate the prospect of this depressing future. When you're depressed, the future is a dark and dismal place, devoid of hope. But that's an imaginary future, since the real future is yet to be written. Having a plan to deal with your worries, one by one, is really a plan to effectively deal with depression.

 Alert

> Living in depression has been likened to doing time in hell. In *The Divine Comedy,* Dante Alighieri wrote, "Abandon hope, all ye who enter here." He placed this inscription above the gates of hell to illustrate complete and utter despair and loss. Yet there's another old expression that serves us better, "Where there's life, there's hope."

You've already constructed the bleak future, so now ask yourself what a good future would look like. It would probably include friends, family, health, and the resources to make life worth living. Again, you've developed your categories. Since you're dealing with depression, begin with the health category, as it influences each of the others. It's time to make a plan for managing your depression. Your first task should be scheduling a complete physical exam. With the information this will give you, you'll be able to target specific behavioral changes to improve the quality of your life. The actions you take now will greatly influence how you feel later on.

Regaining Control

Even if you can only think of one item to add to one category each day, in one week, you'll have begun to construct a blueprint for your life that is of *your* making. There will be seven items you've added and seven can become your lucky number, since you will have begun to retake control. Depression may be a part of your life, but it does not have to define who you are. Only you can define yourself. Need an idea? Go to the friends category and write down, "Send birthday card to Sharon." It can be just that simple. Keeping connections alive is essential to your emotional health. Keeping track of what you have accomplished builds upon itself. Just as with thinking positive thoughts, taking even small, positive actions can bring you out of the doldrums, one baby step at a time.

Identifying Serious Depression

If you've experienced trauma of some kind, you may have heard the following sentiment, or something similar to it, from someone who cares about you: "You can't control what happened. You can only control how you respond to it." Is this true? Not always. Sometimes, your body has its own ideas about how you'll respond, and trying to will yourself to feel differently doesn't work.

Everybody has a different stress (tolerance) level, and everybody has different trigger points. How you respond may be quite different from how someone else does. This doesn't mean you are weak or flawed. It simply means you are an individual.

If you've been the victim of a crime, if you've survived an automobile accident, or even if you've caused an automobile accident, the emotional effects can linger long after the physical injuries have healed. If the situation has resulted in a death, the devastation you feel may be beyond description. No one can tell you what you are feeling or how you are feeling. Even trained psychologists, counselors, social workers, and psychiatrists have to listen to you in order to know how to help.

 ## Question

What is trauma?

Trauma is a Greek word that means wound. In psychology, trauma refers both to the hurtful experience as well as to the body's response to that hurt. When some outside force causes you injury or severe stress, you've experienced trauma. You may be able to see the physical effects immediately, but the emotional effects may not show up for some time.

When an event has occurred that affects a group of people, crisis counselors are sometimes called in to help victims process their feelings. These counselors will visit schools or workplaces and lead discussions, listen, and offer help. Sometimes, however, the impact of whatever has happened doesn't hit one immediately. And later, out of the blue, one will experience shock. The symptoms one encounters then may be diagnosed as post-traumatic stress disorder (PTSD). So when does it get serious?

- When you think that behind every silver lining, there's a dark cloud, it's serious.
- When your depressed mood begins to affect the quality of your life, it's serious.
- When minor annoyances create major reactions, it's serious.
- When you resort to alcohol, tobacco, or other drugs—such as cocaine—to help you get through the day, it's serious.
- When you begin to think that life isn't worth the effort anymore, it's serious.

- When you can't express your feelings, or if you aren't even sure what those feelings are, and if this experience lingers for more than two weeks, it's serious.

When it's serious, it's time to get help. There are all kinds of resources available to you, and many of them are as close as your telephone or your computer. In Appendix B at the back of this book you'll find a list of various agencies. Don't overlook those helping hands closer to home, however. A call to your family physician or family nurse practitioner can send you down the right path for finding support.

The Importance of Friendships

Friendships are the buffer zones for life's ups and downs, and when you're struggling with depression, there is nothing more important than seeking help and support from friends. If you're having a bad day, instead of sulking on the couch alone, pick up the telephone and call a friend. Tell the friend you're feeling down and ask if she would like to go out and get lunch, coffee, whatever. This is a good start. Friends will listen because they care and because they're curious as to the reason why you're depressed. They'll ask what's wrong. You'll take a deep breath, sigh, and tell all. They'll sympathize with your plight and give advice. You'll each commiserate, share stories, have a cup of coffee or a beer, and then the conversation will turn to other topics. It's an effective, practical, and cheap way of working through minor problems that are causing you to feel down. A word of caution, however: Only a trained mental health professional is qualified to provide therapy.

Sometimes, however, even your closest friends reach the breaking point and need to distance themselves for their own well-being. A steady diet of gloom and doom can dishearten even the jolliest spirit.

For friendships to both thrive and survive, there needs to be ample time for both talking and listening by each party. There's an unwritten time limit for each pity party. Each friend listens, each friend shares. Once you've used up your allotted time, you're expected to listen. If you have depression, this becomes more difficult. You may *hear* your friend talk about her problems, but you might not be truly *listening*. It's a fine but important distinction. Do your best to stay on top of this behavior; you don't want to lose the friends who are helping you through your tough time.

Essential

In an intervention, family and friends confront the person whose substance abuse or emotional or mental illness has created the real possibility that suicide may be imminent or that symptoms require immediate professional treatment. They lay out their concerns and often are prepared to take that person to treatment, on the spot. It can be helpful to have a trained professional facilitate an intervention.

Intervention

If things are more dire and you're having trouble even mustering the emotional strength to call a friend or to go out for coffee, your friends and family will likely begin to seriously worry about you. This is when an intervention could come in. Perhaps your friend will show up at your door one day. Perhaps she'll bring along someone else important to you. They'll want to discuss your situation with you and come up with a plan to get you help. While this may make you feel upset and even humiliated at the time, the facts still stand: Sometimes, you have to hit bottom before you can spring back up. If this happens to you, take the advice to get some help.

Even if an intervention doesn't happen, at some point, if you are to regain joy in living and regain a sense of self, you may have to become your own best friend and make that appointment. It's the first step toward managing your depression and moving outside yourself and back into life.

CHAPTER 3

The Physiology of Depression

THERE'S A LOT TO DEPRESSION. It not only affects how you feel but also has implications for your body as a whole. That's where physiology comes in. Physiology is that branch of science that studies living organisms and how they function. So physiologists examine both the physical and chemical processes that affect the human body. What are they looking for? These physiologists are looking for the key that will unlock the mysteries of depression.

It's Not All in Your Head

Diagnostics is as much an art as it is a science. A good diagnostician takes everything into consideration when evaluating a condition. Lab results, patient affect, impressions, and history—all these become integral parts of the diagnosis.

It isn't possible to isolate a specific medical condition by drawing an imaginary line across a given part of the human body. "You've got a headache? We'll just lop off your head at the neck and things will be fine." Of course this is nonsense. Even if you have a definite area of concern, a malfunctioning appendix, for example, the effects of this problem are felt throughout your body. This includes your head! An attack of appendicitis will have certain symptoms:

- Pain
- Elevated temperature
- Elevated white blood cell count

These symptoms, however, are not confined to your abdomen. Your brain tells you that you're hurting. You're running a fever, and you feel awful all over. Perhaps you have chills and are visibly shaking. And those white blood cells have free rein throughout your bloodstream. So, even though the problem is in your tummy, the symptoms of appendicitis permeate your entire body, and no one would tell you otherwise.

One more example to set the stage. A sliver. A little, teeny piece of wood, embedded in your index finger. It hurts, of course. That foreign body is an irritant. And, in addition to the possibility of infection, if you don't dig it out, what else is happening? Are you focusing on that sliver? Is your mood going south? You're irritable. And if you can't find a needle or something else with a sharp point to get that splinter out, it's going to be difficult to ignore, until you can. All in your finger? Technically, yes. However, the spillover effects are felt pretty much everywhere.

How Pain Works

Pain receptors in your finger send a signal to your brain that sends a message via your spinal cord to the affected nerve. You look at your finger and see what's causing the pain. You realize that, to alleviate that pain, you've got to remove the splinter. So, is the pain all in your head? Of course not. If you can accept this fact in minor physical hurts, it makes sense that this truth also applies in more serious hurts, such as depression. You cannot separate your mind from your body.

Your tolerance for pain is highly individualized. What one person experiences as mild discomfort may send another person to the aspirin bottle. That's why hospitals now use a pain index for each patient. You point to the level of pain you're feeling, based upon a facial expression. Personalized pain equals personalized treatment.

It's Everywhere!

When you are depressed, your entire body is affected. You can't compartmentalize. Whether you experience aches and pains, tiredness, irritability, insomnia, or any of depression's other symptoms, it's your mind that takes control and processes the problem. This is the mind/body connection, and it's a marvelous system. Keeping you healthy, keeping you strong, is a major cooperative effort, requiring your body and your mind to be in sync. After all, who else could have more of a vested interest in your health than you do? Trust your body when it tells you it hurts. Trust your mind when it tells you that you're depressed.

Depressive Personalities

Your personality and your temperament may play a role in whether or not you develop a depressive disorder. Researchers in a study conducted at the University of Washington were interested in whether there would be a recurrence of depressive symptoms in patients who had recovered from major depression (*www.apa.org*). Does having had depression predispose you to having it again? They followed seventy-eight patients during the two year study and found that thirty-four participants in the study (44 percent) suffered relapses. The scientists reasoned that if they could identify the risk factors involved in a recurrence they might discover that those same factors might play a significant role in developing depressive disorders in the first place. So they looked at what characteristics those thirty-four individuals shared and found some common traits:

1. Aggressiveness manifested in distrust and hostility toward others
2. Low levels of dependency on others
3. Lower levels of pleasure derived from recreational activities

These are the personality traits, they decided, that may put you at risk for depression. It goes deeper than personality, however. Researchers are now studying whether these traits are linked to genetics. So, if you are morose, gloomy, negative, hostile, or aggressive, you may indeed have a depressive personality, and you might be able to blame it on your genes.

Genetics and Depression

Scientists have already discovered that there is a genetic component to many diseases, such as cystic fibrosis, tuberous sclerosis, certain kinds of muscular dystrophy, Tay-Sachs, sickle cell anemia, and Huntington's disease. Discovering that link is just the first step, however. Isolating that gene responsible for that disease and then finding a way to repair the gene takes time, an enormous amount of money, skill, persistence, and occasionally, luck. For many scientists and researchers, it's the work of a lifetime.

 Alert

If you know that a specific disease shows up in your family on a regular basis, be aware that depression may be a precursor or a symptom of that disease. Keep your medical records up to date, and always keep your annual physical exam part of your health regimen. Know the warning signs and be prepared to act on them.

It's a Long Story

How do you study people? You can observe them, of course, but the data you collect might not be reliable. So, along with observation, researchers conduct physiological tests—blood tests, X-rays, CT scans, and other analytical tools at their disposal. Scientists also study the frequency of specific illnesses in certain families. For this kind of research, longitudinal studies are invaluable.

Longitudinal studies are investigations that follow specific individuals or groups over a period of years. In these studies, researchers are looking for trends and patterns. By gathering information from each generation, through medical records and oral histories, they are able to create a profile of how and when the disease manifests. These studies have to be coupled with lab tests, since memories are notoriously unreliable. Still, longitudinal studies provide important information that scientists might otherwise be hard-pressed to discover.

Seeing Double

Finding twins to participate in research studies is rather like striking gold at Sutter's Mill. Twin studies are rich sources of information for researchers, since identical twins share 100 percent of their genes and non-identical (fraternal) twins, 50 percent. Adoption studies are used to rule out the environmental factor. Stanford University researchers found that depression occurred more often in identical twins than in non-identical twins. They discovered that the risk of developing depression was still greater for adopted twins, if their biological parent had depression. They also found that, if your parent or sibling suffers from major depression, you probably have a two to three times greater risk of developing depression yourself, than if they didn't. This figure may be higher for severe depression.

There are many different kinds of depression, and while scientists have recognized a genetic component for some, other psychological factors, along with physical and environmental factors, also play a role. Whether genetics is totally responsible for some forms of depression, or not responsible at all in others, remains to be determined.

Brain Chemistry

So, where does the brain come into the picture and what does it have to do with this genetic material? The brain is key, although people didn't always know how important the brain actually was.

Ancient Egyptians tossed out the brain when they were mummy-making. They didn't consider it a necessary part of the body. What we've learned since that time is, well, mind-boggling. And we've barely scratched the surface. What do you remember from your biology class? You probably can recall some brain terms, such as medulla oblongata, cerebellum, and cerebrum, but there are more parts, and some of them lie deep within. Scientists are still in the early stages of unraveling the secrets of the human brain. As far as depression goes, the National Institute of Mental Health (NIMH) is a good source of information on brain research, and it reports that two parts of your brain, the amygdala and the hippocampus, are of interest to researchers studying depressive disorders.

The Amygdala

Your amygdala is one of those brain parts located deep in the brain. It's shaped sort of like an almond, and scientists believe it functions as a communications hub between the parts of the brain that process incoming sensory signals and the parts that interpret these signals. For example, if you hear noises in the night, your amygdala serves as a neuro-911. It sends out the danger message, and you experience a heightened sense of anxiety as a result. This is the beginning of the fight-or-flight response. Next, you'll analyze the danger and decide whether to ignore it, confront it, or make tracks.

 Alert

Anxiety that is unrelated to a specific cause is one of the warning signs of depression. If you experience anxiety and can't figure out why you're feeling the way you are, it's time to make an appointment for a physical examination to rule out a physical cause for your symptoms.

In addition to being Mission Control, the amygdala also warehouses these emotional memories. When you experience the same situation again or encounter a situation that's similar, your amygdala kicks in and accesses that prior knowledge, and you become anxious. In essence, your brain's been trained.

The Hippocampus

You also have a hippocampus in your brain, and your hippocampus has been in the news recently. New research has discovered that the dentate gyrus, a specific part of the hippocampus, is the source of the eerie déjà vu effect. Your hippocampus, or your dentate gyrus, works with your amygdala to do some further work on that anxiety-provoking situation you just experienced.

 ## Question

What's déjà vu?
You're doing some activity or thinking about something and you get the distinct sensation that you've done this before and thought this before. Some psychics have attributed this experience to a sort of extra-sensory perception (ESP).

The hippocampus encodes these threatening events into memories. Since memories of traumatic events are the triggers for post-traumatic stress disorder (PTSD), researchers are interested in exploring this further. Also, the hippocampus appears to be smaller in some people who were victims of child abuse or who served in military combat. What causes the hippocampus to shrink? Why does it shrink? These are questions that, when answered, may explain flashbacks and lapses in memory centered around the traumatic event. By learning more about how the brain creates fear and anxiety, scientists may be able to devise better treatments for anxiety disorders and the depression that accompanies them.

The Chemical Process

Your brain is a complex organ, and its chemistry is not yet fully understood. Researchers do know quite a bit, though, and are adding to that knowledge daily. They know that certain chemicals send impulses across nerve endings to other nerves or muscles or organs. These chemicals are called neurotransmitters. When everything is working smoothly, these neurotransmitters operate efficiently and in correct amounts. When things are not going according to plan, neurotransmitter levels may fluctuate. This is not good. The neurotransmitters of interest here are norepinephrine, serotonin, and dopamine. They're the neurotransmitters associated with major depression.

- Norepinephrine is also known as noradrenaline. It has a stimulating effect and promotes alertness and a sense of well-being. If norepinephrine is overproduced, fear and anxiety can result.
- Serotonin is a key neurotransmitter for maintaining mental and emotional health. If your serotonin levels drop, due to prolonged stress or illness or malnutrition, depression can follow.
- Dopamine is the precursor to norepinephrine. It's also a neurohormone (see the next section). Scientists are studying the connection between unbalanced dopamine and schizophrenia and Parkinson's disease.

Essential

The word *neurotransmitter* comes from the Latin *neuro* meaning nerve and transmitto meaning to send across. These neurotransmitters send messages across nerve endings, or synapses.

It may seem strange to think of your brain as a chemistry experiment, but that's exactly how researchers are approaching the problem. They're looking at fear and anxiety as chemically induced responses. If they find out that this is indeed true, then discovering the chemistry behind those responses is the first step toward developing medications to alter those chemicals, reducing the fear or anxiety response, and ultimately curing or even preventing the onset of depression. This is exciting terrain for a scientist.

Add a Hormone or Two

Neurotransmitters have help. They need it! They work hard at what they do. They're aided in their tasks by other chemicals, called neurohormones, that may also play a role in depression. One of these chemicals, corticotrophin-releasing hormone (CRH) gets you on the alert when a real or perceived danger looms. Research suggests that trauma during childhood can negatively affect the functioning of CRH and the hypothalamic-pituitary-adrenal axis (HPA axis) throughout the course of your life.

So much of what people have learned about the brain reinforces the importance of the early years in creating good mental and physical health. Many illnesses, and that includes depression, may have their roots in childhood and in childhood experiences.

Studies have shown that people who have dysthymia (chronic depression) typically have increased levels of CRH. Antidepressants and electroconvulsive therapy are both known to reduce these high CRH levels. As CRH levels return to normal, depressive symptoms recede (*www.everydayhealth.com*).

Neurogenesis

It never pays to be too sure of anything. Science teaches us that fact every day. It used to be common knowledge that, once your brain was injured, that was it. Break your arm, bruise your spleen, and healing is possible. New cells generate and repair the damage. But injure your brain? No way. Too bad. Tough. The brain cells you had when you were born were all you get. That conventional wisdom got thrown out the window when researchers discovered that the brain may indeed be able to generate new cells and possibly have the potential to repair itself, even in adulthood. The implications of this discovery are enormous, especially when you consider what this will mean for sufferers of stroke, Parkinson's disease, and depression.

 Fact

Neurogenesis is a Latin word. As in the Book of Genesis—the beginning of the Bible—genesis means beginning, and neurogenesis means a rebirth of nerve cells in the brain. It's creation, ongoing.

Some Good News

Do you like puzzles? Scientists love them. To understand what's happening in brain research, think of a jigsaw puzzle. The puzzle's not in the box, however. Someone has scattered the pieces throughout the house. There's one under the sofa, a couple are inside the lampshades, and some are inside the pitted olives in the can on the third shelf of the pantry, and the rest? Well, they're somewhere. To make assembling this puzzle more interesting, you don't know how many pieces there are supposed to be. You also don't know what the finished puzzle will look like. Sound like fun? It may not be your cup of tea, but it can help you understand the excitement when scientists find two pieces of research that fit together. That's pretty much what happened during the 1960s and 1970s, when scientists discovered that the axons of the neurons in the brain and spinal cord could regrow, to some degree, after trauma (*http://neurogenesis.iord.org*).

The Depression Connection

Stress, depression, antidepressants, and neurogenesis—research is now focusing on a possible connection. If stress inhibits neurogenesis in the hippocampus, then relieving stress—through the use of antidepressants—may increase neurogenesis, and increased neurogenesis may hold promise in the search for a cure for depression. That's what's in the works. For now, scientists do know that exercise and electroconvulsive therapy (ECT) also promote neurogenesis.

All about Endorphins

The reference to exercise in the last section may have got you wondering about endorphins, those pain-killing chemicals your body produces. Athletes are familiar with endorphins, which are released during periods of strenuous physical activity. Some athletes will tell you that the endorphin rush is almost an addiction.

Finding Those Elusive Endorphins

Medical diagnostic procedures have advanced rapidly in recent years. No longer restricted by clumsy X-ray machines, scientists can opt from a wide variety of new technologies. One of these new technologies is Positron Emission Tomography (PET), an imaging technique that can scan the human body at the cellular level.

Using PET, researchers at the University of Michigan Medical School discovered that the brains of people with severe depression had lower levels of several related molecules that are key to the development, organization, growth, and repair of the brain than did the brains of people without the disease, or those with the bipolar form of depression. Their findings add endorphins to the list of brain systems that appear to be altered in depression.

The Simple Version

In plain English, endorphins are released during periods of extreme physical exercise in order to block pain. Eating chocolate also releases endorphins and is not so hard on your joints. However, to return to the basic idea: Normally, the neurotransmitters would send the pain signal out, and you would feel the pain and stop the activity that was causing it. The endorphins that are released block this signal and so you can continue on and win the marathon or hit the grand slam home run to clinch the World Series. This blocking property is the basis of certain drugs, which you'll read about later. For now, understand that endorphin release varies among individuals, and scientists are continuing their work in this area to understand the role of endorphins in depression. If they can regulate endorphin production, they may be able to get a better handle on treating depression with the body's own tools.

Chapter 4

Depression's Many Faces

THE AMERICAN PSYCHIATRIC ASSOCIATION (APA) refers to disorders that have a disturbance in mood as their predominant feature as mood disorders. Depression is a mood disorder, which can be broken down into the following specific disorders: major depressive disorder, dysthymic disorder, bipolar disorder, cyclothymic disorder (a type of bipolar disorder), seasonal affective disorder (SAD), postpartum depression, mood disorder due to a general medical condition, and substance-induced mood disorders. In this chapter, you'll learn about different types of mood disorders, along with diagnosis and treatment options for each.

Major Depression

Major depression is a serious disorder. It is also known as major depressive disorder or unipolar depression. The National Institute of Mental Health (NIMH) estimates that major depression affects approximately 10 percent of the population, with 20 to 25 percent of the population experiencing at least one episode of major depression during our lives. Symptoms of major depression include the following:

- Anger
- Trouble sleeping or sleeping too much
- Noticeable changes in appetite
- Fatigue and lack of energy

- Feelings of worthlessness, self-hate, and guilt
- Extreme difficulty concentrating
- Agitation, restlessness, and irritability
- Taking no interest or pleasure in what were previously enjoyable activities—including sex
- Feelings of hopelessness and helplessness
- Thoughts of death or suicide

There is an increased risk of alcoholism and drug abuse associated with major depression, and it has been estimated that up to 15 percent of people with major depressive disorder die by suicide. It's serious business and deserves serious attention.

Causes

There is no one, single cause for major depression. Instead, a mix of genetics and psychological and environmental factors seem to be responsible. Depression may also occur spontaneously, that is, without obvious, identifiable triggers such as a stressful life event or physical illness. In any case, the National Alliance for the Mentally Ill (NAMI) considers major depression to be a biological, medical illness.

Diagnosis and Treatment

A diagnosis of major depressive disorder is made based upon your symptoms. The key symptoms are having a depressed mood for at least two weeks, and experiencing anhedonia, a loss of pleasure in all those activities you used to enjoy. If these describe how you're feeling, tell your physician so she can make the proper diagnosis.

NAMI estimates that between 80 and 90 percent of those who have been diagnosed with major depression can be successfully treated and restored to normal life activities. Depending upon the severity of symptoms, treatment may include a combination of antidepressants, psychotherapy, and lifestyle changes. Also, electroconvulsive therapy (ECT) is another treatment option.

 Question

What is psychotherapy?
Psychotherapy is a form of treatment, in which a licensed psychiatrist, psychologist, or counselor works with a patient to help resolve mental and emotional issues that interfere with daily living. It is sometimes called talk therapy. The patient and the psychotherapist talk about the problems and consider logical strategies for dealing or coping with them.

Dysthymia

The word dysthymia is of Greek origin and means bad mood or ill humor. Dysthymia is considered to be a chronic form of depression. Also known as neurotic depression, dysthymic disorder, and chronic depression, dysthymia is characterized by moods that are consistently low. The National Institute of Mental Health (NIMH) reports that dysthymia occurs more frequently in women than in men and affects up to 5 percent of the general population. It may occur alone or with more severe depression.

If you suffer from dysthymia, you'll continue to function in everyday life, but you're miserable doing it. More than half of those with dysthymia eventually have an episode of major depression, and about half of patients treated for major depression have this double depression. Many patients who recover partially from major depression may continue to have milder symptoms that persist for years. This type of chronic depression is difficult to distinguish from dysthymia. Symptoms of dysthymia include the following:

- Sad mood lasting two years or longer
- Changes in eating habits
- Chronic fatigue
- Low self-esteem
- Sleeping problems
- Lack of concentration

- Feelings of hopelessness, guilt, or worthlessness
- Thoughts of suicide

Causes

There may be a genetic predisposition to dysthymia. Researchers are studying neurochemical imbalances in the brain, along with other factors of childhood and adult stress and trauma. Studies show that dysthymia usually has a gradual onset and those individuals who are socially isolated or who lack strong support groups may be especially vulnerable to this disorder. This makes the elderly a population of concern for dysthymia.

Diagnosis and Treatment Options

Dysthymia is diagnosed symptomatically, but is probably not detected as often as it occurs. Some people report a vague list of physical symptoms, which may or may not trigger the correct diagnosis. Also, some people just learn to live with their symptoms, never seeking help.

 Fact

Nearly half those with dysthymia have a symptom that also occurs in major depression, shortened REM latency. This means the rapid eye movement that indicates vivid dreams begins quite early in their sleep cycle. This means that less time is spent in the deeper, more restorative stages of sleep. Researchers are studying a possible connection between shortened REM latency and dysthymia.

Dysthymia is treated with psychotherapy and antidepressant medications. Results tend to vary. Some people experience a full recovery, while others continue to have symptoms. Recovery from dysthymia often takes a long time, and the symptoms often return. In these instances, maintenance therapy and medication may be indicated. The most common drug treatments are selective sero-tonin reuptake inhibitors (SSRIs): fluoxetine (Prozac) and sertraline (Zoloft), or one of the dual-action antidepressants, such as venlafax-ine (Effexor). Some patients may do better with a tricyclic antide-pressant, such as imipramine (Tofranil).

Talk therapies, such as cognitive behavioral therapy (CBT) and interpersonal therapy (IPT), have also been shown to be effective, and the combination of medication and psychotherapy may result in the most improvement.

L Essential

Remember that once you start medication, you shouldn't stop taking it abruptly. Certain drugs must be tapered off under the supervision of a doctor or bad reactions can occur. If you are having trouble with side effects, talk to your doctor. Sometimes taking your medication at a different time of day or just a minor dosage adjustment is all you need.

Bipolar Disorder

You may have heard this referred to as manic depression, an older term that refers to the symptoms of this condition. People with bipo-lar disorder experience an extreme arc of mood swings, ranging from incredible highs to almost unendurable lows, with periods of normal moods usually occurring in between. Sometimes the mood switches are dramatic and rapid, but most often they are gradual. Because the mania (highs) and depression (lows) interfere with normal daily liv-ing, bipolar disorder requires medical treatment for life and usually responds quite well to this.

Mental Health America (MHA) (formerly the National Mental Health Association) reports that over 5.5 million adults in the United States suffer from this disorder, which has a tendency to run in fami-lies. Symptoms of bipolar disorder usually begin in later adolescence or early adulthood. Once the symptoms have manifested themselves, it is important to seek treatment. Manic symptoms include the following:

- Increased energy, activity, and a sense of restlessness
- Euphoria
- Extreme irritability—even aggression
- Jumping from one idea to another, racing thoughts, rapid speech
- Inability to concentrate
- Little need for sleep
- Delusions of power and abilities (the Superman complex)
- Reckless behavior, impulsiveness
- Increased sex drive
- Recreational drug abuse—alcohol, cocaine, sleep medications
- Denial
- Hallucinations—in severe cases

A period of normal behaviors or moods typically occurs between the manic and depressive phases. Depressive symptoms include the following:

- Feelings of despair, hopelessness, anxiousness, extreme sadness
- Feelings of helplessness, inability to cope, worthlessness, pessimism
- Decreased energy, fatigue
- Loss of interest in previously enjoyed activities, including sex
- Difficulty focusing on issues, forgetfulness
- Restlessness, irritability
- Sleeping too little or too much
- Vague aches and pains without physical cause
- Thoughts of death, suicide, even attempts to commit suicide

Sometimes these symptoms of mania and depression occur together. When this happens, it is referred to as a mixed bipolar state.

Different Types of Bipolar Disorder

The *Diagnostic and Statistical Manual of Mental Disorders* (*DSM*), a publication of the American Psychiatric Association (APA), includes Bipolar I, Bipolar II, Cyclothymic, and Bipolar Disorder not otherwise specified within the category of Bipolar Disorders.

- **Bipolar I Disorder:** This is the classic form of bipolar disorder. It involves recurrent episodes of mania and depression.
- **Bipolar II Disorder:** In this form of the disorder, people experience milder episodes of the manic phase alternating with periods of depression. Hypomania is the term used to describe these less extreme manic symptoms.
- **Bipolar Disorder:** This category is for the forms of bipolar disorder that do not fit the criteria for Bipolar I, Bipolar II, and Cyclothymic Disorder.
- **Rapid-Cycling Bipolar Disorder:** When someone has four or more episodes of the disorder within a twelve-month period, the condition is referred to as rapid-cycling bipolar disorder. The National Institute of Mental Health reports that rapid cycling is more common in women than in men and tends to develop later in the course of the illness.
- **Cyclothymic Disorder:** Cyclothymic Disorder is considered to be a milder form of bipolar disorder and its symptoms are essentially the same, although milder in intensity and of shorter duration. Between 15 to 50 percent of people suffering from Cyclothymic Disorder may develop Bipolar Disorder.

Causes

Researchers have studied the occurrence of bipolar disorder in specific families and in studies involving twins. The evidence indicates there is a definite genetic component to this disorder. A 2002 University of Michigan study, "Evidence of Brain Chemistry Abnormalities in Bipolar Disorder," discusses the genetics of the relationship between neurotransmitters, such as serotonin, dopamine, and norepinephrine and bipolar disorder. Even if you are genetically programmed for bipolar disorder, however, whether or not you develop the condition may depend on stresses you encounter on the road to adulthood. Research in this area is ongoing.

Diagnosis and Treatment Options

A diagnosis of bipolar disorder is made by considering the symptoms and family history.

Bipolar disorder cannot be cured; however, it can usually be effectively treated and managed with a combination of medication and psychotherapy. Lithium has been used for many years with good results. Most people who have bipolar disorder take more than one medication. They may take lithium and/or an anticonvulsant, a medication for agitation, anxiety, depression, or insomnia. Carbamazepine (Tegretol), valproate (Depakote), lamotrigine (Lamictal), and gabapentin (Neurontin) are often prescribed.

If you have bipolar disorder, you must treat it for life. Mood changes can still occur, even if you are vigilant in taking your medications. In addition to medications, psychotherapy has proved helpful. In severe cases, electroconvulsive therapy (ECT) may be advised. Your psychiatrist may require you to keep a daily journal to help you take responsibility for managing the disease. With proper care, most who suffer from bipolar disorder can lead full and productive lives.

Seasonal Affective Disorder (SAD)

If you've ever felt dragged down by the weather, or if the dark days of winter cause your usually sunny disposition to go gloomy, you may have experienced seasonal affective disorder, appropriately referred to as SAD. This condition is also known as the winter blahs and The Alaska Effect, a term that relates to that northern state's long, sunless days of winter. This disorder has come into its own and been recognized for what it is—depression. There is also a kind of SAD that occurs in the summer, although this is rarer. Approximately half a million people in the United States are affected by SAD, and it appears to affect more women than men. Symptoms of SAD include the following:

- Food cravings—especially for sweet or starchy foods
- Weight gain
- A heavy feeling in the arms or legs
- No energy
- Fatigue
- Wanting to stay in bed and hide under the covers
- Difficulty concentrating
- Irritability and withdrawal from social situations

Symptoms of summer SAD, discussed in the next section, include poor appetite (and corresponding weight loss) and difficulty sleeping.

L. Essential

Modern office buildings that have few windows or closed-in workspaces—such as a cubicle—can create symptoms of SAD. Even in the summer, extended periods of cloudy weather can trigger an attack.

Summer SAD

There is another form of SAD that operates during the summertime. Summer SAD is almost a mirror image of SAD and may be triggered by the heat. Those cravings for carbs, sleepiness, and weight gain that characterize regular SAD turn into lack of appetite, insomnia, and weight loss in summer SAD. Preferring the shades drawn and air conditioning on, as well as waiting for autumn, are symptoms of summer SAD.

Summer SAD is most common in the southern latitudes. It affects about one percent of the population, with young adult women being the most susceptible. It hasn't received the attention that regular SAD has, but it may be caused by the affect of heat on certain hormones.

Causes

SAD has been linked to a biochemical imbalance in the brain prompted by shorter daylight hours and a lack of sunlight in winter. Melatonin, a sleep-related hormone, steps up production in the dark. It may have a connection to SAD. When the days are shorter and darker, more melatonin is produced. The more melatonin in your system, the sleepier and more tired you will be! Also, the farther from the equator you live, the greater the likelihood you will experience SAD.

Diagnosis and Treatment Options

If you believe you may have SAD, and the symptoms are interfering with daily living, consult your physician, who can make the proper diagnosis. Once you've determined that SAD is the culprit, let the light shine in! Increased exposure to sunlight can improve symptoms of SAD. If you can afford a trip to the Bahamas, this would definitely be in order! Light therapy—bright, white fluorescent light—frequently helps. The *American Medical Association Essential Guide to Depression* points out that although white fluorescent lights are used, they are about twenty times brighter than common household fluorescent lights. Some suggest that full-spectrum lights, which most closely imitate sunlight, are most helpful.

 Fact

A new light treatment is an artificial dawn simulator. This is an electrical device attached to a bedside lamp. It is set to come on automatically, several hours before awakening. The dawn simulator starts with a very dim light and gradually increases to simulate a sunrise.

There are also specific medications, dietary changes, and stress management therapies for SAD. Your doctor may suggest light therapy, either with a light visor, which you wear, or a light box, which you sit down and bask in! Behavior modification therapy can also help.

Postpartum Depression

Whether the pregnancy was planned or unplanned, eagerly embraced or grudgingly tolerated, two things are certain: Having a baby changes your life and motherhood is forever.

For the first week or two after delivery, your moods may swing from joy to sadness, and the tears may flow. You may feel angry at your spouse or partner, your other children, and even at the baby.

These are called the Baby Blues. When the symptoms persist beyond this two-week window, however, you're probably dealing with postpartum depression, a condition that affects about 10 percent of new mothers, according to the National Women's Health Information Center (NWHIC). You may cry, even though you think you should feel happy. It doesn't matter. The tears keep coming. You may feel you have lost, rather than gained—lost your figure, your identity, and your independence. Other symptoms include the following:

- Loss of interest or pleasure in life
- Loss of appetite
- Less energy and motivation
- Sleep difficulties
- Feeling worthless, hopeless, or guilty
- Feeling restless, irritable, or anxious
- Losing or gaining weight
- Feeling like life isn't worth living
- Having thoughts about hurting yourself
- Worrying about hurting your baby

Causes

Changes in hormone levels (estrogen and progesterone) are probably responsible for postpartum depression. Within twenty-four hours of delivery, these hormones drop back to normal non-pregnancy levels, leaving your body to adjust to yet another dramatic change. Also, sleep seems a distant dream now, as baby controls everything you do. If you want to be the perfect mom, that added stress only piles more pressure on your tired mind and body.

If you've experienced postpartum depression after a previous delivery, you're more likely to have it again. Other factors predisposing you to postpartum depression include other forms of depression unrelated to the pregnancy, a history of severe premenstrual syndrome (PMS), and a difficult or unsupportive family situation.

Diagnosis and Treatment Options

Your obstetrician/gynecologist or physician will likely diagnose postpartum depression based upon your symptoms. It's important to seek treatment both for yourself and for the baby. The time after birth is important for infant emotional development, and a mother who is experiencing emotional stress cannot provide her child with all that's necessary at this critical time.

Taking Action Against Postpartum Depression

Talk with your doctor about how you feel. He may offer counseling and/or medicines that can help. If you are breastfeeding, your baby will be exposed to whatever medications you are taking, and you need to discuss this with your doctor. Sometimes, just finding someone to talk to can help immensely. Let people help you. You don't have to do everything yourself. The old advice to "Sleep when the baby sleeps" is good advice. Don't use this time to clean house. Rest. Here are some other good tips:

- Keep a journal. This time will never come again. Writing can be good therapy.

- Find the time to take a short walk every day. Just getting outside and moving will do wonders for you.
- If the weather is inclement, take the time to pamper yourself for at least fifteen minutes every day. Soak in the tub, read a magazine, do something for you.
- Find a new moms' group in your area or go online and find one. Sharing your experiences with others who are also going through them can help immensely.
- Avoid making unnecessary major decisions. This merely compounds the stress.
- Realize that, "This too, shall pass." As your body adjusts and your routines fall into place, you will soon feel better. It helps to understand that you are not alone, and what you are feeling has been felt by millions of women.

Other Sources of Depression

Other physical and mental conditions may predispose you to developing depression, and so can the medications used to treat them, along with some other over-the-counter drugs and substances used for self-medicating.

Mood Disorder Due to a General Medical Condition

If you are coping with a serious or chronic physical illness, such as cardiovascular disease, cancer, or Parkinson's disease, you may find yourself also weighed down by the symptoms of depression. Depression may also be an early symptom of an impending medical illness. You'll read more about these topics later in the book.

Untreated depression may prolong the course of your other illness, negatively impact the quality of your life while you are trying to recuperate, and deplete your energy. If your other illness is serious or chronic, there is another potential risk that depression can bring to the table—suicide. Discuss how you are feeling with your physician and get relief from your depressive symptoms.

Substance-Induced Mood Disorders

The *Diagnostic and Statistical Manual of Mental Disorders* (*DSM*) notes that depression may be caused or precipitated by the use or abuse of substances such as drugs, alcohol, medications, or exposure to toxins. That's quite an extensive list of items that offers depression as a nasty side effect. It's also a side effect you want to avoid.

CHAPTER 5

Who Gets Depression?

PHYSICAL OR MENTAL ILLNESS can strike any of us at any time, and depression is one of the most common forms of mental illness, affecting both men and women, both young and old. Certain risk factors may predispose one to developing depression, but depression does not play favorites. It cuts a wide swath across the American population. In this chapter, we'll take a look at depression and how it affects different groups—from children to the elderly.

A Few Statistics

We already know that depression can happen to anyone, regardless of race, age, gender, and other factors. But there are some statistics that can provide an idea of how common certain depressive disorders are and who is most commonly affected. According to the Depression and Bipolar Support Alliance's depression fact sheet:

- Major depressive disorder affects approximately 14.8 million American adults in any given year.
- Major depressive disorder may develop at any age, but the median age for onset is thirty-two.
- Women are twice as likely to experience depression as men.
- As many as one in thirty-three children and one in eight adolescents have clinical depression.
- People with depression are four times as likely to develop a heart attack than those without a history of the illness. After

a heart attack, those with depression are at a significantly increased risk of death or second heart attack.

- Six million older Americans suffer from depression, but only 10 percent of them will receive treatment.
- Fifty-eight percent of caregivers for an elderly relative experience symptoms of depression.

Now that you have these basic figures in mind, read on through the rest of the chapter to learn how depression affects specific populations.

Children

No two children act the same, and that is what makes childhood such an adventure for both parents and children. Parents and grandparents keep careful note of these developmental milestones and proudly share them with anyone who'll listen! The other milestones, however, those irritating and annoying phases that children go through, sometimes aren't phases at all, but signs of a depressive disorder. How's a parent to know the difference?

Children can suffer from many of the same depressive disorders as adults. Many conditions, including major depression and bipolar disorder, tend to run in families. Mood swings in children with bipolar disorder tend to be more rapid than in adults. Children in the manic phase tend to be irritable and throw temper tantrums rather than experiencing extreme happiness. So, it can be extremely difficult to diagnose depression in children, but generally, behavioral changes offer some clues. Symptoms of depression in children can cover a wide range of territory:

- Marked changes in behavior
- Listlessness, lack of energy
- Bouts of crying that seem endless
- Neglecting school work or hobbies
- Temper tantrums, yelling, shouting

- Withdrawal from friends
- Marked changes in eating habits
- Feeling that nobody likes him or her
- Complaints of headaches or stomach aches or other aches, in order to avoid school or other social situations
- Hyperactivity
- Sleep problems
- Clinging

Diagnosis and Treatment Options

The key to detecting depression in children is change. If you notice changes in your child's behavior, and if those changes continue or worsen, it's important to contact your child's pediatrician to first rule out an underlying physical cause.

It is not normal for a child to have recurrent thoughts of death or suicide. Always take seriously a child's comments about such things and act quickly to get help. Once you have consulted your pediatrician or general practitioner, he may then refer you to a social worker, child psychologist, or child psychiatrist.

Essential

It's always frightening for a parent when a child experiences illness, and mental illness is doubly scary. Your first tendency is to think that somehow you've failed, done something wrong, or been bad parents. Think of depression as you would any other medical condition. Some families have a tendency toward high blood pressure or diabetes. Depression is no different. It's just another illness—and, it's treatable.

Childhood depression usually responds well to proper treatment. Children with bipolar disorder are generally treated with lithium, valproate, or carbamazepine. Other medications may also be prescribed. If the depression has developed as the result of a trauma or abuse, children may benefit from play therapy. In play therapy, your child has the opportunity to work out difficult feelings through role-play, arts and crafts, or other expressive means, while in a safe environment. Your child will attend sessions on a regular basis, perhaps weekly, for a period of time. Play therapy will help your child build confidence and better peer and family relationships. In addition, the family as a whole can also benefit from counseling, to help them through this difficult time.

As a parent, you have a right to ask questions and be informed about every step of your child's treatment, and you should do so. The stakes here are too high not to be included in the information loop. If you don't understand something, ask to have it explained in language you can understand. Be persistent until you are comfortable that you know everything that's going on and what to expect. You and your health care professionals are a team, working together, to help your child.

Adolescents

Adolescence is a time of emotional upheaval. Hormones run wild, and with the onset of puberty, childhood is left behind forever. It's nearly impossible to create a definition of normal in adolescence, for every emotion is exaggerated, every slight—imagined or real—is fodder for drama, and the sexual drive is struggling for control over social constraints. It's a difficult stage of life. It's also no wonder that depression can become a serious problem at this time. Many depressive conditions begin to evidence themselves during adolescence, including bipolar disorder and major depressive syndrome.

Is This Normal?

How to tell what is normal and what is not requires well-developed parental powers of observation. Since adolescents tend to avoid parents and demand their privacy at all costs, it can be difficult to determine what's going on in your teenager's mind. Again, look for marked changes in what's been passing for normal.

Many, if not most, teens adopt a form of dress that visually distances themselves from their parents' preferences. Hair also seems to be the vehicle of choice for expressing this emerging independence. Whether hair is dyed, shaved, grown long, or styled into dreadlocks, the new style can almost be counted on to send your blood pressure skyrocketing—and that is the intent. However, some aberrations are not part of the normal passage into adulthood. Self-mutilation should send those warning signal flares high into the sky. Branding and cutting are visible indicators that your child needs help dealing with some serious issues.

 Alert

Self-injury is not suicidal behavior—that's the good news. It is, however, a warning sign of depression. Burning the skin with cigarettes or other hot objects results in scarring. This is called branding. In cutting, the skin is sliced with a razor blade, knife, or any sharp object. Long sleeves cover the marks. Shame and guilt follow, but it is a mechanism of release and can be a form of self-medicating in adolescents.

Teachers and school counselors can be good sources of information on how your child is faring at school. Depressed teens tend to let schoolwork slide. Nothing seems to be worth the effort it takes, and that includes sports or other hobbies or activities the teen previously enjoyed.

So, what should you watch for? A teen who now sleeps much more than she did previously or who eats a great deal less or a great deal more than had been the habit—these changes should send out danger signals to the watchful parent. Listlessness, lethargy, or extreme agitation and activity are also clues worth following up.

Ruling Out Other Possibilities

Bipolar disorder in adolescents can be hard to tell apart from other problems that may occur in this age group. Drug and alcohol abuse can produce symptoms similar to bipolar depression in teens. Also, prescription medications may have adverse side effects. Reading the warnings for any prescription drug is enough to make even the most even-tempered parent frantic. Most of the side effects never occur, but if one of them describes what you are witnessing, call your pharmacist and physician to discuss the situation.

 Fact

People with binge-eating disorder frequently eat large amounts of food and experience loss of control over their eating. This disorder is different from binge-purge syndrome (bulimia nervosa) because people with binge eating disorder usually do not purge afterward by vomiting or using laxatives.

Eating disorders, such as bulimia and anorexia, can result in marked changes in eating patterns. These disorders are most frequently found in females. In anorexia, a person just picks at food, rearranging it on the plate to make it appear most of it's been eaten, or finds excuses to avoid meals or take them in her room. These meals are often flushed down the toilet. Also, skipping meals and claiming, "I'll pick something up on the way to school," when accompanied by noticeable weight loss, is common in anorexics. In bulimia, the person eats normally, then induces vomiting to purge the stomach contents. Be suspicious if your teen finds excuses to consistently avoid eating meals with family.

Also, attention deficit-hyperactivity disorder (ADHD), which includes ADHD, inattentive type; ADHD, hyperactive type; or ADHD, combined type, will manifest as inability to focus, difficulty following directions, increased (or decreased) activity, aggression, or irritability. These can also be symptoms of bipolar disorder.

Above all, trust your instincts as a parent. They served you well as your child grew from infancy to nearly adulthood. If you sense something is wrong, you are probably right.

Diagnosis and Treatment Options

Adolescents do not respond to antidepressants in the same way as do adults. The use of antidepressants is generally not recommended for this age group. While taking antidepressants, adolescents may experience suicidal thoughts, and the risk of attempted suicide, or actual suicide, is too great.

Adolescents with bipolar disorder generally are treated with lithium, but valproate and carbamazepine are also used. In a study titled "Trends in the Use of Psychotropic Medications among Adolescents, 1999–2004" that appeared in the January 2006 issue of *Journal of Psychiatric Services*, researchers found the trend toward increased prescribing of psychotropic drugs for adolescents to be an area of concern, requiring further study. The researchers questioned whether rapid increases in the prescription of psychotropic medications to youths aged fourteen to eighteen years represented a move toward greater access and more appropriate treatment or whether this represented an overreliance on medications. This issue has broader ramifications. Our society is increasingly turning to medications, rather than to lifestyle changes, to deal with medical concerns. Often, in the rush to get the quick fix, the long-term dangers or side effects and drug dependency are overlooked.

 Question

What's a psychotropic drug?
Psychotropic drugs are a class of medications that effect changes in behaviors, moods, and perceptions. Antidepressants, antipsychotics, mood stabilizers, and anti-anxiety drugs are included in this category.

When medications are indicated, however, they can provide good relief from symptoms of depression. In addition to medications that may be prescribed for your teen, group therapy, individual counseling, and family counseling are helpful in dealing with teen depression.

Women

Women suffer from depression at twice the rate as men. The National Institute of Mental Health (NIMH) reports that this ratio holds true across racial, ethnic, and socioeconomic boundaries. Depression by itself can be incapacitating, but depression can also occur along with medical conditions or can lead to other conditions. Research reported by NIMH has found that depression may increase a woman's risk for broken bones. Mineral density in the hip is 10 to 15 percent lower in women with severe depression than normal for their age. This figure is significant—it translates into a 40-percent greater risk for hip fracture over a ten-year period.

About Those Hormones

Hormones undoubtedly play a role. Beginning with puberty, a woman's body is concerned with reproduction. The onset of menstruation, called menarche, begins around age twelve. The age varies, and some girls do not begin menstrual periods before they're sixteen.

Each month, during the menstrual cycle, estrogen and progesterone levels fluctuate, causing mood swings that can range from mild to severe. For a woman's entire reproductive life, these hormones will play a significant role in her emotional health. When a woman becomes pregnant, hormones again take center stage. (See Chapter 4 for a discussion of postpartum depression.)

It wasn't all that long ago that women who reported symptoms of pain or nausea and other discomforts were told, "It's all in your head." Most women knew differently, but there was no one to listen and so many bore their suffering in a climate of enforced silence.

In some cases, depression resulted. Science has since enlightened the medical profession, and it is now official: Hormonal changes can affect both your physical and mental well-being.

Going Through the Change

Commencing around the age of forty, a woman enters perimenopause, the time before menopause. Once again, hormones run rampant over a woman's psyche. The average woman reaches menopause in her early fifties and can then look forward to bypassing the feminine products aisle in the grocery store.

Essential

During perimenopause, hormone production (estrogen and progesterone) begins to slack off. Your ability to become pregnant also decreases, and you may begin to experience some of the effects of menopause, such as insomnia, hot flashes, and mood fluctuations. Perimenopause can last a few months or several years. These reduced and fluctuating hormone levels can trigger depression.

Beyond hormones, women have the added stress of caring for home, children, and eventually, parents. Technology has both helped and compounded the problem. Women can now do more with less time—and they do. Fatigue sets in, and depression can follow. You need to take the time to take care of yourself. This is not a luxury—it's a necessity. Recognizing depression's symptoms early on and seeking help is something you owe yourself and your family.

Men

Although it's true that men are less likely to suffer from depression than women, it's difficult to know how many men do suffer from depression, as they frequently do not seek help. Approximately 6 million men in the United States are affected by the illness. According to NIMH, researchers have found than men experience depression differently from women and use different means to cope; for example, women may experience feelings of hopelessness, while men may feel irritable. Women may crave a listening ear, while men may withdraw socially or become violent or abusive.

Recognizing the Symptoms

Men who suffer from major depression may not talk about it—even to those closest to them. Men are less likely to admit to depression, and doctors are less likely to suspect it. At least that has been the traditional thinking. As a result, adult males are more likely to self-medicate with alcohol, tobacco, and other drugs—such as cocaine—to alleviate the symptoms of depression.

Signs of depression in men are more often masked as irritability, discouragement, anger, or drug and alcohol abuse. If estrogen and progesterone influence female behavior, testosterone is equally influential in the male. Behavior may become violent and may result in striking out at loved ones or, in the worst-case scenario, at oneself. While more women attempt suicide than men, more men are successful. In extreme cases, pent-up aggression may ultimately result in acts of homicide.

The Role of Stress

Stress plays a significant role in exacerbating physical conditions. With depression, there can be an increased incidence of heart disease and a corresponding rise in fatal heart attacks. While a man may seek treatment for the physical condition, he is unlikely to tell the doctor about his depression. This compartmentalizing can prove fatal.

Breaking through the societal barrier of stoicism is difficult. Even if a man suspects he is depressed, it's more likely that he will self-medicate—increasing consumption of alcohol, tobacco, or recreational drugs. He may exhibit risk-taking behaviors, spend less time at home with family, and spend more time working. The most difficult part of dealing with depression in men is convincing them to seek help.

The GLBT population

Using 2000 U.S. Census data, Harris Interactive Research estimated that 6.8 percent of Americans over the age of eighteen self-identify as gay, lesbian, or bisexual. If this is your demographic, you know that being gay, lesbian, bisexual, or transgender (GLBT) doesn't cause depression. It's the dominant culture and larger society's view and treatment of homosexuality, bisexuality, and transgendered people that causes problems, and those in the GLBT population can suffer from depression to a greater extent than other demographic sectors.

In 2001, the Gay and Lesbian Medical Association (GLMA), in conjunction with the National Coalition for LGBT Health, released Healthy People 2010. They found that, "Many LGBT youth experience feelings of self-hatred, depression, and anxiety as a result of being raised in a society that is condemning and rejecting of mores different from the majority."

Essential

In reparative therapy, a person is immersed in a treatment program designed to reverse a specific course of behavior. GLBT teens are inundated with messages designed to convince them that they really want to be straight and can change if they just put their minds to it.

The Wrong Stuff

Beginning in adolescence, GLBT teens are confronted with a confusing barrage of messages and too few positive GLBT role models. Teens, as a rule, have a difficult time establishing and growing into their identities, regardless of sexual orientation. When your identity, who you are at your core, is something society fears, ridicules, persecutes, or at best merely tolerates, the task of growing into healthy adulthood is made all the more difficult. Since the school culture reflects society at large, GLBT teens may experience harassment and beatings. The sense of being different is reinforced at every turn.

Even family may not accept you, and physical and verbal abuse may occur when one comes out or is even suspected of being GLBT.

There have been cases in which teens have been subjected to conversion therapy or reparative therapy by their families in an attempt to change their orientation to heterosexual.

An Historical Turning Point

It wasn't until 1973 that the American Psychological Association (APA) finally reversed its longstanding position and declared, "The research on homosexuality is very clear. Homosexuality is neither mental illness nor moral depravity. It is simply the way a minority of our population expresses human love and sexuality. Studies of judgment, stability, reliability, and social and vocational adaptiveness all show that gay men and lesbians function every bit as well as heterosexuals."

Depression and HIV/AIDS

With advances in treatment for HIV/AIDS, many more patients are living with these conditions, as opposed to dying from them. Not only the medications, but also the stigma associated with these conditions, may result in symptoms of depression. It is important to be treated for this depression to improve life quality.

Older Members of the GLBT Community

Chronic depression in the elderly may come from many causes. Repressing and denying one's sexuality may ultimately result in depression. If you are a senior citizen, you grew up in difficult times, when your homosexuality was considered a form of mental illness. You may have kept your sexual orientation a secret, perhaps even from yourself. To come out might have been unthinkable. Possibly even your church condemned you, and a lifetime of conflict takes its toll.

Even today, you may not consider this something to share with a physician. However, it's important that your doctor or nurse practitioner be aware of everything that may affect your health. If you're suffering from depression, the roots may go deep.

Tech Support

Technology can play a significant role in providing support for GLBT teens and adults. Resources, including gay-friendly medical services, counseling for college, career, and life issues, and opportunities for networking, are available online. Still, on an individual, case by case basis, depression affects a disproportionately high percentage of GLBT individuals.

The Elderly

Reaching an advanced age means you may have outlived many of your friends and relatives, and perhaps even lost a spouse or long-time companion. Loneliness and grief may at times be overwhelming, but there is a difference between grief and depression. In grief, you mourn your loss but keep your sense of self-esteem or self-worth. In depression, you don't.

As you age, new worries occupy your mind. You may find yourself worrying about losing your independence or mobility and may have serious concerns about how this may affect your quality of life. If you have taken pride in living life on your own terms, this adjustment is not an easy one, and such fundamental changes in life circumstances may trigger the onset of depression.

Diagnosis and Treatment

You'll frequently hear people say that most of the elderly are depressed. This simply isn't true. If you've been happy-go-lucky and well-adjusted your whole life, you'll tend to remain so, as you age. If you were an irritable child, adolescent, and adult, you'll probably become an irritable older person, as well. Your personality—the way you look at and react to life—will tend to remain fairly constant throughout your life.

Certain conditions are often associated with certain age groups. Alzheimer's disease, previously referred to as senility, tends to be the province of the elderly. While this may be the case, it doesn't necessarily have to be. What may appear to be Alzheimer's or some other form of dementia may be something else entirely. Prescription drug interactions may mimic many of the symptoms of Alzheimer's, and so can depression. Since other medical conditions often co-exist with depression, it may be extremely difficult to diagnose depression in the elderly and is often not considered.

When depression develops, it needs to be treated. Diagnosing depression in the elderly requires careful attention to symptoms. As the body ages, the physical symptoms of aging may overshadow the real problem—depression. In some older men, low testosterone levels may play a role in depression. Often, the form of depression that affects the elderly is dysthymia (chronic depression). Treating that depression can lead to renewed interest in life.

Special Considerations for Caring for the Elderly

While many older folks get out and about—keeping mentally and physically active with travel, volunteer work, or other community activities—others with decreased mobility have fewer options. Our society is based on mobility. Relocating—changing jobs and homes frequently—has become the norm. As a consequence of that mobility, the important personal, day-to-day connection that alerted you to changes in your relatives' physical and mental health has been lost. This means that it may be some time before you realize to what extent they may have experienced severe decline.

If you can't be there in person, however, you can be there virtually. Technology can help you to keep in touch. The Pew Internet & American Life Project reports that while 56 percent of all Americans go online regularly, only 15 percent of those sixty-five and older do so. If you are looking for a way to help your older relatives stave off depression, see about getting them connected to the Internet and helping them learn how to go online, send and receive e-mail, and join groups that are of interest to them. Developing online friendships with peers, corresponding with family and friends, and sharing information with other elders, are just some of the ways the Internet can enhance the quality of life for older folks.

CHAPTER 6

What Intensifies Depression?

DEPRESSION IS INSIDIOUS ENOUGH, but unfortunately, some conditions, habits, and influences can make it even worse. Some of these you have control over, and some you don't. In this chapter you'll read about some depression intensifiers—such as alcohol and stress—and learn some strategies to keep them from adding to your discomfort.

Alcohol Use and Abuse

There's a long and strong relationship between alcohol and depression, and the relationship is not a good one. Whether you drink to relieve the symptoms of depression or alcohol triggers symptoms of depression, it's a downer.

Alcohol impairs judgment. When you are under the influence, you may do things and say things that you never would when sober. That's why drinking and driving make such a deadly combination. You may find yourself taking foolish chances and risking your own safety, as well as the safety of others. Some people become more aggressive, and some lose their inhibitions. Severe depression, thoughts of suicide, and alcohol make a deadly cocktail. Before you have a chance to sober up, it may be too late.

The Genetic Factor

Researchers are investigating whether the predisposition to either alcoholism or depression is inherited or something metabolic that causes certain individuals to have either a high tolerance for alcohol

63

or extreme vulnerability to alcohol's effects. There may be something heritable that causes alcohol to affect one person's brain chemistry differently from someone else's. Researchers do know that if depression or alcoholism exists in your family tree, you've got a greater chance of developing either or both than does someone who doesn't have this risk factor. According to Netdoctor.co.uk, 30 to 50 percent of alcoholics, at any given time, are also suffering from major depression.

Association is not causation, but the link between alcohol and depression is too strong to be ignored. If you have a family history of either depression or alcoholism, be aware of your risk factors for developing either or both conditions and be watchful for symptoms that may indicate you are developing either condition—or both.

 ## Fact

When two conditions or diseases occur at the same time in the same individual, they are said to be comorbid. The word derives from the Latin co-, meaning together, and morbus, meaning diseased.

Whichever comes first, alcoholism or depression, they're a deadly combination, and you can be certain that other problems will follow on their heels. While depression wreaks havoc with your sense of well-being, alcohol wreaks havoc with your body. Liver problems, such as cirrhosis and hepatitis, are common in alcoholics. In addition, there is risk of stomach ulcers, anemia, irregular heartbeat, and impotence. In this case, you've got depression, plus alcohol dependency, plus another condition brought on by the alcohol. Not good.

Self-Medicating

Using alcohol to cope with a medical condition is referred to as self-medicating, and bipolar disorder and alcohol dependency often occur in tandem. Alcohol is readily available, it's cheap, and it's legal. Drinking to ease the symptoms of depression or to help you fall asleep may seem logical, but your sleep will not be restful, and you haven't treated the cause of your depression. After a while, your tolerance to alcohol will increase, and you'll need more and more alcohol to achieve the same numbing effect. That's not a good prescription for a cure.

 ## Fact

> When doctors use the term "dual diagnosis," they are referring to a mental health condition and a substance abuse problem occurring together.

Medication and Therapy Options

Antidepressants and psychotherapy cost money. Even if you have good insurance coverage, there are usually a deductible and co-pays to meet. If your job status is on shaky ground, or if you have lost your job because of alcohol dependency, your finances aren't going to be in good shape for very long. In addition, if you have a family to support, marital problems are added to your laundry list of troubles. There will never be a better time to tackle the source of the problem than right now.

Antidepressants are powerful drugs—and so is alcohol. If you read the warning stickers attached to your prescription container, you will probably see some specific cautions against consuming alcohol and driving. What these warnings don't tell you is why these activities are potentially dangerous. Some antidepressants can produce a sedating effect, and some antidepressants are affected by alcohol. Combining these antidepressants with alcohol may over-sedate you to the point of endangering your life. And then there's your liver. The University of Maryland Medical Center (UMMC) explains that some antidepressants are broken down in the liver. Since alcohol abuse can damage your liver, it won't be operating optimally, and you'll have higher concentrations of the antidepressants in your body than your prescribed dose. This puts you at increased risk for side effects.

Warning Signs of Alcoholism

There is no medical test to determine if your consumption of alcohol is excessive. The only way to determine this is to take an honest look at your drinking patterns and assess your alcohol consumption habits. There are many assessments available, but they all cover the same territory. Here is one list. You should probably consider getting help if any of the following are true for you:

- You use alcohol to boost your confidence.
- You drink alone.
- You resent people commenting on your drinking.
- Your drinking has begun to affect your personal relationships or your job.
- Hangovers are now a regular part of your mornings.
- You have no control over how much you drink.
- You have a drink before going to a social function where alcohol will be served.
- You will neglect important matters in order to have a drink.
- You've built up a tolerance, so you must drink more to feel good.
- You've begun drinking in the morning to stop feeling anxious and shaky.

If you've answered yes to any of these statements, it's time to take control of your drinking and your life. In doing so, you'll also be taking steps to help deal with depression.

Teens, Alcohol, and Depression

Depression can set the stage for alcohol abuse among teens. The 2005 National Survey on Drug Use and Health found that young people who have a major depressive episode of two weeks or longer are twice as likely to take their first drink as those who are not depressed. Drinking is not legal for teens in any case, but if you find that your child has begun using alcohol, it's time to take a look at the bigger picture. Alcohol abuse is a symptom you can recognize.

Getting Help

If you've decided that it's time to help your depression by treating your alcohol dependency, good for you. This is a big step, but it's one that will get you back on the road to feeling better and back in control of your life. When depression and alcoholism exist together, your doctor will usually treat the alcoholism first. Often, when the alcoholism is treated, the symptoms of depression subside. Your doctor may prescribe medication to help you over the initial detox period. Remember, though, that ultimately your success is up to you. Alcohol dependency, like depression, cannot be cured. It can, like depression, be treated and managed successfully, and organizations such as Alcoholics Anonymous (AA) are living proof of that success. You'll find their number in your local telephone directory and meetings are advertised in local papers.

Recreational Drug Use

Whether used in social situations or as part of religious ceremonies, people have been using mind-altering substances for as long as there have been people. Alcohol and tobacco remain the drugs of choice for the majority of the population, but they aren't the only drugs on the market. Some of these drugs, such as heroin and cocaine, have been around for a very long time, while others—the "designer drugs"—are relative newcomers.

Marijuana

Marijuana (*Cannabis sativa*) is the most commonly abused illegal drug in the United States, according to the National Institute on Drug Abuse (NIDA). More than a drug, marijuana is a cultural icon of the countercultural and alternative lifestyle. Apart from its association with the peace and love movement, marijuana has properties that make it a plant of interest for the scientific research community, both for its possible benefits as well as its adverse effects on health.

On the positive side, when used as prescribed by a doctor, THC—the abbreviation for delta-9-tetrahydrocannabinol—has been found to be effective for treating nausea and vomiting associated with chemotherapy. Dronabinol (Marinol) is the pharmaceutically manufactured version of THC.

On the negative side, long-term use of marijuana leads to changes in dopamine production, similar to that of other illegal drugs. It's also been implicated in the onset of depressive symptoms. The *Harvard Medical School Family Health Guide* reported on an Australian study that found that young women who had used marijuana weekly as teenagers were twice as likely to have depression as young adults than those who didn't use marijuana. Daily use of marijuana was associated with four times the risk of depression.

Heroin

Heroin use is on the rise, with an estimated 750,000 current heroin users in the United States. Heroin is processed from morphine, and, just as with alcohol, regular heroin use builds up tolerance to the drug, so that higher doses are required to achieve the same high. The effects of the drug harm the body, and withdrawal symptoms can lead to extreme depression and suicidal behavior.

Cocaine

Heavy cocaine use has remained fairly steady since its peak in the late 1980s and early 1990s, with an estimated 600,000 to 700,000 regular users. A University of Michigan study that appeared in the January 2001 issue of the *American Journal of Psychiatry* found that cocaine harms dopamine neurotransmitters—specific brain cells associated with the brain's "pleasure center." Using cocaine can disrupt the dopamine cycle and lead to severe depression.

Ecstasy

Ecstasy is an amphetamine-based drug, originally used in the 1970s to treat depression. It affects the neurotransmitter serotonin. Today it's a party drug used primarily by young adults to allow them to party all night long (rave). The United Nations estimates that its use has risen 70 percent between 1995 and 2000. Ecstasy may not cause depression, but has been implicated in intensifying depression's symptoms. Dutch researchers began a longitudinal study in 1983 in which they followed a group of children who suffered from depression. Results indicated that children who suffered from depression were more likely to use Ecstasy as adults. The implication is that Ecstasy capitalizes on pre-existing risk factors.

Crystal Meth

Crystal Meth, also known as ice, crystal, glass, jib, speed, and tina, is produced in makeshift labs in garages, basements, and even travel trailers throughout the country. It's a cocktail of ingredients including pseudoephedrine and paint thinner. Meth releases high levels of dopamine, is highly addictive, and can cause severe depression.

How This Relates to Depression

Here's the bottom line: Neurotransmitters are affected by different drugs:

- Dopamine is affected by cocaine, amphetamines, and ecstasy.
- Serotonin is affected by ecstasy and LSD.
- Noradrenaline (Norepinephrine) is affected by amphetamines and the opiates, such as heroin and morphine.

Many people use more than one recreational drug, and sometimes they use more than one drug at the same time. Understanding that these drugs do not get along well together is an important first step on the road to realizing that they don't mix with depression at all. Frequently, if you discontinue your use of these drugs, you will find that the symptoms of depression are greatly relieved. If you are currently using recreational drugs and want to get out from under depression's thumb, talk with your psychotherapist or family physician to find out the best way to do this. Be honest about your drug use. Quitting cold turkey may seem the logical choice, but turkeys aren't known for their intelligence. Do this the right way, under the supervision of your physician.

Sleep Disorders

Sleep is important. If you didn't already know this, just watch a few television commercials for various kinds of mattresses. These commercials tell you that you spend about one-third of your life in bed, so it's important for your health to be sure your sleep is restorative. These ads are right on the mark when it comes to underscoring the importance of a good night's sleep.

L. Essential

> "Sleep hygiene" is the new phrase used by doctors to describe all those healthy practices and pre-bedtime routines that can help you achieve a good night's rest: A hot, relaxing bath, quiet reading, a regular time for turning in, and a light snack can help you wind down and enter the embrace of Morpheus. On the other hand, exercising, consuming caffeine and alcohol, and smoking too close to bedtime—within four hours of sack time—can interfere with sleep.

Symptoms

If you have a sleep disorder, you may struggle through the day, fatigued and longing for a nap. You may find it difficult to concentrate and you may feel irritable. Others may call you a grouch and, if you're honest, you'll have to agree with them. When you're tired, every little thing suddenly becomes a big thing. It's like having fingernails scratching across the blackboard of your mind, all day long. The symptoms of a sleep disorder are very similar to the symptoms of depression. Add in headaches, decreased sex drive or impotence, and a serious lack of energy, and you've got a miserable combination.

Insomnia

Having difficulty falling asleep? Perhaps you drift off to dreamland quickly but then wake up frequently during the night. Your mattress becomes increasingly uncomfortable, and there's just no way to get settled and relax. You check your bedside clock at frequent intervals, the minutes drag along, hours pass like snails, morning finally dawns, and you're more tired than when you went to bed. This is obviously not going to give you the energy you need to deal with depression. What to do?

First of all, take an inventory of your pre-bedtime habits. Are you following the recommendations for good sleep hygiene, or are you just trusting luck to get you to sleep? If nothing on the hygiene list seems to apply, it's time to check with your doctor to see if any of your medications might be causing the problem.

A possible side effect of antidepressant medication is drowsiness. Sometimes changing the time of day when you take your medications can help. If you switch from morning to nighttime, you can capitalize on any drowsiness your medications cause and then start practicing some of those sleep hygiene tips to give yourself the best shot at a good night's sleep. Don't read in bed, watch television in bed, or use that computer in bed. Keep all work and everything else out of your bedchamber. Use your bed exclusively for sleep and sex.

 Fact

A Stanford University study found that people with depression are five times more likely to have a breathing-related sleep disorder than non-depressed people. This makes sense, since sleep problems are a symptom of depression.

Sleep Apnea

This condition literally means "without breath." It's a good descriptor. You may snore—many people do—but the snoring associated with sleep apnea is very different from the garden variety kind of snoring. Normal sleep breathing patterns are slow and regular. The breathing pattern of someone with apnea, however, is alarming—a snort and gasp for breath, followed by ten seconds or so without a breath and then a gasp for air again. These events can occur up to thirty or more times an hour while you're sleeping.

There are several forms of the condition, but obstructive sleep apnea is the most common and occurs when the muscles and tissues in the throat and airway relax. Sleep apnea can be treated with a CPAP machine that blows a fixed amount of air through your airway throughout the night, keeping that airway open so that the snoring and gasping don't happen and you get a good night's sleep. Since untreated sleep apnea can be life-threatening, it's important to get a handle on it.

 ## Question

What's CPAP?
CPAP stands for continuous positive airway pressure. If your doctor prescribes a CPAP device for you, you'll wear it across your face, securing it in place with straps around your head. The machine is not silent, and while it usually solves the sleep apnea problem, your bed partner may still seek refuge on the couch or in another bedroom.

The classic profile for someone with sleep apnea is a middle-aged, overweight male. Anyone, however, can have sleep apnea—this includes children. If snoring stops briefly and then resumes, that is a significant indicator of sleep apnea. You may not even know you have it. It's usually diagnosed in a sleep lab, often after a partner has noticed these alarming symptoms.

Danger Behind the Wheel

Feeling drowsy while you're behind the wheel can be a frightening experience, but it may turn out to be a fairly reliable indicator that you've got a sleep disorder, especially if it happens more than once. This is not the time to drift off to dreamland. The consequences of falling asleep at the wheel can be disastrous to yourself as well as to others. This is not a good way to find out that you have a sleep disorder.

Other Medical Conditions

If you've got other medical issues, they may be involved in stealing your sleep. According to the National Center on Sleep Disorders Research, these conditions can affect your sleep:

- Arthritis
- Cancer
- Diabetes
- Cardiopulmonary diseases
- Chronic Fatigue Syndrome (CFS)
- Fibromyalgia (FM)
- HIV/AIDS
- Irritable bowel syndrome (IBS)
- End-stage renal disease (ESRD)
- Obesity
- Temporomandibular joint disorders (TMJD)

Sometimes it's easy to overlook one condition while you're intently focused on another. It's entirely possible, however, to have more than one disorder at a time. You may have asthma and cancer. You may have irritable bowel syndrome and diabetes. What's important here is to be aware that any and all of these conditions may interact with each other to interfere with your sleep.

Over-the-Counter Drugs That Can Hurt

Seemingly benign drugs such as caffeine and pseudoephedrine (commonly found in cold medicines) could be depriving you of much-needed sleep and exacerbating your depression symptoms.

Essential

Be your own record keeper! A health journal is an essential companion and should accompany you to each doctor visit. Write down symptoms, concerns, and questions so you'll be prepared to ask intelligent questions. Don't forget to write down the answers as you get them.

Caffeine

What do coffee, tea, many soft drinks, and chocolate have in common? Caffeine! Caffeine is a stimulant. If you ingest any of these items before bedtime, you may not sleep for quite some time. Caffeine is not an essential nutrient, and you can get along just fine without it. Some prescription medications and over-the-counter drugs also contain caffeine. Fiorinal, Fioricet, Esgic, Medigesic, and Phrenilin, prescribed for pain relief during migraine attacks, are examples of prescription drugs containing caffeine. Excedrin, Midol, and Cafergot are examples of over-the-counter drugs that contain caffeine. If you want to sleep, stimulants aren't the way to go.

Ĺ. Essential

If you're confused by the labels on drugs you find in stores, talk to your pharmacist. You can get a mini-course in understanding how these drugs interact and also learn how to use them properly to get the most benefit from them. Sometimes just taking your prescribed drugs earlier or later in the day can be all that it takes to solve the sleep problem. Check with your doctor or pharmacist to see if this is an option.

Pseudoephedrine

Pseudoephedrine, a decongestant, can also disturb sleep. You can find this in cold medications, nasal sprays, allergy medications, and prescription diet pills. If you are taking heart medication, beta blockers can interfere with your sleep. Thyroid hormones and some drugs used to treat Parkinson's disease also can affect sleep.

Stress

Stress is part of living. When you feel overwhelmed by the commitments you've made to family or friends or by the extra assignments you've agreed to take on at work, you're experiencing stress. Stress enters your life in many ways. Running late for an appointment, being overdrawn at the bank, or fighting with a friend or loved one—any and all of these can create stress and elevate pre-existing stress to difficult levels. Even positive stress—getting that job promotion, or achieving retirement, falling in love or achieving a life goal—can affect your body.

 Fact

According to Psycheducation.org, stress hormones, trauma, and depression may have a link at the cellular level. Researchers are looking at how trauma, experienced early in life, causes subtle changes in brain function. Stress hormones within the brain may be the basis for these changes and may be responsible for creating anxiety and depression.

Effectively managing stress is essential to good health and treating depression. Fortunately, healthy practices designed to get your body operating at optimal levels can also work to keep stress under control. It's like getting a two-for-one return on your investment. Try some of the following strategies:

- Listening to music
- Yoga exercises
- Relaxation tapes
- Breathing exercises
- Dancing
- Walking
- Meditation
- Sports

Anything that refocuses your attention and your body to something soothing, energizing, or restorative will help you conquer stress.

Trauma

While stress may be ongoing and even chronic in nature, trauma is usually sudden and severe. Trauma is a shock to the system that can leave both your body and your mind reeling. Researchers are now looking into how trauma actually can change brain function. This has direct implications for depression. Feelings of hopelessness and despair may arise after a traumatic incident, and these are symptoms of depression. Both children and adults can experience trauma, but childhood trauma is especially insidious.

Childhood Trauma and Depression

In 2005, the *Journal of Family Practice* reported that "Childhood trauma may lead to neurobiologically unique mood disorders." The research indicates that stress and trauma, incurred during childhood, have long-lasting effects on brain development. Those effects, according to the *Journal of Clinical Psychiatry* (2004), are long-term changes in various neurotransmitter systems.

As you read earlier, scientists rely to a great extent on twin studies, as they formulate theories that apply to larger populations. Some twin studies have now proven that trauma experienced in childhood, such as child abuse and child neglect, as well as the death of a parent, are predictors of major depression. Further, depressed women who experienced sexual abuse as children experienced earlier onset of depressive symptoms than did women who had not been abused as children.

Adult Trauma and Depression

You've read that certain medical conditions can occur in tandem. For example, alcohol dependency may go hand in hand with depression. Likewise, post-traumatic stress disorder (PTSD), an anxiety disorder, may accompany depression. If you've been the victim of a sexual assault, an automobile accident, or a natural disaster, for instance, the feelings of helplessness you felt during the experience may linger on. If you find yourself dwelling on the incident to the point that you are unable to get beyond it and resume your normal life, you may find that you're now suffering from depression, as well as PTSD. Seeking relief from the symptoms of depression that have developed as a result of trauma can free you to address the anxiety disorder that accompanied the depression.

CHAPTER 7

Seeking Professional Help

YOU'VE DECIDED TO take a major step and get some help. That takes an enormous amount of courage. See this step for what it is: part of your personal plan to achieve a healthy life. In this chapter you'll discover who does what, how they do what they do, and what you can expect from these health care professionals. Your access to any of these professionals will depend on where you live, your insurance company's policies and coverage, and the general economy of your area. The more hospitals your area has, the more likely you will have access to clinical psychologists, psychiatric nurse practitioners, and psychiatrists. But even in more remote areas, help is available.

The Historical Figures Behind Modern Therapy

Modern psychotherapy has its roots in behavioral therapy, which is also referred to as behaviorism. This school of thought teaches that all human behaviors are conditioned responses to external stimuli—what we'd refer to as our environment. A pioneer in this field was Ivan Pavlov, a Russian researcher whose name became a household word. He trained dogs to salivate at the sound of a bell, because they had been conditioned to receive food after the bell rang. Another pioneer was B.F. Skinner, an American psychologist who carried this work over into human subjects. His theory of operant conditioning held that living creatures operate on their environment. If the results of their operating produce a desirable result, they'll continue doing whatever caused the good thing. If the results turn out to be bad, they'll stop whatever caused the bad thing. Behavior modification is a current form of therapy that draws on Skinner's work. Essentially, you change your behavior and you get different results. If you're suffering from depression, lifestyle changes are an important component of therapy. But perhaps the two biggest names in the field of psychology are Sigmund Freud and Carl Jung, who you'll read about in the following two sections. (You'll read about two more important figures, Albert Ellis and Aaron Beck, in Chapter 8.)

Sigmund Freud

Sigmund Freud was a medical doctor specializing in neurology. Freud was fascinated with the workings of the unconscious mind—those thoughts that occur when you are sleeping. According to Freud, adult depression and anxiety were related to childhood experiences, and dreams held the answers for treating these disorders. During REM sleep, the rational and reasoning portion of the brain is not at the helm, so all inhibitions can break loose. That means that you can think about very painful experiences that your awake mind keeps repressed. Analyze your dreams, and you can relieve the symptoms of depression. This was the theory Freud discussed in his *Interpretation of Dreams*. Freud also found that when his patients discussed their symptoms, problems, and concerns with him, their depression symptoms decreased.

Freud also studied the sexual causes of psychological disorders; but, in this regard, his work has largely been bypassed, as medical breakthroughs have begun to unravel the neurochemical aspects of depression.

Carl Jung

Carl Jung is considered the father of analytical psychology. With a more spiritual bent than Freud, Jung believed that there was a "collective unconscious" shared by all humanity. Where Freud focused on sexuality and aggression, Jung focused on the spirit. Jungian psychoanalysis, therefore, takes a holistic approach to therapy and is used widely today. Jungian therapy is not open-ended; the goal is to be able to function without long-term therapy.

Jung's philosophy had much in common with yoga's meditative aspects, which also seek collective consciousness. Jung also developed the concepts of the extroverted and the introverted personality styles.

Counselors

High school counselors, often called guidance counselors, offer advice as you choose your career path. If you've ever been party to a law suit or needed help with legal problems, you've sought legal counsel from an attorney. Financial counselors offer advice with investments and help you make good decisions for your stock portfolio. There are counselors who provide mental health services, as well.

According to the report *Mental Health, United States, 2002,* published by the U.S. Department of Health and Human Services, there are more than 100,000 professional counselors licensed or certified for independent practice in the United States. One of these is sure to be just what you're looking for! There are many kinds of counselors, filling many kinds of needs.

Tailored to Your Needs

Since counselors have a certain area or areas of practice, such as family counseling, substance abuse counseling, codependency counseling, and so forth, be sure your prospective counselor works in your area of need.

Clinical social workers, licensed professional counselors, and mental health counselors all offer counseling services in the area of depression. Each can diagnose and provide individual or group counseling.

- Clinical social workers will have a master's degree in social work (MSW), and they'll be licensed by the state in which they practice. Their professional organization is the Academy of Certified Social Workers. These social workers practice in family service agencies, community mental health centers, private practice, and outpatient clinics attached to general or psychiatric hospitals.

- Licensed professional counselors will have a master's degree in counseling. They will also be licensed by the state in which they practice.
- Mental health counselors will have a master's degree, along with a minimum of two years' post-master's clinical work under the supervision of a licensed or certified mental health professional. They will be licensed by the state in which they practice. Their professional organization is the National Academy of Certified Clinical Mental Health Counselors.

Medical Professionals

In addition to counselors, who work in the lay sector, the medical field has many types of professionals who can treat depression. You may find some of these folks engaged in private practice, or they may be associated with a hospital or medical clinic. Your best resource is your family health care provider. Ask who is available in your area to help you get started tackling the symptoms of depression.

Psychiatric Nurse Practitioner

A psychiatric nurse practitioner (PNP) is a registered nurse who is trained in the practice of psychiatric and mental health nursing. The professional organization is the American Psychiatric Nurses Association. Psychiatric nurse practitioners are licensed by the state in which they practice. They're trained to diagnose and provide individual and group counseling. Psychiatric nurse practitioners are frequently affiliated with psychiatric hospitals or may be in private practice.

Psychologist

A clinical psychologist is a therapist with an advanced degree from an accredited graduate program in psychology and two or more years of postgraduate supervised work experience. Most states require a doctoral degree and a state license for psychologists. Clinical psychologists are trained to make diagnoses, administer psychological testing, and provide individual and group therapy. Previously, only medical doctors could write prescriptions, but in 2002 New Mexico granted prescription privileges to psychologists, and in 2004 Louisiana followed suit. Psychologists in the Armed Forces also have prescription privileges. Otherwise, psychologists are required to consult with a physician before prescribing. These psychologists are required to have advanced training in order to qualify for this designation.

Essential

If you are having difficulty locating a therapist, finding one just got a whole lot easier. Simply dial 1-800-Therapist. That will get you on the right track to finding someone who can help you.

Psychiatrist

A psychiatrist is a medical doctor with special training in the diagnosis and treatment of mental and emotional illnesses. Like other doctors, psychiatrists are qualified to prescribe medication. A psychiatrist should have a state medical license and be board-eligible or board-certified by the American Board of Psychiatry and Neurology.

Specific Therapy Options

Depending upon the causes of your depression, you and your therapist will decide what approach will be most effective for you. All licensed therapists are trained in a particular approach, and some therapists are skilled in more than one. You may choose to try cognitive behavioral therapy, interpersonal therapy, or psychodynamic therapy, all of which are described in this section.

Cognitive Behavioral Therapy

Cognitive behavioral therapy (CBT), which is usually done on an individual and not a group basis, has proven to be very helpful in treating depression. The National Institute for Mental Health's *Science Update* from May 2007 reports that for those who were unsuccessful in treating depression with an antidepressant medication, switching to or adding CBT is generally as effective as switching to or adding another medication. You'll read more about CBT in a later chapter of the same name.

If you choose CBT as a treatment option, you can expect weekly therapy sessions that are supplemented with practice exercises you do on your own.

Interpersonal Therapy

Interpersonal therapy (IPT) is frequently used to treat depression. When you are depressed, you aren't able to relate to others as well as you did before depression set in. IPT helps you reach out beyond yourself, and ending those feelings of isolation. You'll work on communication skills, appropriate expression of feelings, and learn how to speak up for yourself so you get what you need. Another goal of IPT is to help diffuse conflict.

Psychodynamic Therapy

"How did you feel about that?" asks the psychiatrist, as the patient reclines on the couch, reaching deep inside to pull out the situation that started his downhill slide into depression. That's the Hollywood image of psychodynamic therapy, also known as psychoanalysis. It's been the basis of more than one movie—the most recent being *Analyze This* and *Analyze That* with Robert DeNiro as the conflicted mobster and Billy Crystal as the long-suffering but empathetic shrink.

This sort of pseudo-psychiatry has been the subject matter of all kinds of jokes and parodies. These portrayals do not represent the way this kind of therapy really works. In psychodynamic therapy, you and your therapist will work together to find the unconscious processes that are shaping your behaviors.

Psychotherapy

In general, psychotherapy involves talking about how you're feeling. In fact, it's often called "talk therapy." Your therapist is there to guide you and help you. How you feel affects how you act. When you are feeling better, you are able to interact more positively with those around you, be they family, friends, or work associates. Your therapist guides you on your journey to sort out what's important from what's not. Then, you'll get an action plan to help you act on what you've learned.

Choosing the Right Therapist

Cost of services will probably be a primary concern for you. Therapy can be expensive, but most insurance companies will cover a specific portion of the costs. Check with your insurance company to see what services they will cover and what your co-pay will be. If you do not have insurance, check with your local hospital to see what mental health services are available to you at reduced costs or on a sliding fee schedule.

 Alert

With the advent of the computer age, it is now possible to find therapists with online practices. Some of these are reputable, and others are not. Before you sign up and sign on the dotted line, do careful research. Don't be taken in by Internet scams.

Even with glowing recommendations by satisfied patients or clients and the referral of your primary physician, finding the right therapist for you make take some time and a little leg work. Your first contact will probably be with the receptionist when you call to make an appointment for a consultation. It's been said that secretaries and receptionists reflect the culture of their work environment, and this is a good analysis. Your request should be handled professionally, and you should be treated with respect.

Entering the Inner Sanctum

You've made the appointment for your consultation and you've prepared a list of questions to ask. You're both looking forward to the session and dreading it at the same time. It's that fear of the unknown acting up. But you've persevered, and now you've been shown into the office.

At this first session, you and your counselor will spend some time getting to know each other. You will discuss your personal history, medical history, and any other areas of your life that have relevance. This helps in firming up the diagnosis of a depressive disorder and gives the counselor information as to the best course of treatment for you. You are building trust, essential for a good working relationship.

Conducting Your Own Interview

This is also the time for you to interview the counselor to be sure you are both a good fit. Remember, you are hiring a professional to do some work. Ask what experience your counselor has in addressing your particular issues. Ask what kinds of therapy she offers. Will you opt for individual or group sessions? Ask how long your treatment is likely to last. Ask what you can expect from treatment. Most therapists are trained in several different approaches. They then combine techniques from these various approaches that fit their own style and personality. There are also various formats in which therapy may be held. These include individual, group, and family psychotherapy.

Ethics and Confidentiality

You may be ill at ease, at first, and find it difficult to talk about your family relationships or your personal history. Whatever you reveal during your counseling session is confidential. Counselors abide by a strict code of ethics, which states in part that "Personal information is communicated to others only with the person's written consent or in those circumstances where there is clear and imminent danger to the client, to others or to society. Disclosure of counseling information is restricted to what is necessary, relevant, and verifiable" (American Mental Health Counselors Association).

If It's Not the Right Fit

Perhaps you decide that this first counselor is not going to do it for you. You just don't see a rapport developing between you. There's no blame involved on either side, and you don't have to apologize. You're dealing with people, and everyone is different. If there's a personality clash, if you aren't comfortable with your first choice of counselor, move on to the next prospective therapist on your list. It's important that you feel comfortable if you're going to make the best use of your time and money.

L. Essential

> You don't want to hurt your therapist's feelings, but the situation isn't working out. How do you go about telling your therapist that you're going to go somewhere else? Just say, "I'm not making the kind of progress I need. Thank you for your help, but I'm going to end my sessions." Then do it! But don't stop there—keep looking until you find the right therapist for you!

You're Hired!

You've found the therapist that you're comfortable with. This is the one. Perhaps it was the first one you interviewed, maybe it's the third. Whatever the case, it's settled, and you're ready to begin.

You'll tell your therapist just that: "I think I'll be comfortable working with you. I'd like to get started." The next thing that will happen, most likely, will be that you and your therapist will agree on a specific date and time for your first official session. You may ask how many sessions you can expect to have, and your therapist will discuss this with you. You may be given some homework right at the start. For example, you've told your prospective therapist that you're struggling with specific symptoms. Your therapist may ask you to start keeping a log in which you'll write down when you experience one of these symptoms, and perhaps what you're doing when it happens. You'll get some instructions, regardless, so that when you arrive for your first session, you'll be ready with some specific information.

Working with Your Therapist

Right away, you'll set goals for your therapy. This is not going to be a passive relationship. Depression won't fall by the wayside without you being the one to make sure it gets left behind. You are the one who will have to do the hard work, with your therapist right at your side giving encouragement along the way.

 Question

How many goals should I set? Are these like New Year's resolutions?
These goals are definitely not like New Year's resolutions—everybody breaks those before the week is out. Start with one goal, such as overcoming a symptom like insomnia that's causing you distress. Then work out specific objectives for meeting that goal. You'll find that success breeds more success, and you'll be ready to move on from there.

Goals and Strategies

Your ultimate goal, of course, is to free yourself from depression. The strategies you develop to achieve this goal will vary, depending upon the type of depression you are dealing with. For example, if you are struggling with sleep issues, you and your therapist will work together to develop strategies to help you relieve this symptom. Your therapist may ask you to keep a journal in which you write down all your pre-bedtime habits and routines, along with notes on how the course of your sleepless night plays out. For example, if you wake frequently, can't fall asleep easily, or can't get your mind to relax, these are all useful bits of knowledge that you and your therapist can make use of at your next session.

Will I Be in Therapy Forever?

No. That's why you've set goals. You'll set up your schedule at the first visit. You'll usually meet once a week for a specific period of time—three months is not unrealistic. Each session will probably begin with reviewing your progress relative to your goals. You'll also continue to evaluate how well you're relating to your therapist. Your progress should be moving forward. If you feel you're getting stuck, talk to your therapist about the best way to get going again.

Prescriptions from Your Psychiatrist

Psychiatrists are physicians, and they can prescribe antidepressants for you take in conjunction with your psychotherapy. A combination of antidepressants and psychotherapy has been shown to be the most effective means of dealing with many forms of depression.

 Alert

It's good practice to have one regular pharmacy where you get your prescriptions filled. That way, the pharmacist has easy access to your records and can advise you quickly if there is a potential problem with mixing your medications.

However, before you fill that prescription for an antidepressant, be sure your psychiatrist knows what other medications you may be taking. Side effects and dangerous drug interactions can occur with medications prescribed for certain medical conditions, so be aware and be safe.

If your doctor has prescribed an antidepressant, ask the doctor what to expect when you begin taking it. Some medications have initial side effects that go away as your body adjusts to the medication. Once your questions have been answered, be sure to take the medication as directed. If you miss a dose, ask the pharmacist what you should do.

Sometimes it's best to wait until the next scheduled dose; other times, you may be able to take the missed dose right away. And don't stop your medications without checking with your doctor. Some can cause potentially serious side effects if you stop taking them abruptly.

CHAPTER 8

Cognitive Behavioral Therapy

COGNITIVE BEHAVIORAL THERAPY (CBT) is among the most popular and most effective forms of psychotherapy for dealing with depression. You got a brief introduction to CBT in the last chapter; now it's time to delve into the details. An important thread throughout this book has been the mind/body connection. Once again, you'll see it at work in CBT, which holds that the way you think affects the way you feel, and the way you feel impacts the way you behave or act. When you are suffering from depression, your thoughts are not focused or channeled toward positive, constructive ideas, and the world becomes a dark and gloomy place. CBT helps depression sufferers reframe those maladaptive thoughts into more positive ones.

Origins of CBT

CBT's origins can be traced back to the mid-1950s, when Albert Ellis and Aaron Beck developed the basic principles of this form of psychotherapy. CBT made a radical departure from psychoanalysis, which sought to probe and understand how past events shaped the workings of the unconscious mind. Beck and Ellis understood the significance of the past but decided the cure lay in working in the present and being focused on the future. They developed similar methodologies and shared many of the same beliefs. Today, CBT is the fastest-growing type of psychotherapy, with one in four practitioners employing it. CBT is based upon the concept of personal responsibility: How we think and the way we feel are responsible for our behaviors. External events and other people are not.

Aaron Beck

Psychiatrist Aaron Beck is considered to be the father of CBT, which he called cognitive therapy. His early work was in psychoanalysis or psychodynamic therapy, but as he saw more and more clients who described their depression in ways that didn't fit into psychodynamic theory, he sought another approach. As he explained in a conversation with Albert Ellis, hosted by PBS in 2004, he believed in the Give/Get balance of life: Output in terms of worries, obligations, and other actions needed to equal the input of satisfaction and happiness. If this balance was out of whack, depression could ensue.

Essential

In psychodynamic therapy, depression is considered to be a result of misdirected or pent-up anger. CBT holds that depression results instead from distortions in thinking.

As he studied his client sessions, Beck discovered that his depressed patients harbored irrational thoughts that drove their behaviors. He called these thoughts *systematic distortions*. Beck was a student of the Greek philosopher Epictetus, who taught that it's not things that make us either happy or unhappy. It's in the way that we *perceive* these things that create happiness or depression. The key is to stop trying to change the world, and instead, change our perceptions of the world. Once we've mastered this, we have corrected those *systematic distortions*.

Beck worked with his patients to help them discover what thinking distortions they harbored. He found that depressed people weren't aware of how these "automatic thoughts"—habitual negative beliefs—influenced their behavior. As with any habit, these thoughts came readily and easily. Patients were accustomed to them, didn't question them, and were victims of them.

Once the patient recognized one of these automatic thoughts, the next step was to test it out to see if it was accurate. If it proved to be inaccurate, then it needed to be corrected. For Beck, the therapist became a coach, actively involved in the patient's progress.

Albert Ellis

Ellis was a practicing psychoanalyst when he began to develop his own approach to cognitive therapy. In an article published in the *New York Times* in 2004, he explained that, while much psychotherapy helped you *feel* better, you weren't necessarily *getting* better. He labeled his approach to psychotherapy rational emotive behavior therapy (REBT) and said the most important aspect of it was simply work, work, work. At the American Psychological Association's conference in 2000, REBT was recognized for its pioneering approach to psychotherapy and as the foundation of all modern cognitive behavior therapies. In 2003, the American Psychological Association named Dr. Ellis the second most influential psychologist of the 20th century, second only to Carl Rogers.

L. Essential

Ellis may have rubbed many of his colleagues the wrong way, but he was a strong believer in the power of the human mind. "You largely constructed your depression," he wrote. "It wasn't given to you. Therefore, you can deconstruct it."

Albert Ellis drew on personal experience as he formulated his approach to CBT. He used himself as a guinea pig, working to cure his shyness by forcing himself to make social contact with a specific number of women while he sat on a park bench in the New York Botanical Gardens in the Bronx. Once a woman sat down, he began to talk. It worked. He attributed the effectiveness of his experiment to its causing him to think, feel, and act differently. He became so successful at approaching women that he became a sexologist (a scientist who studies human sexual behavior) and wrote books in that field, incorporating that knowledge into his therapeutic approach.

Ellis was confrontational in his approach to psychotherapy. He would tell patients to stop complaining and deal with the problem. He used the term *awfulise* to describe the tendency of people to make a difficult situation worse than it was. His approach, in simple terms, was "Deal with it." During Friday night meetings at the Albert Ellis Institute in New York, to which he invited guests and colleagues, he'd conduct two half-hour sessions of "stand-up therapy" with volunteers chosen from his guests. He encouraged the audience to comment during these sessions. He could be abrasive and vulgar, characteristics that came to define him.

Like Beck, Ellis believed that irrational thoughts led to self-destructive feelings and behavior. Ellis held that you can control your feelings if you make a conscious effort to do so. You must confront those events that have challenged you and rework the way you think about them. Events are neutral. It's your interpretation of these events that causes all your problems. He believed that rational people know this and operate accordingly. A person who is depressed, doesn't. However, everyone still has the choice as to how to react. You control your response because you can't control the event, and you go on with your life by deciding to go on with your life.

Characteristics of CBT

CBT has been the subject of extensive scientific testing and has been found to be highly effective for a number of mental disorders, including depression. Nobody really understands exactly how CBT works to alleviate depression. However, new brain research shows that certain areas of the brain are significantly altered as a result of CBT treatment. It has appeal among both clinical practitioners and patients for three important reasons: It's specific, it's focused, and it's immediate.

Specific

When you're depressed, your thoughts can be muddled and incorrect. Since your thoughts control your behaviors, they may also be inappropriate or ineffective. Breaking out of this vicious loop is essential to managing depression. According to Albert Ellis, there are three components to this distorted kind of thinking:

1. I must do well.
2. You must treat me well.
3. The world must be easy.

CBT works to change this. First, you learn to recognize that your thinking is distorted. You can't always do well. People won't always treat you well. And, finally, the world is a far from easy place. Then you learn how to change these cognitive distortions into rational thought patterns, which allow you to act in healthy ways.

Focused

Problem solving is at the heart of CBT. You may have had an unhappy childhood, issues with parents, or other longstanding concerns, but the problems you're dealing with are in the here and now. While CBT understands the importance of your past, it focuses on solving present-day problems by giving you coping strategies and a plan for managing your life—now. What symptoms are you experiencing that are causing you distress? What will you need to accomplish in order to alleviate your depression? This is the focus of CBT. You'll set goals and develop problem-solving strategies to allow you to meet those goals in a timely fashion.

Immediate

In dealing with depression, especially severe cases of depression where suicidal thoughts have created a crisis situation, therapy needs to get to the heart of the problem quickly and provide relief immediately. This immediacy is important in other situations as well; for example, in addressing depressive issues for children and adolescents. Getting well, as quickly as possible, is the goal. And in today's medical climate of HMO-managed care and spiraling costs of medical insurance, there really isn't time for anyone to engage in lengthy, open-ended therapy. This is where CBT fills the bill.

CBT for Young People with Depression

Parenting a child or adolescent with depression can be a difficult, frustrating experience. This is where a licensed psychotherapist trained in CBT can provide invaluable assistance. The therapist has the benefit of emotional distance from your child and can handle therapy from an objective point of view.

There are several reasons why CBT is an effective psychotherapy for children and adolescents, but one seems paramount: CBT employs characteristics of a familiar setting for young people—school. The therapist initially is seen as teacher, and there is homework. Where CBT differs from most school situations, however, is in the degree of autonomy the young person can expect to encounter and the sense of empowerment that this encourages. It's actually closer to the ideal model of mentor and student than it is to school in American society today.

Research from the University of California at Los Angeles

In a UCLA study of CBT's effectiveness on young people with depression, researchers found that in fourteen of sixteen clinical trials, CBT therapy had measureable, positive effects. Researcher John Weiss, speaking on National Public Radio's (NPR) *All Things Considered* in June 2004, explained that, of the available psychotherapies, CBT is the most reliably beneficial treatment for young people. CBT works fast—in twelve to twenty sessions. That's the time span of just a few months. And what it accomplishes in that short time is nothing short of remarkable. Young people take away with them a "menu of coping skills: problem-solving behaviors, thoughts that are less self-critical, and enjoyable activities." With such a good assortment, young people find several that work well for them.

Research from the University of Texas at Austin

Researchers at UT Austin decided to study how helpful CBT would be to even younger groups of people—elementary and middle school girls. Their study, funded by the National Institute of Mental Health (NIMH), was reported on during that same series on depression and young people that ran on NPR during June 2004. Researchers already knew that, starting with adolescence, girls experience depression at a rate three times that of boys the same age. The researchers wanted to see if early work with CBT would help reduce that rate, so they set about to create a therapy that was gender-specific. The girls in the study had their CBT sessions at their school. They met twice a week for a period of ten weeks, and early data collected suggested that 87 percent of the girls were no longer depressed after therapy. This was extremely exciting news.

Snapshot of CBT Problem Solving in Young People

The worries of children and adults can be wide-ranging. In children, depression can ensue as the result of experiences at home or at school. A child who is depressed and feels that no one likes him will withdraw more and more, and the depression will worsen. A therapist trained in CBT will help the child articulate that belief and let the child explain why he feels that way. Perhaps no one talks to him. The therapist will ask the child for possible reasons why no one is speaking to him. Then, the child may offer that he doesn't speak to them. That provides the opening for the therapist to teach communication strategies to tackle the problem. From there they can work together to build successes.

What to Expect from CBT

CBT is an interactive form of psychotherapy. You will work with your psychotherapist as an active partner in your treatment. At first, your therapist will carry most of the session's responsibilities, but as you progress and learn how to use the coping skills and strategies you are shown, you will take more and more responsibility for your therapy. The goal is independence.

A Typical First Session

It's the fifty-minute hour, and you'll want to make the most of every minute. At the first session, you'll explain your issues to your therapist, and your therapist will explain CBT and how she approaches it. You'll probably see the CBT manual on her desk. Basically, you'll establish your comfort level. You may fill out certain forms and inventories to get a better handle on your moods. Once you've narrowed your focus, you'll set goals for your therapy and decide on a schedule of appointments. You'll probably receive your first homework assignment. This may be tracking your moods—finding out what times you feel which way. You'll record everything in a notebook, which you'll bring to every session. At the beginning, you'll likely see your therapist weekly. As you progress, there's a gradual winnowing down, until you both agree that you're ready to strike out on your own. Even then, there's the security of follow-up appointments—perhaps quarterly visits to keep you on track.

Subsequent Sessions

Judith Beck, Ph.D. is the director of the Beck Institute for Cognitive Therapy and Research, founded by her father Aaron Beck. Information about the Institute and its services can be found at the Web site: *www.beckinstitute.org*. Dr. Beck explains that sessions begin with a mood check. The therapist will ask how you felt during the previous week, compared to weeks before. She'll ask what problem you want on the current session's agenda, and will elicit your input as to what happened of importance since you last met. You'll discuss your self-help assignments (homework) and make any needed adjustments to your therapy protocol.

These are the preliminaries. Next, you'll get to work on this week's problems. You'll begin to assess your thinking and beliefs and determine if they are cognitive distortions. It's a brainstorming process. You'll look for alternative explanations for difficult situations and will be taught some new skills to deal with them. Your therapist will summarize what you covered, and you'll take your homework with you to provide material for your next session.

Snapshot of CBT for Adults

The workplace is full of opportunities for stress and subsequent depression. If you are dreading going to work because you feel overwhelmed and unable to cope, you'll need to find out just what's at the heart of this belief. Your therapist will ask you to explain why you are overwhelmed—what's causing this feeling of inadequacy. You may reply that the work keeps piling up and you never get caught up. You're afraid you'll lose your job over it. When your therapist asks you why your workload is so heavy, you may realize that you can't say *no*. That realization can lead to learning strategies for asserting yourself and not taking on more than you can handle.

Your Responsibilities in CBT

You are not a passive observer in CBT. Quite the contrary. You are half of the team, and just showing up for the game is not enough to get the job done. There are certain obligations and responsibilities that you must fulfill in order to get better:

- Develop specific goals for your therapy.
- Come to your sessions prepared.
- Do your homework.
- Practice your new skills.
- Reflect on your progress and analyze and report your findings to your therapist.
- Keep your appointments.

Your therapist will actively engage with you, so you must be willing and able to engage with your therapist. Your CBT notebook will be important both as a record of your progress and a handy reference for the specific tools, skills, and strategies you will learn. You'll chart your daily moods, negative thoughts, and track how pleasurable activities helped you cope.

The Long-Term Picture

Fighting depression is a long-term commitment. Just as you would manage a heart condition, diabetes, or lupus, you manage depression. Slacking off and slipping back into patterns of distorted thinking or maladaptive behaviors can happen gradually, without your being aware of it. Just as weight management requires constant vigilance, so does managing depression.

Broadening Horizons

Judith Beck recommends that you consider other areas to pursue to improve the quality of your life. Spiritual, intellectual, and cultural activities will feed your mind. Exercise and proper nutrition will feed your body. Reach out to others. Resist the inclination to retreat back into yourself. By expanding your circle of interests and circle of friends, you'll help to ensure that your depression remains under control.

Therapy Forever?

When you began your CBT, you and your therapist created a roadmap of recovery. You considered how many sessions might be necessary to achieve maximum results. Once you've made noticeable progress, and that can come as early as three or four sessions with CBT, you'll want to reassess and re-evaluate your therapy schedule. If your symptoms are straightforward, you may find that six to eight sessions are enough to give you the coping skills you need. If your problems are more complex, it may take several months to get where you want to be. Just remember, the goal is to taper off therapy so that you can use your skills and receive feedback from your therapist before you're ready to tackle your problems alone.

Reconnecting with a Therapist

If you relocate or need help finding a certified cognitive therapist in your area, Dr. Beck recommends checking out the Academy of Cognitive Therapy (ACT) Web site: *www.academyofct.org*.

CHAPTER 9

Pharmaceutical Treatments for Depression

THERE IS NO one perfect course for treating depression. There are many kinds of depression, and each one presents its own challenges. The traditional methods of managing depression have included antidepressant medications, psychotherapy, and lifestyle changes. In this chapter, you'll learn about what the pharmaceutical world has to offer in the form of antidepressant medications. You'll also read all about the restrictions, side effects, and other details that come with these medications.

Pharmaceuticals—Marvels of Modern Science

After psychotherapy became an established protocol for treating depression, interest turned to finding medications that would also help defeat the symptoms of this condition.

It takes quite some time—years in fact—to get a new drug on the market. From concept to market takes twelve to fifteen years, on average, and may cost up to $500 million. At any step along the way, the drug can be pulled and the project either modified or abandoned. It's a high-risk endeavor. Whether you believe pharmaceutical companies are agents for the public good or corporations primarily concerned with market share and profits, the world can't move along without them.

It Starts with an Idea

Scientists are always asking questions, and that's very important for the rest of us, who benefit from their insatiable curiosity. The questions they ask lead to breakthroughs in treatment of disease. Often, it's having witnessed a loved one struggle with an illness that becomes the motivation that fuels someone to pursue a lifetime of research. One researcher, obsessed with finding a cure for diabetes or cancer or depression, may spend an entire career in the pursuit of answers, hoping the payoff will come during her shift.

It's not random chance that leads to discoveries. Even before the research begins, however, a great amount of work has already been accomplished. Researchers have selected a medical condition and examined the biochemical processes involved in that condition. Next, they begin to develop drugs that will interact with those processes.

Compounding the Research

Plans for clinical trials begin in this earliest phase, along with the Investigational New Drug (IND) application that is sent on to the Federal Drug Administration (FDA). The IND lays out specific procedures that must be followed by the researching entity. It also specifies what the researchers can and cannot do. If the IND is approved by the FDA and by an Institutional Review Board (IRB), the manufacturer may begin the first phase of development.

 Fact

Somewhere between 5,000 and 10,000 different compounds may show up and try out for this preclinical phase. Just as with tryouts for a Broadway production, however, most of the hopefuls won't even get the chance to finish their audition before they're yanked off the stage or, in this case, banished from the lab. Suddenly, the number of candidates has dropped to about 250!

Into the Lab

The lab and animal studies come next, and this phase reduces the number of drugs under consideration to about five. While it is uncomfortable to know that animals may die because of reactions to drugs that they receive, federal regulations do mandate that all animals used in laboratory testing be treated humanely. Using animals in drug research raises ethical and moral concerns for sure, and there are no easy answers. Before humans are permitted to undergo drug trials, however, lab tests, which may include animal testing, are required. From here, the potential drug moves through three phases of testing that include humans.

Phase I Testing

Having successfully cleared the hurdles to this point, the drug now is tested on healthy individuals. The purpose of this is to discover the drug's basic properties and establish its safety profile. During this time, researchers will be examining the effects of one dose, increased dosage, and dosage that corresponds with a short-term course of treatment. Phase I will typically last from one to two years, and by the time it's complete, only one compound remains.

Phase II Testing

Now it's time for the target population to become involved. In Phase II, the drug is administered to volunteers of the target population to see how effective the drug is, or if it's effective at all. This is also the time for observing side effects of the drug. These trials are small scale, involving anywhere from 100 to 250 patients. This is the nail-biter phase, because at the end of Phase II, the drug manufacturer meets with FDA officials to discuss the future of the drug in question. If the FDA is satisfied with progress to date, the plans for the final stage, Phase III are laid out. Phase III—Going for Broke

This is large-scale testing and is the most expensive part of the process. The paperwork submitted for each drug can reach over 50,000 pages.

⌐, Essential

If things are going exceptionally well, the manufacturer can obtain accelerated development/review of the drug. This has important economic repercussions for the manufacturer and, if the need for this particular drug is urgent, can literally mean the difference between life and death for a patient.

While Phase III studies are in progress, preparations are made to submit the appropriate application forms to either the FDA or the Center for Drug Evaluation and Research (CDER).

This review can take from one to two years. Once the application has been approved, the manufacturer can put the drug on the market with FDA regulated labeling.

The Role of the FDA

The Food and Drug Administration (FDA) is an agency of the United States Department of Health and Human Services. It's responsible for regulating food, dietary supplements, drugs, biological medical products, blood products, medical devices, radiation-emitting devices, veterinary products, and cosmetics. And just like every other government agency, the FDA is a bureaucracy whose rules, regulations, and requirements continue to expand. In 1980, the typical drug underwent thirty clinical trials involving about 1,500 patients. By the mid-1990s, the typical drug had to undergo more than sixty clinical trials involving nearly 5,000 patients.

Ongoing Oversight

The FDA continues to monitor the drugs for which it has granted approval. It gathers safety information on side effects and potential hazards as they arise. Occasionally, the FDA will recommend changes in labeling that reflect these new concerns. The FDA also releases periodic news bulletins to alert the public when a serious problem has arisen. The FDA reserves the authority to withdraw a drug from the market if the drug proves to be harmful when used as prescribed.

Alert

The most severe FDA alert, short of withdrawing a drug from the market, is the "black box" alert. This warning provides additional cautions for use of the drug in question. After concerns about potential risks of suicide in teenagers and children who used antidepressant medications, the FDA issued a black box advisory, cautioning about antidepressant use in these populations.

Shortening the Process

Everything seems to be moving faster in our technologically driven world, and the FDA is no exception to this. In January 2006, the FDA announced plans to streamline the process of getting a drug through the earliest stages of clinical development. The Secretary of the Department of Health and Human Services pointed out that nine out of ten experimental drugs fail in the clinical trials because researchers cannot accurately predict how these drugs will affect people based solely on animal and lab studies. To address this problem, the FDA will permit small amounts of experimental drugs to be tested on human subjects before Phase I trials begin. This will not only cut time, it will also cut back on expense.

Antidepressants Enter the Picture

It took a great amount of time, energy, resourcefulness, and a not inconsiderable portion of luck to discover and develop the first antidepressants. There are now three main classes of medications for depression: selective serotonin reuptake inhibitors (SSRIs), tricyclics (TCAs), and monoamine oxidase inhibitors (MAOIs).

Introducing Lithium

Back in 1949, an Australian psychiatrist by the name of John Cade introduced lithium into the pharmacopeia as a treatment for bipolar disorder. He'd noticed the sedating effect that lithium had on guinea pigs in the lab and decided to become a guinea pig himself. He self-administered lithium and then sat back and waited to see what would happen. Nothing happened. At least nothing bad. He didn't experience any ill effects from the drug, and so he began prescribing it for his patients with manic symptoms. Today, nearly sixty years later, lithium is still the drug of choice for the treatment of bipolar disorder.

MAOIs

Lithium was only one drug, but it opened the door and opened some minds. It so happened that a drug being used to treat tuberculosis (TB)—iproniazid—was found to significantly increase the energy levels of TB patients. This side effect led to its use in treating unipolar depression. As researchers continued to study the drug they found it had the ability to block the activity of monoamine oxidase, the enzyme that destroys the monoamine neurotransmitters norepinephrine, serotonin, and dopamine. Iproniazid was the first of the monoamine oxidase inhibitors (MAOIs). However, a nasty side effect of iproniazid was jaundice, and the drug was withdrawn from the market. MAO inhibitors (MAOIs) are now the most rarely prescribed type of medications for depression, because of their potentially serious side effects. Fortunately, these early setbacks didn't discourage the researchers, and the push was on. In 1952, chlorpromazine, the first generation drug for treating schizophrenia, came on the market.

Tricyclics

The tricyclics came on the market in the 1960s. The first tricyclic antidepressant was imipramine, discovered in 1950 by researchers who were looking for a new class of antipsychotic drugs. Impramine didn't do much for schizophrenia, but it did have antidepressant qualities. Researchers determined that the tricyclics increased the activity of the monoamine neurotransmitters norepinephrine and serotonin by inhibiting their reuptake into neurons. TCAs can cause side effects such as dry mouth, constipation, bladder problems, sexual dysfunction, blurred vision, dizziness, and drowsiness. Because of their side effects, they have fallen out of favor and are not commonly prescribed. Elavil, Tofranil, and Anafranil are members of the tricyclic family of antidepressants.

SSRIs—The Breakthrough!

Finally, in 1971, a researcher at Eli Lilly began working on the neurochemistry angle. Previous drugs had affected more than one neurotransmitter, so his objective was to produce a drug that would specifically target a single neurotransmitter. He discovered that one compound, fluoxetine hydrochloride, blocked reuptake of serotonin but did not block other neurotransmitters. Fluoxetine hydrochloride was approved as a treatment for depression and came on the market in 1987. Its trade name was Prozac, and soon the drug became a household word. Side effects for SSRIs include weight gain and sexual dysfunction. SSRIs are now the most commonly prescribed class of antidepressants. You'll find a list of these drugs in Appendix C.

Brand Names Versus Generics

Once the pharmaceutical company has released the drug to the consumer market, the race is on. Recouping its financial investment and making a profit before the patent expires is essential, since the day after the patent expires, generic drugs will show up on the drugstore shelves. Before 1995 a drug patent was effective for seventeen years. Legislation passed that year, however, extended the term to twenty years. Since patents are often obtained before the drugs are ready to market, the actual patent term is frequently less.

What the FDA Requires of Generics

Even though generics aren't bound by the same procedures of development as innovator drugs, there are still some requirements:

- The generic must contain the same active ingredients as the innovator drug.
- The generic must be identical in strength, dosage form, and route of administration.
- The generic must have the same use indications.
- The generic must be bioequivalent to the innovator drug.
- The generic must meet the same batch requirements for identity, strength, purity, and quality.
- The generic must be manufactured under the same strict standards the FDA requires of innovator drugs.

So, what's the problem? Sure sounds good enough. Generics are cheaper, and that's important. A generic is the same as the brand name drug, right? Wrong.

Essential

The term for the inactive agents in a drug is excipient. Additional excipients used include binders, emollients, lubricants, and preservatives. Common excipients include cornstarch, lactose, talc, magnesium stearate, sucrose, gelatin, calcium stearate, silicon dioxide, shellac, and glaze. Among their functions: They keep a drug from dissolving too soon or breaking into particles when handled.

A Small World of Difference

First of all, since the law requires that you need to be able to visually distinguish the generic from the innovator drug, its appearance will vary slightly. Next, the inactive ingredients—the flavors, fillers, and dyes—may be different from the brand name drug. Just because something is inactive doesn't mean you won't react to it. If your body doesn't absorb the fillers used in generic products the same way it handles name brand drugs, you may get different amounts of the medication than you did when you used the brand name product.

Also, since you don't know what those inactive ingredients are, it's possible that you may be allergic to one or more of them.

Don't Make Assumptions

The FDA assumes that generic drug manufacturers will abide by the same constraints as the innovator drug companies. In fact, some of these innovators have bought into the generic market, to ensure they will be able to continue profiting from their research investment. Most American companies do conform, but if your generic drug is manufactured outside the United States, you can't be sure of anything.

The Loophole

There's a loophole for the generic companies, and it's big enough to drive a truck through. The FDA uses the plus or minus 20 percent test to determine blood serum availability. That means the amount of the active ingredients in your bloodstream, after you have ingested a generic drug, has to come within plus or minus 20 percent of what those levels would be if you had ingested the innovator drug. Twenty percent may not be important or medically significant for certain conditions, but it can be of vital significance in others. Also, the math gets more complex once you analyze what can happen.

Suddenly, It's Serious

Here's a scenario to chew on. Suppose you are on heart medication, and your physician has had you on a specific brand name drug. That drug was produced at the higher end of the plus or minus 20 percent allowability. Your insurance company has balked at paying for the brand name and will only cover a generic. So, you have your next prescription filled with the generic. If that generic had been produced at the lower end of the plus or minus 20 percent allowability, you are now getting 40 percent less medication than previously. The same scenario could have the numbers flip-flopped, so now you're getting 40 percent more than you should. This can be extremely dangerous for you.

Equivalence Doesn't Mean Equal

All the generic company has to do in order to meet FDA requirements is to produce a drug that has chemical equivalence (similar quantities and availability of the active ingredients to the innovator drug) and bioequivalence (defined by absorption parameters that fall within the plus or minus 20 percent regulation). Similar and equivalent do not mean *the same as*. If you need an example of this, just think: margarine is similar to butter. It's got a similar color, caloric equivalence, and similar uses. Or, how about siblings? If you have a brother or a sister, you probably share some similarities. In fact, the list can be quite long; however, are you the same person? Are you different enough to make those differences statistically significant? Even if you are an identical twin, there are differences enough between you to tell you apart as individuals. The drug descriptors work exactly the same way.

What to Do?

Your physician knows what the therapeutic level of your prescription must be. Before you decide to go generic, discuss this with your doctor to see if it's a good move on your part or an invitation for problems.

If the generic will work for you and not be a source of potential problems, it may be a logical choice. If it won't do the job, however, hold your ground. Your health is what's important and, at the very least, your prescription medications should first and foremost do you no harm.

Generic Antidepressants

You knew this was coming next, didn't you? Generic antidepressants are beginning to appear en masse, as the patents on the innovator drugs expire. Generic Prozac has been available since 2001, generic Paxil since 2005, and generic Zoloft since 2006. Joining them will be generic versions of Wellbutrin XL, Paxil CR, Lexapro, and Celexa.

New and Improved

Manufacturers have been working on the innovator drugs to increase their attractiveness and give them an edge up on the generics. If they can change the drug enough to keep the patent, it's well worth the additional time and money investment. Extended-release formulas is one tactic the manufacturers are using and the other strategy is separating out one function from a drug that has mixed forms. In many cases these improvements are not just to enhance profits but actually do enhance the drug's performance.

 ## Question

How does an extended-release formula help?
These new formulas increase the amount of time it takes for the medication to dissolve. As a result, the drug gets a chance to go lower in the digestive tract and reduce the occurrence of certain side effects, such as nausea. Also, you don't have to take these drugs as often, and that may help you remember to take them when you should.

Surfing the Net for Meds

Generic drugs can save you a considerable amount of money. Buying your drugs online can save you even more. Some folks even travel to other countries to purchase their medications, but is this safe? The FDA advises that buying medication over the Internet from foreign sources, from storefront businesses that offer to buy foreign medicine for you, or during trips outside the country may not be safe or effective. Even if the packaging and labeling seem identical to what you'd find in the United States, the FDA cannot attest to the cleanliness or safety of purchases made outside the United States, as its jurisdiction stops at the borders. If you buy online, be sure the site requires a prescription and also has a pharmacist available to answer any questions you may have about your medications.

Save Time, Don't Do Time

The U.S. Department of Justice Drug Enforcement Agency (DEA) has issued a warning to consumers about buying controlled substances online. Federal law prohibits the purchase of controlled substances without a valid prescription from your doctor. The existence of a real patient-doctor relationship is the criteria used here, and this, according to most state laws requires a physical examination. The DEA warns that prescriptions written by "cyber doctors," who rely on online questionnaires to gather information, are not legitimate under the law.

Controlled substances dispensed in this fashion may include the narcotic pain relievers such as OxyContin and Vicodin; sedatives, such as Valium, Xanax, and Ambien; and stimulants, such as phentermine, phendimetrazine, Adderall, Ritalin, and anabolic steroids (e.g., Winstrol and Equipoise). Be aware that the DEA is targeting illegal Web sites for prosecution and is shutting them down. If you aren't sure about a Web site's legality, check with the National Association of Boards of Pharmacy before you make a purchase. You can find them at *www.nabp.net*.

CHAPTER 10

Is Alternative Therapy Right for You?

IF YOUR SYMPTOMS are mild or if you're looking for something to give your prescribed medications and psychotherapy a boost, you may be interested in alternative and complementary therapies. Alternative therapy refers to a wide variety of treatment options other than prescription drugs and psychotherapy. Complementary therapies, which will be covered in the next chapter, are those treatments used in conjunction with conventional medicine. Today you may hear the term integrative medicine used. That's the name given to treatment protocols that employ the best of traditional as well as complementary therapies. You'll discover, as you read the chapter, that many of these therapies share a common objective: restoring balance.

Acupuncture

The practice of acupuncture goes back over 2,000 years in traditional Chinese medicine, but the word acupuncture comes from the Latin words acus ("needle") and punctura ("prickling"). In this case, that's as close to a crystal clear description as you can get. Prickling needles.

If you decide upon acupuncture to help treat your symptoms, the acupuncturist will first interview you to gain an understanding of your complaint. Then he will insert needles at certain points on your body, creating a specific pattern. The points selected depend upon the nature of your ailment. You may feel a slight pricking sensation, but the procedure is not painful. Once the pattern has been completed, you will rest quietly for a period of time, perhaps half an hour. Then the acupuncturist removes the needles and sends you on your way.

The Tradition

The Chinese believe that energy, known as *qi*, flows throughout the body along specific meridians or pathways. If you become ill, it is because this energy has become blocked in some fashion. This blockage disrupts the natural balance between yin and yang, the body's opposing forces. Acupuncture brings the yin and yang back into balance, the normal flow of qi is unblocked, and health is restored.

The Modern Version

According to the National Center for Complementary and Alternative Medicine, acupuncture needles act upon the central nervous system (CNS), which then responds by releasing endorphins (the body's "feel good" hormones) and immune system cells that diffuse throughout the CNS, promoting healing. In essence, acupuncture uses the body's own capacity for healing.

What's the Connection to Depression?

The connection to depression is a logical one. A 1998 study at the University of Arizona, funded by the NIH's Center for Complementary and Alternative Medicine (NCCAM), found that, following acupuncture treatment, 43 percent of those participating in the study reported a reduction in depressive symptoms. The control group reported a 22 percent reduction in symptoms.

Acupuncture may play a role in altering brain chemistry by effecting changes in the release of neurotransmitters and neurohormones. This accounts for the general feeling of well-being and mood elevation that occurs following an acupuncture treatment.

Are There Any Risks?

As with any invasive procedure, there is risk. Using a licensed acupuncturist is one way to lessen the chances of any mishap. Acupuncture inserts fine needles into the skin, so if the needles are not inserted properly, there is a possibility of hematoma, nerve, or organ damage. Needles that have not been properly autoclaved (sterilized) may transfer diseases such as HIV and hepatitis. To prevent that possibility, most practitioners use one-time use needles and dispose of them after that one use. The other option is to autoclave needles after each use.

 Alert

The National Certification Commission for Acupuncture and Oriental Medicine (NCCAOM) provides testing for acupuncturists. Since many states require acupuncturists to be licensed, passing this test is a prerequisite for licensing. Check with NCCAOM to learn the requirements for licensing in your state. Their Web site is *www.nccaom.org*.

Finding an Acupuncturist

Your health care provider may refer you to a licensed acupuncture practitioner, or you may be pleasantly surprised to learn that your doctor is trained in this discipline. More and more practitioners of traditional western medicine are becoming trained in acupuncture. Also, your insurance may cover part or all of the costs of this treatment. Check with your insurance carrier to see if preauthorization is required. Just as you inform your primary health care provider about any alternative or complementary protocols you are following, be sure to inform your acupuncturist of any prescription medications you are using.

Yoga

If you've seen pictures of people practicing yoga, you may have wondered how they got into such impossible positions or why they even wanted to. What's the attraction with yoga? Perhaps it might be the element of control involved. Just as acupuncture considers depression to result from a blockage of the body's qi, yoga believes that depression is the result of the body's separation from its source—its connection to a sense of self.

Yoga is all about regaining that balance and reuniting the body with that sense of self. Whereas acupuncture is passive, meaning that you're lying on the treatment table while the acupuncturist attends to you, yoga is active. In yoga, you take control of your body. And when you're dealing with depression, taking an active position, pardon the pun, can be a healthy step forward in your depression management plan.

The Tradition

While Western medicine works to alleviate symptoms and cure the disease, Eastern medicine takes a more holistic approach and operates from the premise that mind, body, and spirit are one.

L, Essential

Eastern medicine is considered to be those healing arts that have their origins in China, India, and other countries of the Orient. Eastern medicine developed independently of the West, separated from it by geography and language.

Yoga probably originated in the Indus Valley civilization some 4,000 to 8,000 years ago, so it's even older than acupuncture. It's not a religion, but rather it's a discipline that seeks to unite body, mind, and spirit. The Yoga Sutras, an ancient Indian text, explain the postures and the philosophy behind the system. Yoga works to cultivate *prana*, which equates with qi. This is the body's energy or life force on its quest to achieve consciousness—understanding. Ultimately the goal is to reach a union between one's own consciousness and the universal consciousness. Yoga is a means to attain that consciousness.

The Modern Version

Yoga is a non-aerobic exercise that teaches precise postures, breathing, and meditation. According to a report by the National Institutes of Health (NIH), yoga may help relieve anxiety, stress, and depression. Practicing yoga helps you focus your concentration, work with your body, and open yourself to the strength within you.

 Fact

> Aerobic exercise is intense physical activity, such as running or swimming. The heart and lungs must work harder to fulfill the body's increased need for oxygen. Non-aerobic, or anaerobic, literally means "in the absence of oxygen." In non-aerobic exercise, such as yoga or weight training, the nature of the activity doesn't require the heart and lungs to work overtime.

Usually, you'll practice yoga in the morning or at the close of the day. The benefit of yoga is that you can do the exercises on your own, in your own home. There are books you can read to gain a clearer understanding of how yoga works. In *Yoga for Depression: A Compassionate Guide to Relieve Suffering Through Yoga*, Yogi Amy Weintraub provides a look at specific ways to use yoga to relieve the symptoms of mild depression. She stresses that yoga is a supplement to conventional therapy. It is not a replacement for that therapy.

Of course, there are classes you can take, as well as CDs and DVDs you can purchase. You can find classes through your YMCA or YWCA, local community center, or check with your local hospital for the location of the nearest site.

What's the Connection to Depression?

You got a hint of the connection in the last section. It's control—learning how to use your body to achieve peace and relaxation. When you've had some time to practice your postures, you may begin to see positive changes in your blood pressure, heart rate, and breathing. The postures, breathing exercises, and meditation all work together to help your body achieve a sense of self and union.

Research has confirmed the benefits of yoga. A Boston University School of Medicine study found that yoga practitioners' brain scans showed a 27 percent increase in levels of the neurotransmitter gamma-aminobutyric (GABA) immediately following a one-hour yoga session. Low GABA levels are associated with anxiety and depression, so if yoga can raise those levels, that's exciting news. There's more research on the way.

Are There Any Risks?

You may hear yourself saying, "Don't all those postures hurt? Anyway, I'm too old for yoga." You are never too old to take control of your body. That's why you start slowly and build gradually. Yoga sessions can last from twenty minutes to an hour. You begin with stretching. As you progress through the postures, you will concentrate on your breathing. Some postures may be uncomfortable at first, especially if you suffer from arthritis or have joint problems. Discuss your plans with your doctor before you begin a yoga regimen.

Meditation

Have you ever tuned anyone out? Have you ever become so engrossed in something that you were oblivious to your surroundings? Did you ever have the unsettling experience of driving and suddenly realizing you weren't aware of those past few miles? In each of these examples, your awareness—your mindfulness—was redirected. More accurately, you have redirected that awareness or mindfulness. Learning how to do that when you want to and when it will serve you is fundamental to meditation.

Concentrate!

There is an aspect of meditation in yoga. While you are practicing your sun salutations or assuming the lotus position, you are using the power of your mind to transcend your perceived limitations of your body. So, how do you meditate? Is it like thinking? Actually, it's more about not thinking. At least, not thinking about the things that cause you stress. It's learning to refocus your thinking through visualization, relaxation, and breathing.

In meditation, your attention is focused and concentrated. How you focus your concentration is up to you. Choose a particular word—such as "om"—or a phrase or visualize a specific scene or concentrate on your breathing. The object is to clear your mind of distractions, so you actively work to exclude anything else that tries to butt in. Distraction breeds stress, and stress breeds depression. When you clear your mind of distractions, you are not stressed. You're aiming for a relaxed physical state. The logical end of this, of course, is to manage that depression. To accomplish this, you'll probably want to use a combination of therapies that work just for you and your needs.

As you practice meditation, you'll learn to isolate the stressors in your life. In this regard, meditation can be a useful addition to your arsenal in fighting depression. It can help you reframe the way you see your world. That's also the object of psychotherapy—to help you change your outlook—that's why meditation is a good adjunct to psychotherapy.

Breathing Lessons

If you've ever studied voice, then you know that much of a vocalist's training centers on learning how to breathe properly—from the abdomen instead of the diaphragm. Deep, regulated, and controlled as opposed to rapid, shallow, and fast. Why breathe differently? One thing that's happening, when you're concentrating on your breathing, is that you're not concentrating on your depression. You're teaching your brain to re-focus. That's good. You have the power within you to effect change.

The second thing that happens when you're breathing correctly is that you're getting more oxygen into your bloodstream, nourishing all those red blood cells. It's the ripple effect—a chain reaction of health.

Spirituality

Defining spirituality is difficult at best. It's a highly personal concept. Is spirituality the same as religion? No. That part's easy, although for some people, religion is a means of expressing their spirituality. However, you can be a spiritual person without being a religious person. In a way, it's rather like art. You know it when you see it.

The word religion comes to us from the Latin verb *religio*, meaning "to bind back" or "to bind together." There's a reason for the term "organized religion." Religion organizes people to worship a divine being or beings and uses certain protocols or ceremonies for this worship. These ceremonies are usually held in a building—such as a temple, synagogue, or church—specifically designed and built for the purpose. Religious denominations also fulfill important social functions, carrying out rites of passage, caring for the sick and elderly, educating children, and generally providing a sense of community. For many people, religious faith is sufficient to see them through the hard times in life. They take comfort in the knowledge that God is watching over them and they feel supported by the members of their congregation.

In some churches, depression has historically been viewed as something sinful—a sign of lack of faith in God. This belongs to the "Get over it" school of thought, and fortunately is fading away, as research demonstrates that depression is not a character flaw, but a medical condition. If your religious affiliation supports you as you deal with depression, this can be a positive component of your health management plan.

Relevant Religion

A study conducted at the Durham Veterans Affairs Medical Center in 1999 examined the effects of religious practices, coping mechanisms, and social support on recovery among individuals diagnosed with major depression. The researchers found that religion served a vital purpose in helping patients cope with depression and advised doctors to keep their patients' religious beliefs and spiritual concerns in mind, as they treated those patients' depression.

Just As I Am

Not everyone has a church affiliation, however. If you do not have a religious faith, spirituality provides many of the same benefits of religion. Spirituality can be achieved on your own, without groups, without ceremony, and without "going public."

What's involved in spirituality? First, there's a belief in a Higher Power—something bigger than yourself. This Higher Power doesn't have to be God, spirit, or even anything specific. Whatever you're comfortable with works. Then, there's a sense of purpose. Your life has meaning because there is a purpose to it. You are here on earth to learn, to do, and to grow. Finally, there is a sense of being connected to all life. Here's the connection to the universal consciousness!

⌐ Essential

> If you have a church affiliation, you may find that your rabbi, minister, or priest can help you find the right kind of counseling to deal with depression.

Letting Go and Getting Free

Why is the concept of a Higher Power important? Sometimes the feeling that you need to control everything adds to your stress to the point you can't function. However, some things are beyond your understanding and control. So, accepting the Higher Power, however you define it, can relieve your stress and ease your mind. There's a line in Max Ehrmann's famous poem, "Desiderata," that's worth noting: "And whether or not it is clear to you, no doubt the universe is unfolding as it should." Accepting that premise frees you. It allows you to let go.

A Little Help from Your Friends—The Big Book

If you are coping with depression, "One Day at a Time" and "Just for Today" take on special meaning. These are the familiar slogans from Alcoholics Anonymous (AA), the very first twelve-step program.

AA also uses the term "Higher Power." For members of AA, relinquishing control to a Higher Power and accepting your humanness are essential to achieving the goal of sobriety. There's some valuable insight here for managing depression, as well.

AA operates from the premise that the body, mind, and spirit are inextricably intertwined. Treating the mind is just as important as treating the body. Dealing with the source of the problem involves sharing experiences and gaining strength from others who are going through similar experiences. In group counseling, individuals suffering from depression find the same type of support.

Finding Your Focus

So, is religion or spirituality a crutch? No more so than ibuprofen is. In the Judeo-Christian tradition, the Bible serves as a guidebook for dealing with adversity and depression. It would be difficult to conjure up an individual more depressed than Job, and the lesson in Scripture is "Hang in there." But the message extends beyond those faith systems. Buddhism teaches that all human life is suffering and that we must work to rise above our limitations to achieve peace. The message is clear: "You can do it. Don't lose hope."

A spiritual focus can include religion, yoga, and any other method that helps you find resources to manage your depression. Back to yoga, for a moment. A study in the February 2007 issue of *Journal of Gerontological Nursing* found that those seniors involved in the yoga program showed a significant decrease in depression. According to Shirley Telles, the study's senior author, "the seniors particularly enjoyed (and felt better with) the bhakti yoga sessions—singing devotional songs to no particular deity." It evoked "a sense of faith in a Power greater than themselves."

Understanding that you are not alone or abandoned is essential to good mental and emotional health. Life's journey is not always an easy one. Spirituality—that connection to a higher power—can be a powerful help as you work to manage depression.

Hypnosis

Quick! What comes to mind, when someone mentions the subject of hypnosis? Unless you've undergone hypnosis to help you with weight control or to quit smoking, you probably think of a magician of sorts, on a stage, swinging a chain with a gold coin, or something like it, in front of someone's eyes, intoning "You are getting sleeeeepy..." Inevitably, the person ends up crowing like a rooster, barking like a dog, or doing something else that's embarrassing and demeaning, but harmless.

Watching someone lose control over his or her actions is disconcerting and so you laugh. It's a nervous reaction. You're just glad it's not you. Is this what hypnosis really is? No, it's not. Hypnosis is an altered state of consciousness. In self-hypnosis, you induce this state in yourself. Otherwise, it's induced by another person. While you're hypnotized, you have a heightened receptivity to the power of suggestion. That's the technical definition.

 Alert

> Don't fall for those Internet or magazine ad scams that guarantee results with a hypnotist who has graduated from some bogus school. Always get a reference from a physician or licensed counselor or psychotherapist.

Hypnotic History Lesson

Once again, those Greeks were involved. The term *hypnosis* comes from Hypnos, the Greek god of dreams, although hypnosis really isn't about sleep, at all. The Greeks and others, in ancient times, used hypnosis as a healing tool. No one really understood how it worked.

Freud Facts

Sigmund Freud, the father of modern psychiatry, used hypnotherapy in his work but discovered that hypnosis was more powerful than just a tool for working with phobias. Under hypnosis, his patients brought all kinds of troubling emotions to the surface, and Freud backed off. Eventually, he stopped using hypnosis altogether. Since Freud's time, however, hypnosis has enjoyed something of a resurgence and is used to help individuals quit smoking or quit drugs. It's also used to treat simple phobias.

 Fact

Franz Anton Mesmer, an 18th-century Austrian physician, used what he called "magnetic healing" to treat a variety of disorders, such as hysterical blindness and headaches. He believed this animal magnetism passed from him to the person being hypnotized. His name, Mesmer, gave us the word mesmerized—meaning "caught up in a trancelike state."

Entering the Subconscious Mind

Psychiatrists don't completely understand how hypnosis works. They do know that it's a trance state in which subjects are relaxed and have heightened susceptibility to suggestion and an increased imagination. This trance state has been compared to that moment between wakefulness and sleep. You're relaxed and open. Hypnosis may be the key that unlocks the door to the subconscious mind. Think of it like this: When you're conscious, you're aware; when you're unconscious, you're on auto-pilot. You're unaware of your subconscious mind, but it's very aware of you.

In hypnosis, your conscious mind takes a breather and lets your subconscious control the show. Since memories are stored in the subconscious, hypnosis can bring them to the surface. If these memories are the source of anxiety or phobias, through hypnosis, you can work through them and alleviate the symptoms you have been experiencing.

How Does It Work?

In order to be hypnotized, you must want to be hypnotized. You must also believe that you can be hypnotized, and you must feel comfortable with the idea. Usually, the hypnotist brings on the trance by speaking to you slowly, in a soothing voice. The goal is to bring about that state of utter and complete relaxation. You can also learn to hypnotize yourself!

Who Does This Kind of Hypnotherapy?

Psychiatrists, regulated by the American Psychiatric Association (APA) and the American Medical Association (AMA), and licensed psychologists who have gone through advanced training courses in hypnosis are qualified to perform hypnotherapy. Check with your physician for a referral, as anybody who has watched an instructional video or read a book on the subject may call herself a hypnotist.

Regression Therapy

You may have heard of regression as a form of hypnosis that seeks to discover past lives. A while back, it was quite a fad for people who wanted to go back in time to see if they might have been Cleopatra or Caesar or some other historical figure, in a previous life. This was the frivolous aspect of regression. It is important to understand that this practice may result in the creation of false memories, resulting from the subject incorporating the hypnotist's suggestions into remembered scenes or events. Be aware of the risks these false memories may create.

The purpose of regression therapy, however, is not frivolous. This is a form of hypnosis that seeks the source of trauma. Since post-traumatic stress disorder (PTSD) results from trauma, returning to the source of that trauma allows the therapist to help the patient confront and deal with PTSD.

As Mark Wolynn, director of the Medical Hypnotherapy Center, explains, "A belief in past lives as real is completely irrelevant to this therapy. All we really know for sure is that each of us carries within us an image that has the power to help us heal." It is the function of regression therapy to access that image of healing.

Chiropractic

Practitioners of chiropractic believe that manipulation and adjustment of the spinal column can result in the healing of various complaints. Chiropractic assumes that the nervous system coordinates all of the body's functions, and when that system is not optimal, disease results. Most practitioners use the Palmer Method, named after the founder of chiropractic, Daniel David Palmer.

Essential

Palmer was an Iowa grocer, not a medical doctor, and performed his first chiropractic adjustment in 1895. The term chiropractic is of Greek origin: chir for "hand" and prassein for "manipulate." Palmer founded the Palmer College of Chiropractic in Davenport, Iowa, in 1898.

Outside the Umbrella

The traditional medical establishment did not endorse chiropractic for many years, primarily based upon the prevailing chiropractic belief that all diseases, including cancer, could be treated by chiropractic. In 1978 the American Medical Association (AMA) modified its position on chiropractic, accepting its use in some musculoskeletal disorders. A doctorate of chiropractic (DC) requires minimally two years of college and four years in a school of chiropractic.

Risks of Chiropractic

The greatest risk appears to be in cervical neck adjustments. Individuals with medical conditions that cause insufficient blood flow to the brain should not have chiropractic treatments, as there is a risk of stroke. Apart from relieving stress, which may occur as the result of painful back spasms and that may contribute to depression, chiropractic has not been shown to be of any benefit in the management of depression.

Biofeedback

Biofeedback is an interesting way of harnessing the mind's power to control what previously had been thought to be involuntary body functions, such as blood pressure and brain wave activity.

Biofeedback is now used to treat a number of medical conditions, and stress is one of them. Since stress is involved in depression, biofeedback may provide some benefit.

How Does It Work?

Scientists aren't totally sure how biofeedback works. The University of Maryland Medical Center explains that, during a biofeedback session, electrodes are attached to the skin. Then readings, or information, are relayed via the electrodes to a monitor that translates the physiological data into a tone, a visual meter with varying degrees of brightness, or a computer screen that shows the data as lines moving across a grid. The biofeedback therapist then guides the patient through a series of mental exercises, looking for the ones that will create positive change, which is then shown on the monitor. As patients focus on relaxation, positive changes in blood pressure and brain waves occur.

L. Essential

Neal Miller, an American experimental psychologist, did the groundbreaking work in biofeedback during the 1950s and 1960s. At the time, no one believed that the human mind could be taught to control the autonomic nervous system. Miller proved them wrong!

Benefits for Depression

As with other therapies you have read about in this chapter, biofeedback gives you control over how your body responds to different situations. There is a significant feeling of loss of control in depression, so by using biofeedback techniques, you can regain that sense of mastery over your body and its reactions. Control your reactions, manage your stress levels, and you may be able to relieve the symptoms of depression.

Massage

If you've had massage therapy previously, you know its benefits. There are many forms of massage, but they all have the objective of manipulating muscles and connective tissue to promote relaxation and well-being. Therapeutic massage can ease tension and reduce pain. Massage therapists use their hands, their fingertips, and their elbows to get at the source of your pain and discomfort.

Back to the East

Massage comes to us from Eastern Medicine. The Chinese used therapeutic massage some 2,500 years ago, and it was also practiced in India. The word itself is of Arabic origin—from *mass'h*, meaning "press gently." Later, the Greeks made use of it, and Hippocrates used massage to treat sprains. Perhaps massage is as old as the human race. It's a natural reaction—to rub where it hurts!

The Healing Touch

The power of human touch cannot be overestimated. A series of studies conducted by the Touch Research Institute at the University of Miami School of Medicine found that massage therapy lowered the stress hormone cortisol levels by up to 53 percent. It also increased levels of serotonin and dopamine, neurotransmitters that help reduce depression. Simply stated, massage relieves the symptoms of depression.

As you've seen, there are many forms of alternative therapy. Some have proven their effectiveness, while others have not. Any form of alternative or complementary therapy should be approached with caution and should be discussed with your physician before you add it to your treatment protocol. This chapter focused on practices; the next chapter covers herbal and supplement alternative therapies.

CHAPTER 11

Complementary Therapies: Herbals and Supplements

HERBS WERE OUR FIRST MEDICINES. The use of herbs is a time-honored approach to strengthening the body and treating disease. Since the earliest times, people have turned to Mother Nature's pantry to cure their ailments. In this chapter, you'll see what herbs may be useful for treating depression's symptoms, along with what supplements are available on the market. Herbs, however, contain components that can trigger side effects and interact with other herbs, supplements, or medications. For these reasons, herbs should be taken with care, under the supervision of a health care provider qualified in the field of botanical medicine.

It's Only Natural

In traditional Eastern medicine, herbs have always played an important role. In Western medicine, however, they've taken a back seat to the pharmaceuticals produced in scientific labs, where their quality and uniformity can be monitored. Still, many medications used today have strong roots in the plant world. Consider the most wonderful of the wonder drugs—aspirin and its plant ancestor, the willow. Native Americans chewed on willow bark to relieve headaches and other pains. The active agent in willow, salicin, is the word from which aspirin is derived.

A Warning Note or Two

Some herbs have the power to soothe your nerves, and some have the power to relieve pain. Others, however, contain deadly poisons and can cause illness and death. Before you go off into the woods or the meadows picking plants to brew into a tea, consult a good herbal (the name given to an authoritative work on herbs). *Rodale's Illustrated Encyclopedia of Herbs* is the plant bible and provides sound information to the curious mind. After you've done some homework and determined that your herb of choice is not potentially harmful, consult your physician or pharmacist. Some herbs have negative interactions with prescription medications, and you could find yourself in some serious trouble if you inadvertently create a deadly mix. Always clear your proposed regimen with your physician and pharmacist before you go native.

Essential

> Botanical is the term used to refer to any plant. You may see botanical used interchangeably with herb or herbal. It relates to the word botany.

You're On Your Own

The warning above also holds true for any non-herbal supplements you decide to make part of your health management plan. Just because you can buy it at the natural foods or health foods store doesn't mean it's harmless or even good for you. Also, the Food and Drug Safety Administration (FDA) considers herbs and supplements to be dietary supplements—that means neither a food nor a drug—and that means the FDA stays out of the picture until a product has proven to be unsafe.

Learn the Law

According to the Dietary Supplement Health and Education Act (DSHEA), a dietary supplement is a product other than tobacco that:

- Supplements the food you eat
- Contains one or more dietary ingredients—including vitamins, minerals, herbs or other botanicals, amino acids, and other substances
- Comes in pill, capsule, tablet, or liquid form
- Is labeled as a dietary supplement

So What Does All This Mean?

Many supplements have specific health benefits, but you never can be sure exactly what you're getting, so consistency of product strength and purity are concerns. The difficulty is in quality control. You need to read the labels with an educated eye and become a knowledgeable and confident consumer. Here's why: Consumer-Lab.com tested eleven brands of echinacea to run a quality control check. They found that only four samples contained what was stated on their labels. About 10 percent had no echinacea at all; half were mislabeled as to the species of echinacea in the product; and more than half of the standardized preparations did not contain the labeled amount of active ingredients.

 Alert

Caveat emptor! It's an old Latin saying, but it holds true today just as it always has. Buyer Beware! The burden is on you, the consumer. If you want to make a purchase, know the whole deal. After all, your health is your most precious possession!

Herbs and supplements are available at the warehouse superstores, health food stores, regular grocery stores, and pharmacies. Don't try to save a few pennies by buying an off brand or an unknown brand. Choose a company with a proven track record. Again, your pharmacist can give you good information and recommendations. Before you get to the store, know in advance the common name and the scientific name of the herb or supplement you're seeking. Since common names vary by geographical region, the scientific name is the way to be sure you're getting what you want.

Essential

The scientific name consists of two Latin words—the first indicates genus and the second, species. It was the work of Carolus Linnaeus, a Swedish scientist, and provides a means for categorizing all species, in a uniform manner. It eliminates confusion and allows for clear communication.

Holding That Brown Bottle in Your Hand

The color, by the way, is to keep sunlight from degrading the contents of the bottle. Now that the label is staring up at you, read the warnings. If nothing there applies to you, check the ingredients. If you have allergies to certain products, be sure they aren't on the ingredient list. Then check the expiration date, storage instructions, and dosage information. Finally, look to see what kind of fillers are used. Sometimes these are called "flowering agents." How much herb or supplement are you actually getting and how much filler? Okay! It's time to take a look at herbs and supplements that may help with the symptoms of depression.

Traditional Remedies

Believe it or not, there's a lot to be said for folk wisdom and old wives' tales. While they may not always be completely true, they may have origins in fact, or part of their history might be relevant today. One such topic in which this often holds true is the healing power of herbs.

It must have been a challenge, learning which parts of plants to use and which to avoid. The common rhubarb plant is a good illustrator of that. The stalks are fine, the leaves are poisonous, and some people eat rhubarb pie without a second thought because they know what's what. Same thing with the potato. People eat the tubers and don't eat the leaves. Trial and error—maybe fatal error—is a fast teacher. The benefits of plants, however, have stood the test of time. And here are some that may be helpful in treating the symptoms of depression.

- **Angelica** (Angelica archangelica): Angelica has been used to treat insomnia. The medicinal use is to drink angelica as a tea. The recommended amount is one teaspoon of the roots or seeds boiled or steeped to a cup of water. Warning! Angelica resembles the poisonous water hemlock, so it's best not to go off and harvest your own.
- **Basil** (Ocimum basilicum): Basil is a common herb that you may already have in your cupboard. Basil has been reported to have a mild, sedating effect. If you wish to give it a try for treating anxiety, you can either drink it as a tea or use it in your cooking. Basil is a member of the mint family, so it's an easily recognizable plant. It's considered quite safe.
- **Betony** (Stachys officinalis): Betony contains glycosides, which, in one Russian study, were shown to have a moderating effect on blood pressure. It has been used for mild anxiety attacks. Betony's leaves can be used in a tea. It's generally considered to be safe.
- **Borage** (Borago officinalis): Borage has pretty blue flowers, so just looking at it can lift the spirits. The leaves, stems, and flowers are all edible, and borage has been used to treat depression. You can make a diffusion of the flowers for a soothing tea.
- **Catnip** (Nepeta cataria): Catnip is another member of the mint family. Just like its cousin, basil, catnip is used in tea for insomnia. It has a mild, sedating effect, just the perfect nightcap.
- **Goldenseal** (Hydrastis canadensis): Goldenseal has been used to treat both stress and depression. It's extremely expensive.

Warning! Hydrastine, goldenseal's main component, can be quite toxic and is considered dangerous.

- **Mint** (Mentha ssp.): You've seen mint before in the catnip and basil sections. Any member of the mint family makes an excellent tea and is considered a safe treatment for insomnia. If you're skeptical about mint's sedative qualities, just offer some to your cat and watch what happens!

- **Rosemary** (Rosmarinus officinalis): Rosemary has been used to treat insomnia and depression. It has a nice fragrance, which is soothing. Its leaves can be used as a diffusion to make a tea.

- **Saffron** (Crocus sativus): Saffron has been used to treat insomnia. Its vibrant yellow color resembles sunshine. It is quite expensive. Warning! Saffron can be toxic, even in small doses.

- **Serpentwood** (Rauvolfia serpentina): Serpentwood has been used to treat insomnia, and it is a crossover herb used in pharmaceuticals. The drug reserpine, which is used as a tranquilizer, is extracted from serpentwood root.

Essential

Herbs lose their potency over time. Plan to use your herbs within six months of purchase and store them in a cool place, away from moisture and light. Be sure to reseal the cap tightly, before returning it to the cupboard.

Herbs in the News

Two popular herbs, Echinacea and St. John's wort have gotten more than their share of recent publicity. Echinacea has been defrocked as a common cold preventative, and St. John's wort has come up short in the safety sector. A third perennial favorite, ginseng—sold as Ginkgo biloba—has also been demoted. Ephedra has also received bad marks, in this case, an F.

Echinacea (Echinacea ssp.)

Echinacea is also known as purple coneflower and is grown in many perennial and herb gardens. The Native Americans used it for a variety of ailments. Echinacea is sold in extracts, tinctures, tablets, capsules, and ointments and in combination with other herb products. However, a study published in 2005 in the *New England Journal of Medicine* busted the myth that echinacea could ward off the common cold. Researchers found that echinacea just didn't make any difference.

Warning! Echinacea is not the benign herb that you may have been led to believe, and its use is contraindicated in people with tuberculosis, leukemia, diabetes, connective tissue disorders, multiple sclerosis, HIV/AIDS, autoimmune disease, or liver disorders. People taking autoimmune suppressants should not use echinacea. If you have asthma or certain allergies, you may experience an allergic reaction to echinacea, ranging from mild to life-threatening.

Ephedra (Ephedra ssp.)

Ephedra looks like a stubby pine tree or a horsetail plant. It's been used extensively in Chinese medicine, where it's known as *ma-huang*. A tea made from the dried branches has been used to treat stress and depression. Warning! The FDA published a final rule on April 12, 2004, banning the sale of dietary supplements containing ephedrine alkaloids. The principal active ingredient ephedrine is an amphetamine-like compound. The FDA found that these supplements present an unreasonable risk of heart problems and stroke.

The National Center for Complementary and Alternative Medicine (NCCAM) has reported that calls to poison control centers revealed a disproportionate rate of reactions to ephedra relative to other herbal products. There is strong evidence that ephedra is associated with an increased risk of side effects, possibly even fatal ones.

Ginseng (Panax quinquefolius)

Ginseng, also known as ginkgo biloba, has been used to treat stress and depression and is widely used both in the United States and Europe. It's a staple in the Chinese pharmacopeia, and like soy, it's been touted as a cure for just about everything. It comes in pill form. Ginkgo biloba extract (GBE) is manufactured from the plant's leaves.

Warning! Children under age twelve, as well as pregnant and nursing women should not consume ginkgo biloba. If you are scheduled for surgery, discontinue use of ginkgo biloba at least thirty-six hours prior to surgery to avoid the risk of bleeding complications, according to the University of Michigan Medical Center.

Warning #2! The University of Michigan Medical Center advises that ginkgo may negatively interact with some prescription and over-the-counter drugs, including selective serotonin reuptake inhibitors (SSRIs) fluoxetine (Prozac), sertraline (Zoloft), paroxetine (Paxil), and escitalopram (Lexapro). Ginkgo may cause serotonin syndrome, which is characterized by rigidity, tachycardia (fast heart rate), restlessness, and diaphoresis (sweating). Ginkgo may enhance the effects (both good and bad) of antidepressant medications known as MAOIs, such as phenelzine (Nardil). There has been a report of an adverse interaction between ginkgo and trazodone (Desyrel), an antidepressant medication that resulted in an elderly patient going into a coma. Before you consider using ginkgo biloba, consult with your physician. If you are taking any medications—prescribed or otherwise—be sure ginkgo biloba will not cause adverse reactions with them.

St. John's Wort (Hypericum perforatum)

St. John's wort is an attractive plant with pretty yellow flowers. It's been used for centuries to induce a sense of well-being, and for that reason it's commonly used to help alleviate the symptoms of depression. It can be toxic in large doses. It's used more in Europe than in the United States. Warning! The Food and Drug Administration (FDA) issued a Public Health Advisory in February 2000 noting that St. John's wort appeared to affect an important metabolic pathway used by specific medications, including antidepressant medications. Before using St. John's wort, you should consult with your prescribing physician.

Aromatherapy

What's the difference among smell, odor, and aroma? Of course, smell is one of the five senses, but a smell has a distinctly negative connotation—as in, "What's that smell?" Odor also has an unpleasant affect—as in, "That's certainly a noxious odor." Aroma, however, conjures up a palette of pleasing fragrances. And it is for just this reason that aromatherapy—the use of specific herbs for their calming properties—has a place in soothing the mind and treating at least one of the symptoms of depression: stress.

⌷. Essential

The sense of smell is one of the most powerful of your senses. Just catching a whiff of a perfume, a roasting chicken, or scorched hot chocolate can transport you back in time. The associative nature of the sense of smell can bring childhood memories to the forefront in the time it takes to catch your breath. If those memories are good, that's wonderful. If they're not, they can become stressors and compound the symptoms of depression.

Aromatherapy has ancient origins. It can be traced to religious ceremonies and the burning of incense to purify the ceremonial chamber. The Egyptians practiced aromatherapy, as did the Indus Valley civilizations. The ancient Greeks used olive oil, a plentiful agent, to bind the essential oils. The Romans used aromatherapy to scent their bath water. So the history of aromatherapy stretches back into time.

Today, concentrated oils from various parts of specific herbs are used to create healing lotions, sprays, or compresses. These concentrated oils are called essential oils, since they are believed to capture the essence of the desirable plant. Then these oils are mixed with water or alcohol to create a spray and with oil, if the goal is to create a lotion. Aromatherapy products are for external use only. Aromatherapists believe that the essential oils are absorbed through the skin or inhaled and create the desired calming effect in this way. Lavender is a perennial favorite for aromatherapists, and its recommended use is as a stress reliever. Aromatherapy is considered safe—and it smells good!

Omega-3 Fatty Acids

Omega-3 fatty acids are necessary for maintaining good health. Your body needs omega-3 fatty acids but does not have the capability to produce them; therefore, you need to look elsewhere for a source. Fish is an excellent source for omega-3 fatty acids, and so are certain plants. Why are omega-3 fatty acids so important? If you don't maintain a good balance of both omega-3 and omega-6—another essential fatty acid—you may be at increased risk for depression. It makes sense, then, if you are suffering from depression, to get that balance back.

L. Essential

You've learned how important neurotransmitters are in preventing depression. Omega-3 fatty acids are important components of nerve cell membranes. They help nerve cells communicate with each other. Once again, balance is the key word. Maintaining a healthy balance is essential for optimal health.

Omega-3 fatty acids are being studied to gain further information about the roles they play in preventing depression. There's a great deal of interest in these substances, and the more scientists learn, the more they realize how important these essential fatty acids are. Here's a summary:

- In a study of thirty people with bipolar disorder, those who were treated with EPA (eicosapentaenoic acid) and DHA (docosahexaenoic acid) for a period of four months, in combination with their usual mood stabilizing medications, experienced fewer mood swings and recurrence of either depression or mania than the participants who received placebos.

- The University of Maryland Medical Center reported on a study of patients hospitalized for depression. Researchers found that levels of omega-3 fatty acids were measurably low and the ratio of omega-6 to omega-3 fatty acids were particularly high in those patients.
- In another study of people with depression, researchers found that those who ate a healthy diet, consisting of fatty fish two to three times per week for five years, experienced a significant reduction in feelings of depression and hostility. If you don't love fish by now, you haven't been paying attention!

EPA and DHA are found in cold-water fish such as salmon, mackerel, halibut, sardines, and herring. ALA (alanine) is an amino acid that is found in flaxseeds, flaxseed oil, canola (rapeseed) oil, soybeans, soybean oil, pumpkin seeds, pumpkin seed oil, purslane, perilla seed oil, walnuts, and walnut oil. These substances are also sold in the form of fish oil capsules.

Question

What's an amino acid?

An amino acid is one of the twenty building blocks of protein. The functions of amino acids are determined by the genetic code in your DNA. It was during the late 19th and early 20th century that German biochemist Albrecht Kossel determined that amino acids were these "building blocks."

Warning! If you bruise easily, have a bleeding disorder, or take blood-thinning medications, check with your physician to determine a safe amount of omega-3 fatty acids for you. In any case, it's always best to check with your doctor before adding any kind of supplement to your diet, even essentials such as omega-3s. Alanine, the amino acid, provides a nice segue to the next section.

SAM-e

SAM-e (S-adenosyl-L-methionine), is one of those serendipitous discoveries that keep scientists encouraged as they plow through the mysteries of the human body. This discovery happened in Italy during the 1970s. Doctors gave SAM-e to patients suffering from schizophrenia. The schizophrenia didn't improve, but the symptoms of depression did. SAM-e became a prescription drug in Europe, after that, and has been available in the United States as an over-the-counter drug since 1996.

So what is SAM-e? SAM-e is another naturally occurring substance in your body. It's made from an amino acid, but as you age, your body produces less of it. Researchers were able to make a synthetic version that seemed to work well as a supplement. Next, U.S. researchers wanted to see for themselves just how good SAM-e was.

Study Says . . .

A study of SAM-e's beneficial effects in treating major depression was carried out at the Depression Clinical and Research Program at Massachusetts General Hospital in Boston.

What researchers found was exciting. When the dietary supplement SAM-e was added to the patients' medication protocol, half of the patients with major depression improved, and 43 percent went into remission. They learned that SAM-e boosts the neurotransmitters serotonin and dopamine, and that has a positive effect on depression, as reported by WebMD. That's the function that researchers will continue to study. The NIH is supporting further research into the therapeutic effects of SAM-e.

A Warning

Even though SAM-e is available at health food stores and other places where dietary supplements are sold, you still need to follow the necessary precautions regarding its use. If you have bipolar disorder or Parkinson's Disease, you should not take SAM-e. If you have heart disease or are at risk for heart disease, check with your physician before making SAM-e part of your medical regimen.

CHAPTER 12

Your Diet

How you eat has tremendous impact on the way you feel. Developing good eating habits is one of the lifestyle changes you can make to help yourself as you fight depression. Since eating too much or too little are symptoms of depression, it's important to understand the role food plays in your life, apart from feeding your body. Adult eating habits and patterns develop in early childhood, so recognizing the way you use food—or the way food uses you—is crucial to making those good nutritional choices.

Changing Habits

One of the key factors in ensuring success in changing habits is to tackle one thing at a time. It's important to have goals, of course, but you can't wake up one morning and decide that today you're going to completely revise your eating habits, lose ten pounds or gain twenty, and totally revamp the way you've always looked at nutrition and your diet. You're bound to end up feeling overwhelmed by the whole idea and before you know it, you've decided the entire project is hopeless, tossed your good intentions into the trash, and resigned yourself to the status quo. With no forward progress, depression tightens its grip. Be reasonable and realistic, and you're much more likely to be successful.

Reclaiming Your Food Rights

Here's your opportunity to set things right. Spend some quality time with yourself and take a journey backwards through your mind.

You're looking for clues as to why you eat the way you do. Once you can see where the patterns began in your own life, you can begin to do something about changing them. If you can enlist another family member in this little discovery session, you'll be accomplishing more than ferreting out your food history. You'll be engaged on a social level, and that's a healthy way to pull yourself out of depression. Reminiscing can be healing and restorative!

⌐. Essential

If you don't have a journal, it's time to get one. They're easy to find at the drugstore or the grocery store in the school supply section. Loose scraps of paper are easily lost. Once you've got that little notebook, write down your goals. Give each one its own page. That way, as you meet each goal, you'll have a record of how far you've come. Looking back through the pages of your journal can give you the strength to keep moving forward in your life.

Goal Setting

It's essential that you separate goals from objectives. This has such a positive sound that it's energizing just to think about it. Goals. This means that you believe in the future and in your ability to change your own future. That's the ticket! Your goals don't have to be extreme. In fact, if you're just starting to lift yourself out of the quagmire of depression, getting out of bed and even considering eating a healthy breakfast can be a laudable goal. The key here is to make goals that have meaning for you. Nobody else can do this for you. So, take a piece of paper and a writing implement of your choice and write down one goal you'd like to meet. It can be short-term (the getting out of bed), mid-range (meeting all of your work obligations every day), or long-term (kicking depression out of your life). Got a goal? Good!

Objectives

Suppose your goal is to eat a healthier diet. Your objectives are the strategies that you'll use to meet your goals. Think of objectives as steps on a ladder. For each goal, you may have several objectives. For now, just write them down, as they come to you. You can arrange them in order of importance later. Here's one woman's plan for eating better:

1. Dump the junk cereal.
2. Buy some whole grain cereal.
3. Buy some fresh fruit.
4. Buy reduced or low-fat milk.

You'll notice she hasn't decided to tackle every aspect of her food intake in this example, but she has taken care of the most important meal of the day—breakfast. She's also eliminated a source of too much sugar in her diet and replaced it with something healthy. She's done something about trimming her fat calories, as well. Also, in our example, the lady has done some shopping. That means she's gotten out of the house and taken control. She's made that first step—commitment. You can do that too. It doesn't have to be a chore to eat better. The key is not looking back, but looking forward.

 Alert

Don't fall for the mistake of buying the high-fat granola, thinking it's healthier than the junk cereal you just tossed out. Read the label. Ouch! You're cutting back on saturated fats! Bad choice, here. Put it back on the shelf.

Shopping Lessons

Breaking long-standing dietary patterns takes a bit of work, along with your desire to make food your ally in your struggle with depression.

To eat right, you must shop right, and there's a science to smart shopping. Next time you're in the grocery store, take a stroll around the aisles and check the layout. You'll probably be in for a surprise. If you're used to shopping at one store, you know where the items you buy are located. It's convenient. You zip in, zip around, and zip out, without giving much thought to where stuff is. Everything in the store, however, is where it is for a reason, and that reason is to maximize profits for the store. Period.

Traffic Patterns

Want milk? Want bread or eggs? Prepare to walk all the way to the back. Everybody wants these items, so the store's made sure you'll have to pass by a host of other products on your way to your objective. Instead of falling prey to the ploy, however, think of this as a chance for a short power walk. Eyes straight ahead, mind focused on the goal—whole grain bread and reduced fat milk.

 Fact

In the *Beck Diet Solution,* Judith Beck, Ph.D., director of the Beck Institute for Cognitive Therapy and Research, offers insight into how to use your brain as your ally in good nutrition. Based on clinical research in cognitive therapy, this book explains how you can retrain the way your brain thinks about food. The logical extension here is that if you can change the way you think about food, something so fundamental to life, you can also change the way you think about those stressors that aggravate depression.

The Perimeter

Walking around the perimeter of the store should lead you to the produce section. While you're stocking up on the fruits and veggies, however, you'll undoubtedly see the endcaps, those cute arrangements at the end of the counters, where the strawberry glaze for the shortcakes is displayed, along with other complementary items. Had you really intended to buy that high-fat specialty salad dressing that's presiding over the lettuce display? It's amazing the items that end up in your shopping cart, and many of these can sabotage your efforts, if you're not vigilant.

Eye Level

Consider the example of the junk cereal. You're not going to have to search for it, because it's staring at you, smack dab in the middle of the case, right at eye level. That whole grain cereal will either be at the end—the far end—of the aisle, or on the very top or bottom shelf. If you want it, you're going to have to bend down or stretch up to get it. Perhaps the makers figure that the junk cereal buyers can't bend or stretch, while the healthy folks can.

 Fact

> Manufacturers pay for optimal shelf space in stores. Prominently displayed products sell faster and garner more profits. Smaller companies are relegated to the less desirable spaces.

Impulse Purchases

The kids are tired and whining. They want this and they want that. They've been conditioned by the commercials they watch on television, and you must wait patiently for your turn to check out, while the frazzled parent ahead of you either gives up and gives in or tries to ignore the screaming of the thwarted mini-consumers at her side. Tuning them out, you absentmindedly pick up a pack of gum or breath mints or possibly a magazine. You're just as much a victim of impulse shopping as the kids. Look at what's displayed—candy and other high-sugar and high-sodium snacks. Have you ever seen an apple display at the checkout stand?

Finding the Fish Counter

Fish, such as salmon, is high in omega-3 fatty acids. Scientists know that these essential fatty acids have positive effects on brain health, so make sure to include a fish purchase while you're at the store.

Strategies for Beating the System

Heading out on your summer vacation without a destination in mind may sound impulsive and romantic. However, gas is expensive and camping sites and motels fill up quickly during the peak season. If you don't plan ahead and prepare, you may find yourself not having a very good time. Also, as the old saying goes, "If you don't know where you're going, how will you know when you get there?" The same holds true with foiling the marketing plans directed at taking your money and compromising your health. How to do this? Know what you want before you get to the store. Make a list, if there are several items you need, and remember to take the list with you, get the items on the list, and get to the checkout as quickly as you can. Don't buy what you don't need. And never, ever shop on an empty stomach.

Sugar

How's your sweet tooth? If you're like the majority of people, you have one. Back in early times, back before agriculture and urbanization, humans were hunters and gatherers. They reaped a natural harvest of seeds, nuts, and fruit. They found that fruit tasted good. They didn't know that fruit was healthy—they just knew it satisfied a craving. Today, however, through the marvels of science, you can get that sweet fix in a multitude of other, less healthful ways. You can satisfy your sugar craving through candy, gum, and other nutritionally bankrupt foods. You get the carb surge, and then you crash. This is a deadly mix for depression, since you're already dealing with a depressed mood.

Just How Bad Is Sugar?

Pretty bad. Research hasn't come up with a whole lot of benefits for sugar, but it has found sugar implicated in a host of medical problems, including depression. That's one important reason to limit sugar in your diet. Also, that sugar high that kicks in shortly after you've consumed a sweet soon dissipates, leaving you feeling tired and spent. With depression, fatigue is probably high on your list of symptoms. You don't need to increase that fatigue factor. In *Lick the Sugar Habit*, Nancy Appleton, Ph.D. explores the damaging effects of sugar. What does sugar do? She explains:

- Sugar raises the levels of the neurotransmitters dopamine, serotonin, and norepinephrine.
- Sugar can lower the amount of Vitamin E (alpha-ocopherol) in the blood.
- Sugar can interfere with the absorption of protein.
- Sugar can increase the body's fluid retention.
- Sugar can cause hormonal imbalance; some hormones become underactive, and others become overactive.
- The body changes sugar into two to five times more fat in the bloodstream than it does starch.
- The rapid absorption of sugar promotes excessive food intake in obese subjects.
- Sugar induces salt and water retention.

What to do? Reducing your consumption of sugar and products containing refined sugars is one giant step forward in relieving the symptoms of depression. You'll feel less tired and more able to exert control over your depression. It's also better for your teeth!

Where Is All This Sugar Coming From?

It's everywhere! Or at least it seems to be everywhere. You'll find it on product labels for canned fruits, cereals, puddings, cakes, powdered milk, cookies, brownies—all kinds of desserts.

Once you start reading labels and becoming aware of what you're eating, you'll get a good idea of why sugar is so addictive. Watch for sugar under the names of fructose, corn syrup, heavy syrup, or light syrup. Make a commitment to get your sugar fix the natural way, with fresh fruits.

Salt and Sodium

Salt is probably our oldest food preservative. By removing moisture from foods, it allows those foods to be kept safely for future consumption. Today, however, salt is used primarily as a flavoring agent in foods, and its ubiquitous presence can cause some real hardships for people who need to restrict salt intake.

 ## Question

What's the difference between salt and sodium?
Salt is the common term for sodium chloride (NaCl). This is what fills up the salt shaker on your kitchen table. Sodium is an essential mineral the body uses to regulate fluid balance, muscles, and for conduction of nerve impulses.

Sodium Sleuthing

Just like sugar, sodium is just about everywhere. You can even find it in some prescription and over-the-counter medications. It's another reason to become a careful label reader. Back when humans did more cooking "from scratch," people determined how much salt was added to recipes. To be honest, people weren't all that careful about restricting their sodium intake even then. Recipes might call for a "pinch" of salt or might even specify a much greater amount. People have always consumed more sodium than they should. Today, however, you take what you get when you're shopping. Convenience foods are loaded with sodium—just take a look at a typical frozen dinner. Even one that advertises being "low-fat" may contain more sodium than you should be consuming at one meal.

Some common foods with their sodium content include the following:

- Tomato sauce, 1 cup—1,482 mg
- Sauerkraut, 1 cup—1,560 mg
- Parmesan cheese, 1 cup—1861 mg
- Dill pickle, 1 pickle—928 mg
- Chicken noodle soup, canned, 1 cup—1,106 mg

Look for lower sodium products when you shop. You won't miss the sodium, guaranteed!

 ## Alert

If you reach for the salt shaker before you've even tasted your food, you may be a salt addict. Reduce the amount you use, and you'll find that you can taste the food—not just the salt. If you're brave, remove the salt shaker from your table, or at least make it a bit more inconvenient to locate! Try some of the salt substitutes and herb blends. Each step that you take in a positive direction builds confidence, and that confidence has a ripple effect, extending far beyond your food. It extends into your greater life arena and helps you become more able to exert control over depression.

Recommended Daily Allowances

As a nation, we're addicted to salt. Sodium is necessary for good health, but some people overdo it. An adult needs 500 to 1,000 milligrams of sodium, daily. Excessive sodium consumption has been linked to high blood pressure and the risk of stroke and heart attack. Again, dealing with these conditions while also coping with depression means it's essential to cut back on the sodium. U.S. Department of Agriculture (USDA) and the Department of Health and Human Services Dietary Guidelines for 2005 recommended that adults decrease their sodium consumption to 2,300 milligrams per day.

Caffeine

Caffeine is found in coffee, tea, chocolate, soft drinks, and some nuts. It's not an essential nutrient, but try telling that to someone who hasn't had that first cup of coffee in the morning. Caffeine has a stimulating effect upon the central nervous system (CNS), and even though researchers keep trying to implicate caffeine in heart disease, the American Heart Association (AHA) reports that no studies have been conclusive in linking moderate caffeine consumption to coronary heart disease. Moderate drinking was defined as one to two cups per day.

 Alert

If you drink caffeine on a regular basis and then abruptly stop drinking it, you may experience "caffeine withdrawal." Symptoms include primarily headache, along with anxiety, fatigue, drowsiness, and depression. Interestingly, researchers have found that the post-surgery headache many people experience has nothing at all to do with the operation. It's caffeine withdrawal! You head into surgery on an empty stomach—no food or drink after midnight, has been the standard protocol. Now, to relieve that symptom, many hospitals will permit you that cup of java.

Consuming caffeine up to eight hours before bedtime, however, can adversely affect your sleep. Since insomnia and other sleep disorders are symptoms of depression, it makes good sense to limit your caffeine intake to earlier in the day. Also, caffeine is an appetite suppressant, so if your depression is keeping you from eating well, you may want to limit your intake of caffeine.

Cholesterol and Depression

Here's the mini-course on cholesterol. Do you know your numbers? Cholesterol is classified as HDL (good) and LDL (bad). You have both kinds. You want your HDL levels up and your LDL levels down, and you want their combined numbers to be less than 200. This lowers your risk for heart attack and stroke. The healthier your cardiovascular system, the more energy you have for battling depression.

Essential Fats

That may seem like a contradiction of terms, if you've decided that fats are the enemy. With all the discussion about low-fat this and nonfat that, you may think that fat *is* the enemy. It isn't. Well, at least certain kinds of fat aren't the enemy, and the bottom line is that your body needs fat in order to operate effectively.

Saturated Fats—The Bad Guys

Potato chips, fried chicken, French fries, and all their friends and acquaintances are not good for you. Stop eating them! They're bad, bad, bad! Saturated fats are the main dietary cause of high blood cholesterol, according to the American Heart Association (AHA). These are the animal fats and they're found in milk (whole and two percent), butter, cream, cheese, lard, and meat products. In the plant world, you'll find them in coconut, coconut oil, palm oil, and cocoa butter.

Polyunsaturated, Mono-Unsaturated Fats, and Omega-3 Fatty Acids—The Good Guys

Researchers at Harvard University found that increasing your intake of omega-3 fatty acids by eating fatty fish, such as salmon, can help lift symptoms of depression. These omega-3s are believed to raise serotonin levels, in the same fashion that antidepressants, such as Prozac, do. So, where to find these gems? Avocados, olives, walnuts, salmon, trout, and herring are good sources. And for cooking? Try soybean, corn, safflower, canola, olive, and sunflower oils. Stock your cupboard and pantry with the good guys.

Alert

Even though there are good fats, too much fat of any kind isn't good. Keep your total fat intake between 25 and 35 percent of your daily calories.

Pyramid Power

For years, you followed all the rules for good eating. Well, even if you didn't actually follow them all the time, you knew what they were—so many servings of bread and milk and all the other foods every day. Then the government came out with the Food Pyramid, and all of a sudden, it got very confusing. Once you figure out the new arrangement, however, you'll see that color is the key. Instead of layers of food groups, the new Pyramid has a vertical layout, and each food group has been assigned its own color. It looks something like a rainbow.

Essential

The U.S. Department of Agriculture has a Web site specifically designed to assist you in understanding the Pyramid. The site also includes options for tracking your food and physical activity choices. Go to *www.mypyramid.com*. As you work through this, you may see a connection between what you will do here and the notebook and homework exercises you've been assigned as part of cognitive behavioral therapy (CBT).

The Bottom Line of the Pyramid

According to the USDA, here's what you should include in your healthy, depression-fighting diet:

- Fruits, vegetables, whole grains, and fat-free or low-fat milk and milk products

- Lean meats, poultry, fish, beans, eggs, and nuts
- Low amounts of saturated fats, trans fats, cholesterol, salt (sodium) and added sugars

It's what you've been reading all along, isn't it? And now you've got the U.S. government right behind you!

Still Confused About the Pyramid?

You're going to need a set of measuring cups and spoons, and a scale that weighs in ounces. Even if you're not up to measuring and weighing everything you eat, the colorful pictures on the Web site are cheerful, so at least make a start and bring up the Web page. And if you persevere and enter your age, height, gender, and weight into the program, you'll get a diet tailor-made just for you. You can also get a meal tracker to keep track of how well you're doing. It's worth investigating. Just as with other goals you set for yourself, keep track of your eating habits, chart your successes, and have that visual record posted somewhere prominent to remind you to stay focused.

Putting It All Together

There's a great deal of complexity to food. There's the nutritional component, the emotional factor, and the power of tradition. Knowing which aspect of this you're dealing with at any given time is important to your physical and mental health. Knowing how you use food, or sometimes, how food uses you, is also important.

Comfort Foods

What's your comfort food? Is it meatloaf? Macaroni and cheese? Chocolate cream pie? This is the emotional context of food. Food not only fuels your body, it soothes the hurts life tosses at you. Once again, it's all things in moderation. If you've gotten a traffic ticket and eating a few spoonfuls of chocolate ice cream makes you feel better, go for it! However, if you sit down and eat the entire half gallon, that's not such a good idea. Then there's eating out of boredom or because you're tired. You're not hungry, but you reach for the comfort foods because they're there. They're reliable—the trusted old standbys. When you are struggling with depression, it's easy to reach for the comfort foods a little too often. This is the time to remember your goals, take a deep breath, and stop with a spoonful or two.

Eat When You're Hungry, Drink When You're Dry

There are many kinds of diet programs out there, in the world. Some are good, some are not so good, and some are downright dangerous. It's your nickel, but spend it wisely, and think twice before choosing to invest in a plan that promises miracles. Balance is really the key to nutritional health. And if you start making good nutritional choices, you'll have no need for a "diet." Let each day build on the successes of the previous one. Set your goal for the day, write down objectives that will help you meet it, and develop good habits. That's the key to both nutritional health and fighting depression.

Choices

Ultimately, the choice is up to you. Learning to change bad eating habits into good ones takes time and energy. Time may not be a problem, but the energy may be in short supply right now. Still, the payoff is worth the effort, and there is some help to be found in another of those wise sayings that are part of our culture, such as "just for today," which comes from Alcoholics Anonymous (AA), an organization that knows its stuff. You have to eat, so you might as well eat something that's good. You can choose to fuel depression or to fight it. It's up to you. Just for today, eat healthy. Then tonight, you can look back at what you accomplished. It will feel good. Little steps, one at a time, can cover a tremendous amount of distance if you make up your mind to keep walking. You've got to eat. Feed your body well and reap the benefits of the mind/body connection.

CHAPTER 13

Essential Exercise

MUSTERING ENOUGH ENERGY to even think about exercising may wear you out, but exercise is one of the most important components in your anti-depression arsenal. You've really nothing to lose and everything to gain. The secrets to making exercise work for you are simple: Have a plan and work that plan. In this chapter you'll see what kind of plan can work for you and how you can make exercise your personal prescription for working through depression.

How Exercise Helps Fight Depression

Exercise taps directly into the mind/body connection to work its wonders against depression. For the body, exercise does the following:

- Helps regulate your weight
- Strengthens joints and muscles
- Increases energy and stamina throughout the day
- Reduces the risk of heart disease
- Helps prevent or control type 2 Diabetes (adult-onset diabetes)
- Reduces the risk of arthritis and alleviates the symptoms associated with arthritis
- Helps lower cholesterol
- Helps lower high blood pressure
- Improves sleep
- Helps protect you from certain cancers

And, if all those benefits haven't got you thinking seriously about locating your gym bag or your sneakers, here are some ways that exercise benefits your mind:

- Relieves the symptoms of anxiety and depression
- May help in preventing a relapse of symptoms of depression
- Builds a healthy self-image and promotes confidence
- Gives your mind something else to think about
- Promotes social interaction
- Provides healthy coping strategies
- Promotes positive thinking and reduces negative thoughts

Fact

While antidepressants can take up to three weeks to reach effective levels in your system, exercise has an almost immediate positive effect. In our impatient, fast-paced world, that's an added plus for exercise.

Endearing Endorphins

Endorphins, those "feel good" hormones, are activated when you exercise. They're your body's natural pain-fighters, and they can help you keep on track with your exercise program. Athletes actually speak about the addiction they have to endorphin release, and while you may not decide to take your treadmill on the road professionally, it's nice to know that your body will give you a reward for making it work. Endorphins also give your immune system a boost and improve your sense of well-being. Not bad for a free prescription!

Don't Forget Neurotransmitters

Norepinephrine is a neurotransmitter in your brain, and it gets a jump start from exercise. Once it's been activated, it seems to work directly on improving your mood. If you feel better, you'll start to look better, act better, and actually get better.

A Good Night's Sleep

Insomnia and other sleep disorders are also parts of depression's laundry list of symptoms, but exercise can scrub them right off. Regular exercise can help you fall asleep more quickly and give you deeper, more restful sleep. There's a natural dip in body temperature five to six hours after your exercise, so if you exercise later in the afternoon, you can take advantage of that dip and get to sleep more easily. Scientists believe that this dip in body temperature works like a kind of trigger mechanism that tells your body it's sleep time.

A Natural Mood Lifter

Exercise reduces feelings of depression and anxiety. A couple of things are at work here. You're stimulating those neurotransmitters (more about them a little later in the chapter), and you're also re-establishing a sense of control over your body. You determine when you exercise, how much you exercise, and where you exercise. Your mind is working with your body now, not against it. Also, you're burning calories, toning your body, and gaining stamina. It's a neat and tidy package.

 Alert

Doctors believe that depression relapses may be tied to thought patterns that still exist in the brain, even after treatment. Sometimes people stop their antidepressants too soon. If you find yourself experiencing depressive symptoms, after a period of time in which you'd been symptom-free, contact your physician and get back on top of your depression.

Scientific Proof That Exercise Works

Scientists love to watch people. They're good at it, and they especially seem to enjoy watching other people exercise! In a study published in the *Archives of Internal Medicine* in 1999, researchers divided 156 men and women with major depression into three groups. The first group followed an aerobic exercise regimen, the second group took an antidepressant drug, and the third group exercised and also took the antidepressant. At the end of the sixteen-week study, 60 to 70 percent of the total participants no longer showed the symptoms of major depression. Exercise had been shown to be as effective as the antidepressant.

There's also evidence that exercise can help prevent a relapse of depression. In a follow-up to the study mentioned above, researchers found that those people who continued to exercise after the conclusion of the study were less likely to relapse into depression. That was very good news, since relapse is not uncommon.

Wary of Workouts?

You may be thinking that exercise isn't for you. You've never cared for it all that much, even when you weren't dealing with depression. Exercise sounds like work—too much work. But it doesn't have to be! It's all in the way you go about it. If you've successfully pushed thoughts of exercise to the back of your brain, it's time to drag them out into the open. Rethink exercise as a way to counteract several of depression's symptoms.

Has it been a while since you looked in the mirror and liked what you saw? When you're so tired that it's a struggle to lift a finger, maintaining your fitness level is probably not high on your priority list. Would you be interested in getting rid of that fatigue? Of course, you would! And light to moderate exercise, such as walking, can do that for you. You've got all the equipment you need, and you're in control, every step of the way.

 Alert

Before beginning any kind of exercise regimen, check with your doctor. She will give you some tips to make exercise work for you, especially if you have certain medical conditions, such as arthritis, that can make movement painful.

If you're worried about the high cost of a gym membership, fancy workout clothes, and exercise equipment, worry no more! You don't need to empty your bank account to reap the benefits of exercise. You can incorporate exercise into your daily life for next to nothing. Read on to find out how.

Setting Goals

Your goals don't have to be pie-in-the-sky dreams. No one is going to expect you to race out the door and sign up for the Boston Marathon, the Tour de France, or a spelunking adventure to Carlsbad Caverns. Your goals are personal and, if you wish, private. What's your goal? To regain some energy? To drop some pounds? To get to looking and feeling better? If you're feeling too tired and listless to even think of a goal, start small and work up. How about simply having the energy to face each day without dread? The hardest part of anything is the getting around to it. Depression is an energy zapper, and once it starts zapping, it doesn't let up until you're zapped out.

 Essential

> Write down your goals and keep them in a place where you can see them frequently. Tape your list to the fridge or tack it onto the bulletin board above your computer. Out of sight means out of mind, so keep the list clearly in view. Keep your focus, and you'll get results.

Start with Something Easy

Easy is a relative term. What's easy for you might be difficult for someone else, so only you can be the judge of easiness. The secret here is to think of the next step. For example, if you're lying down while you're reading this, sit up. If you're sitting, stand. If you're standing, walk. If you're ready to run—good for you! Small increments can add up quickly. Remember: "The longest journey begins with a single step." Bottom line: Get moving and keep moving.

Essential

Just as easy is a relative term, so is pain, and everybody has a different pain threshold. Genetics is involved here, but by now you've already recognized that genetics plays a role in practically everything! It used to be common knowledge that women withstood pain better than men, and the example used to prove the point was childbirth. Recent research, however, shows that pain tolerance is more complicated than simply being male or female.

A Peek at Your Genes

If you've been called a wimp, take heart! If you pride yourself on your toughness, take a humility lesson! According to News.bbc.co.uk, researchers have identified a specific gene that regulates the brain's signals involved in response to pain. This gene comes in two forms, and everyone inherits one copy of the gene from each parent. The study found that people with two copies of one form of the gene felt pain more intensely than did people with two copies of the other form of the gene. People with one copy of each form had pain responses somewhere in between. The study was published in *Science* magazine.

Alert

Too much exercise too soon is not a good idea. You want to work up to and work into a new and improved you. Remember, you're in this for the long haul. You want to make exercise part of your daily routine—just like brushing and flossing your teeth. It takes a certain amount of time to break a bad habit and establish a good one (the usual time frame given for this is three weeks). You can't rush the process.

How Much Is Enough?

If this exercise business is new to you, it's best to start slowly. Generally, beginners should exercise for twenty minutes a day, three times a week. Gradually increase that to thirty minutes a day, three times a week. It's more fun, and you'll stay motivated, if you alternate activities. Use your treadmill one day, then bicycle or choose another outdoor activity the next. According to Everydayhealth.com, your goal should be mild to moderate exercise four to five times a week.

Exercise Explained

There are basically just two kinds of exercise: aerobic and anaerobic. Each kind of exercise has a place in your antidepression workout kit. Aerobic or cardio workouts primarily improve the cardiovascular system, targeting the heart and lungs. Anaerobic workouts, such as weight training or strength training, improve muscular strength and flexibility, and stretching exercises improve overall mobility and coordination.

 Fact

Aerobic and anaerobic are not mutually exclusive states. In other words, your body will never fully switch from an aerobic state to an anaerobic state. Think instead of aerobic and anaerobic as transitional phases in metabolism, where the proportion between aerobic and anaerobic are conversely related to the intensity of the exercise. It's more accurate to say: The greater the intensity of the exercise, the greater the need for anaerobic energy production to supplement the aerobic energy production.

So which type of exercise is best? It depends upon your goals. Different types of exercise offer different benefits. The difference between aerobic and anaerobic exercising is the presence or absence of oxygen. Anaerobic, by definition, means *without air.* Most human body cells use oxygen to receive the energy they need and fuel their metabolism. Oxygen helps the muscle cells to repeatedly contract, without fatigue, during exercise. Conversely, while exercising under anaerobic conditions, muscle cells now need to rely on secondary reactions that do not require oxygen to fuel muscle contraction. However, this anaerobic cell metabolism produces waste molecules that can impair repeated muscle contractions. These impaired contractions are called *fatigue.*

You may be thinking, "But I'm already fatigued!" This is different. Think of it as housecleaning on a cellular level. Fatigue causes muscles to lose power and become weak. The direct effect will cause the body to slow and create a need for a decrease in the intensity of the exercise. Decreasing the intensity of the exercise allows the muscles to once again contract without fatigue and remove the wasted molecules that are produced. All the time, you're gaining strength.

 Alert

Do not stop taking your antidepressant medications, just because you've begun exercising. This is something you need to discuss with your psychotherapist or physician. Sometimes the combination of medications, exercise, and psychotherapy is the right combination.

Isometrics

Isometrics is a type of strength training that uses static positions rather than dynamic ones. This means the angle of the joints being exercised does not move. The exercise is accomplished by holding the muscle in one fixed position. Isometric contractions can be achieved with or without weights, and one of the most popular kinds of isometrics is yoga.

 Question

What does the word *isometrics* mean?
Isometrics comes from the Greek iso-, meaning "equal," and metron, meaning "measure." In isometric exercise, you essentially use a law of physics—for each action there is an equal and opposite reaction—to create resistance and strengthen your body.

Isometric exercises have several important characteristics:

- Isometrics has the same benefits as other strength training exercises, as well as a few more.
- Isometrics helps increase strength faster than traditional training. This is due to the greater intensity of the exercise over a shorter period of time. It is possible to finish a full isometric workout in as little as fifteen minutes.
- Isometrics can be done anywhere. Because they do not require weights, any space where your body can fit can be utilized. It is simply a matter of using the resources around you effectively.
- Isometrics are safer than traditional training. Because there are no weights, you don't have to worry about being injured by a weight falling on you. Also, the less movement involved, the less chance for injury. This is also why isometrics are commonly used in physical rehabilitation.

Here are three examples of isometric exercises to get you started and show you how the principles work. The first two exercises target the chest and the last one works your biceps.

1. If you have a door in your home, you've got all it takes for this exercise. Open the door and, centering your chest, stand in the middle of the doorway and place your hands on either

side of the door. Press each hand against the door, as if you were trying to crush the door and make your hands touch. You should almost look as if you are praying. Hold this position as tightly as possible for thirty seconds. Make sure to concentrate on the chest and breathe.

2. This time, you'll need a floor. Simply put yourself in a push-up position. Slowly maneuver your body halfway down and hold your body steady. Again, be sure to concentrate on the chest and breathe throughout the exercise.

3. A great isometric exercise for the biceps can easily be done at any desk or table. Position your chest at table level. Now, either sitting or standing, place your hands under the table, with your palms facing up. Apply pressure through the table, as if you were trying to push your hands through the table. Concentrate on the biceps throughout the exercise.

Essential

As people age, it's often useful to reclaim the kinds of physical activities you enjoyed in your youth. Back then, you did them because they were fun. Today, they still have that positive connotation and may still have the power to make exercise enjoyable. The added benefit is that you can call up that old muscle memory and not have to learn a new skill.

Aerobics

If the word aerobics conjures up nightmare images of sweaty people jumping about to a driving primal musical beat, take heart. There's more to aerobics than that—much more. Walking is perhaps the most popular and well-known aerobic activity. Not the casual stroll, however, but a firm, purposeful stride that gets your heart rate up and pumps that good, oxygenated blood throughout your system. That, after all, is the reason for the invention of the treadmill. If you can't get outside to walk, the treadmill is the next best idea. Once you've gotten the walking action firmly in place, it might be a good time to see what else is out there in the aerobic world. Perhaps you like to dance or garden or ride a bicycle. Branch out!

Getting Serious

If you've decided to reactivate that gym or health club membership, you're going to be faced with an array of machines and devices. Which ones you decide to use will depend on what goals you're aiming for. Which is better—free weights or machines? Both have advantages and disadvantages. Free weights are better for the more advanced exerciser. Free weights will allow you to create your own range of motion, which will allow maximum growth and stimulation of the muscle. Machines will constrict the range of motion but will also reduce the chance of injury. Machines are often used for rehabilitation purposes, as they follow a specific program and can be regulated for intensity. Here's where it's important to consult with a fitness trainer, to develop the program that's right for you.

 Alert

Always speak with a trainer on staff regarding questions about proper use of exercise machines. You'll get more out of the experience, you'll learn how to best use the equipment, and you'll reduce your risk of injury.

Self-Help Strategies

You can become your own ally in the antidepression war, and it's important that you do. It's so easy to engage in negative self-talk when it comes to fitting exercise into your daily schedule, but you know that's not going to benefit you. There are ways, however, to get the job done.

Get a Dog

Really. Actually, any pet can help you combat the symptoms of depression, and animals are frequently used in therapy. Stroking an animal can lower your blood pressure, decrease feelings of isolation and loneliness, and keep you on track with your exercise program. Why? You've got to walk the dog. You can't explain to him why this isn't the best time for you. You are forced to think beyond yourself. Don't cheat and just let the dog out into the backyard. Take the opportunity to get some exercise for you both. He needs it and so do you. Having a companion has been proven to help people stick with an exercise regime. So, partner up!

Do Power Housework

Sweeping the floor? Put your whole body into it. Dance. Twirl. Act stupid. Nobody's watching, anyway, and so what if they are? Run that vacuum cleaner as if it were the most complicated weight training device in the health club. Get your arms moving, and while you're at it, this is the perfect time to do some furniture rearranging. Just remember to lift with your knees bent—don't use your back. Get the window cleaner, some clean rags or newspapers, and let the light into your home. Sparkle and shine dispels the gloom.

 Alert

While it's a good plan to exercise the next day, if you've missed your regular day, it's not a good plan to double your normal time and intensify your workout. Keep a steady course to get the most benefit from your routine and to avoid injury.

Be Flexible

If you've got a migraine, if you're not feeling up to snuff, or if something has come up and you just can't fit in that thirty-minute walk or two-hour trip to the gym, recognize this for what it is—the reality of everyday life. There will be times when you won't be able to follow through with your plans. At that moment, walk over to the calendar and pencil in an exercise time for the following day. You'll feel better having dealt constructively with the problem, and the notation will remind you that you've made a commitment to yourself.

Establish a Routine

Your days are already packed to the max. There isn't an extra minute, let alone a half hour to squeeze in your exercise time. That's a perfect, or not so perfect, example of negative self-talk. There's always time, it's just that depression has you thinking there isn't. Here's where you give depression a stern talking to and let it know exactly who's in charge. It's not wrong to have time during the day just for you. In fact, it's essential to your mental and physical well-being. So, what to do? Want to find a way to exercise every day?

- Set the alarm thirty minutes earlier.
- Turn off the television.
- Dovetail tasks into your exercise program.
- Walk during your lunch hour at work.
- Park the car a little farther away from the entrance to the store, mall, or health club, and walk. Increase this distance every week.
- Take the stairs instead of the escalator or elevator.
- Keep a pair of walking shoes in your car.

You'll undoubtedly come up with good strategies of your own once you get into the exercise habit. Once you get to feeling better, you'll find that you actually miss your exercise sessions if you have to skip one. Honest!

Should It Hurt?

"Feel the burn!" and "No pain, no gain!" Nonsense. Exercise doesn't have to leave you doubled up on the floor with cramps and shin splints. Learning to pace yourself is part of the program and moderation in all things definitely applies here. Does this mean that you won't feel some discomfort? No. You will. But this will pass, and you'll be getting stronger and more fit each time you lace up your tennis shoes. Listen to your body. If it's screaming at you to stop, you're doing too much. Time to back off a bit and regroup at a gentler pace. There's an exercise regimen suited just for you. It's simply a matter of finding out what it is.

Setting the Pace

Remember, "Lead, follow, or get out of the way?" If you do, forget you ever did. You are the only one who matters, here. Whatever your pace is, it is the right one for you at this time. You wouldn't think of throwing a non-swimmer into the deep end of an Olympic pool or putting an unlicensed driver at the wheel of a semi truck. So why would you think that exercising requires that you start out at peak fitness levels? What's important now is to formulate a plan that fits your current fitness level and use that as your baseline. Improvement will come quickly and before long, you'll be ready to make some adjustments.

Picking Up the Pace

After you've been exercising for a couple of weeks, you'll notice some important changes. The initial soreness has gone away and you're beginning to feel better. Your energy and stamina levels have increased, and you no longer feel so tired all the time. Now is the time to increase your reps, your time on the treadmill, or your walking speed to keep those benefits coming. Your goal should be thirty minutes of moderate exercise four or five times a week. And you'll want to *cross-train*—that is, to alternate between aerobic and anaerobic exercises. Also, by now exercise has become part of your routine, and you're on your way toward establishing it firmly among your good habits. You never realize just how bad you felt, until you start feeling better. And once you start feeling better, you'll never want to look back.

Chapter 14

Other Illnesses and Their Role in Depression

NOTHING EXISTS IN A VACUUM, and that includes depression. Certain other medical conditions and the medications used to treat them can create depressive symptoms. This means you've got to fight the battle on two fronts. If you don't have enough ammunition at the ready, the struggle can be long and arduous. In this chapter, you'll discover what some of these diseases are and how they fit into the depression picture.

The News: You've Got Something

When you first receive the bad news that you've got something, everything changes in that instant. You may have gone in for your annual physical, expecting routine tests with routine results. This time, however, you get the phone call asking you to come to the office to discuss your test results. Or, you're sitting on the exam table in that fashionable, yet drafty, paper garment, and the nurse comes into the room, asks you to get dressed, and meet the doctor in his office. You know immediately this is not good, and you wish that you'd taken better care of that body while it was still in A-1 condition.

Whatever the diagnosis turns out to be, it will most likely involve you making some lifestyle changes. You're going to need to change your diet, go on medication, maybe have surgery. For the rest of your life, that condition will always be either on your mind or very close to the surface. And just when you didn't need anything else on your mind, along with the condition comes stress. It's like a one-two punch—you may begin to experience depression because of the condition or the medications used to treat the condition may cause depressive symptoms. Either way, you're not feeling really great.

You're probably familiar with Elisabeth Kübler-Ross. She's the one who discovered the five stages a person goes through when faced with the prospect of death. The stages are denial, anger, bargaining, depression, and finally, acceptance. But it's not just terminal patients who experience these stages—anyone who receives a life-changing diagnosis may have to work through them. Even if you've gone to the doctor with a suspicion, confirmation of that suspicion may first result in denial. It's the depressive stage, however, that's of concern here. Let's take a look at some common medical conditions and see where depression enters in.

Cardiovascular Diseases (CVD)

The American Heart Association (AHA) reports that cardiovascular disease (CVD) ranks as the number one killer of Americans, accounting for a 36 percent share of annual deaths. In addition, 79.4 million people in the United States are living with some form of CVD.

 Fact

Cardiovascular diseases include arteriosclerosis, coronary artery disease, heart valve disease, arrhythmia, heart failure, hypertension, orthostatic hypotension, shock, endocarditis, diseases of the aorta and its branches, disorders of the peripheral vascular system, and congenital heart disease.

CVD and Depression

You already know that about one in five people have an episode of major depression in their lifetimes, but that number climbs to about one in two for people with CVD. That means that 3 to 5 percent of the general population is depressed at any one time. With heart patients that figure is 18 percent. That's a significant statistic. One of the positive consequences of being the number one killer is that there's no shortage of studies looking into the problem, both here in the United States, as well as abroad. Several of these studies considered the role of depression in CVD.

Studying the Old Ticker

Think depression is just an annoyance? Recent studies have investigated the role depression can play in heart attacks and found that depression turns out to be a reliable indicator of risk, equal to previous heart attack. Here's what some studies uncovered:

- A Montreal Heart Institute study found that depressed patients who'd had heart attacks were four times more likely to die within six months than those who were not depressed.
- A Washington University study found that depressed people with newly diagnosed heart disease were twice as likely to have a heart attack or require bypass surgery.
- A Johns Hopkins study found that those who were depressed were four times more likely to have a heart attack within fourteen years than those who were not.
- An Ohio State University study found that depressed men were 70 percent more likely to develop heart disease. The number was only 12 percent for women but increased to 78 percent for cases of severe depression.
- A Queen's Medical Center (UK) study found that depressed men were three times more likely to develop ischemia (heart damage from blockages of blood).

In spite of the research findings, heart patients are not routinely tested or treated for depression. The focus has primarily been on the primary condition of CVD. In light of the research, however, this may change.

Alert

> If you have cardiovascular disease, be sure to talk with your cardiologist about what you can expect to experience, regarding symptoms. If you find yourself becoming overly tired, even though your medication has been carefully monitored, you may be experiencing symptoms of depression, and you should tell your doctor about this.

Depression in CVD

If you've been used to living life on your own terms, a diagnosis of CVD may turn everything upside down. That body that you've been taking for granted suddenly seems to have become a betrayer, and you're brought up short by the realization that being in control is an illusion. So you take a long, hard look at that physical shell of yours and you may not like what you see. You may also feel some guilt for having treated it with a cavalier attitude in the past. Life as you've known it is about to change. The upshot? You're experiencing the symptoms of depression.

Overcoming Depression in CVD

Tell your cardiologist how you're feeling. Not just the shortness of breath, the palpitations, sweats, dizziness, or fatigue—although these might be related to depression—but everything about how you're feeling. Go back to review the list of depression's symptoms. If you see yourself there, it's time to discuss this with your physician. It might seem simplistic, but depression is often overlooked.

It's important to feel better while you're getting better! Antidepressants can help you deal with the downside of your CVD, and psychotherapy can help you make positive changes in your life. If you've survived a heart attack, you've got a second chance to get it right. Sometimes, just sharing what you're going through is enough to take the edge off. Take all the opportunities you can find that will help.

Medication and Side Effects

The American Heart Association (AHA) reports that some medications used to treat CVD may have depression as a side effect. These medications include the following:

- Beta blockers: Acebutolol (Sectral), atenolol (Tenormin), metoprolol (Lopressor), nadolol (Corgard), pindolol (Visken), propranolol (Inderal), or timolol (Blocadren)
- Peripheral adrenergic inhibitors

L. Essential

Beta blockers act upon the autonomic nervous system. They block substances such as adrenaline (epinephrine) to relieve stress on the heart, lessen the force with which the heart muscle contracts, and reduce blood vessel contraction in the heart, brain, and throughout the body.

If you are taking any of these medications and are experiencing depressive symptoms, work with your cardiologist to get to the heart of the problem!

Stroke

If you are a stroke survivor, you have beaten the odds, but you may be faced with a host of issues. Stroke can be devastating. You may find yourself unable to communicate, get around without assistance, or even use your hands. The American Stroke Association's (a division of the American Heart Association) statistics on stroke are grim.

- About 700,000 Americans suffer a new or recurrent stroke every year. That translates to a stroke occurring every forty-five seconds.

- Stroke is the third leading cause of death behind heart disease and cancer.
- Someone dies of stroke about every three minutes. Of every five people who die from strokes, two are men and three are women.

The effects of stroke depend primarily on the location of the obstruction and the extent of brain tissue affected.

Essential

A stroke occurs when normal blood flow to the brain is interrupted by a blood clot or a rupture. When brain cells are deprived of the oxygenated blood they require, they die.

Since the right side of the brain controls the left side of the body, and vice versa, a stroke occurring in the brain's right side will affect the left side of the body (and the right side of the face). The American Stroke Association notes that, in this case, there may be paralysis on that left side, vision problems, a sharp and inquisitive behavioral style, and memory loss. If the stroke occurs on the left side of the brain, the right side of the body (and the left side of the face) will be affected. There may be paralysis on the right side of the body, speech and language problems, a slow, cautious behavioral style, and memory loss.

Depression in Stroke Survivors

Just as with CVD, having your body turn on you is not only frightening, but it's a reminder of your mortality. If you can't trust your own body, what is there to trust? It may all seem hopeless.

Stroke happens quickly, but frustration afterwards builds slowly and there's no outlet when you've experienced some of the more serious effects of a stroke. If recovery turns into a slow process with little headway, depression is likely to add to your difficulties. Also, the stroke can create some biochemical changes in your brain and make it impossible for you to experience positive emotions.

The American Stroke Association reports that about 40 to 50 percent of stroke survivors experience depression, which can occur soon after the stroke or several months later. So whether it's in response to what you have lost or as a result of brain injury, your depression should be treated.

Treating Depression in Stroke Survivors

Before treatment for depression can begin, the diagnosis has to be made. With elderly stroke survivors, other physical conditions may hide depression's symptoms. And if the stroke survivor can't articulate how he feels, diagnosis becomes doubly hard. Treating depression, however, leads to improved thinking skills which enhances physical recovery. If an elderly stroke survivor is unable to effectively communicate, family members or close friends may notice changes in behavioral patterns that they can share with the medical or mental health professional to aid in making or ruling out a depression diagnosis. If you are a caregiver or relative of an elderly stroke survivor, ask the attending physician if treatment for depression would improve quality of life. It's important to persist and find out if depression is a factor that's complicating recovery.

Cancer

Cancer is the second leading cause of death in America, responsible for 23 percent of annual deaths. The good news is that the five-year cancer survival rate is increasing: 68 percent for whites, 57 percent for African Americans, according to data supplied by the American Cancer Society (ACS). Still, a diagnosis of cancer is not what you want to hear. Mostly, you fear the unknown. You don't know what the future holds, or even if you're going to have much of a future. Uncertainty, fear, and pain can all contribute to depression.

Risk Factors for Depression

Cancer and depression seem to be logical partners. The National Cancer Institute (NCI) notes these risk factors for depression, associated with a diagnosis of cancer:

- Depression at the time of cancer diagnosis
- Poorly controlled pain
- An advanced stage of cancer
- Increased physical impairment or pain
- Pancreatic cancer
- Being unmarried and having head and neck cancer (a strange combination, it would seem, but probably is related to a lack of emotional support that marriage may supply)
- Treatment with some anticancer drugs

If you've been diagnosed with one of the so-called "good cancers" such as thyroid, prostate, or some forms of breast cancer, you may be grateful that it's not any worse, but that doesn't mean you are worry free. If you've gotten the really bad news, all you know is that you're in for a siege. At this time, depression is probably the most normal emotion you can feel, apart from anger.

Reacting

To say that you're going to have a reaction to a cancer diagnosis is the understatement of understatements. Whether or not this reaction develops into depression depends on many factors. Reactive depression is the term given to the way you feel after you get the diagnosis. You may withdraw from your normal activities, feel moody, and find your daily routine beyond your abilities. This usually passes and the coping mechanisms come into play. If the symptoms don't show signs of letting up after a couple of weeks, it's time to consider that depression has settled in.

You're going to be tired. Just adopting a new routine of doctor visits and treatments will take the stuffing right out of you. About 25 percent of all cancer patients are depressed, but only about 16 percent receive medication for the depression. If you're undergoing chemotherapy and radiation, you will experience fatigue. But if that fatigue becomes overwhelming, talk to your doctor to rule out depression. Antidepressants can help you get through the toughest parts of chemotherapy and radiation.

Medical Causes for Depression

Not all depression associated with cancer is the result of psychological changes. Pain that isn't under control can cause depression. So can abnormal levels of calcium, sodium, or potassium, thyroid hormone, or steroids in the blood; anemia; vitamin B_{12} or folate deficiency and fever (American Cancer Society). Your oncologist can help you here—but only if you explain what you're feeling.

Finding Strength

Finding a support group can greatly help in managing depression associated with cancer. A Stanford University study of advanced breast cancer patients found that those who attended a weekly support group lived twice as long (eighteen months) as those who didn't. A UCLA study of patients with malignant melanoma found that those who attended support groups were three times more likely to be alive five or six years later.

When you're with others who are experiencing what you are, all the barriers are down. You can share and know you won't be judged. You'll be accepted and supported—after all that's what a support group is for. Loneliness and isolation can't live where there's camaraderie at the deepest levels.

Depression and HIV

People living with HIV deal with their condition and also with the stigma still associated with it. While other medical disorders garner understanding and sympathy, HIV/AIDS is viewed with suspicion, distrust, and even a sense that those living with it somehow "deserved it." About 30 to 40 percent of men with HIV and 40 to 60 percent of women with HIV experience significant depression.

Recognizing Depression in HIV/AIDS

The symptoms of AIDS and the side effects of the drugs used to treat AIDS may cause depressive symptoms. One of these drugs is Sustiva. In advanced symptomatic HIV disease, a number of opportunistic infections, as well as HIV itself, can produce symptoms of depression. Also, HIV-positive men can have low testosterone levels, which may cause feelings of depression. If the symptoms of depression last more than two weeks, and especially if they begin after starting a new medication, let your physician know.

 Fact

AIDS—Acquired Immunodeficiency Syndrome—was first reported in the United States in 1981. Since that time is has become a worldwide epidemic. It is a virus and is spread through contaminated blood, unprotected sex with someone who is infected, or using needles or syringes that have been used by infected persons. Also, an infected mother may pass the virus to her unborn child.

Coordinating Treatment

Treating your depression will have positive effects on your daily functioning as you cope with your condition. If you are seeing a psychiatrist for your depression, be sure he knows all the medications you are taking. Your psychiatrist and your HIV physician should work as a team to help you manage your health care.

Parkinson's Disease

Parkinson's disease (PD) is a progressive, chronic illness, and it's really difficult to maintain a cheerful demeanor when your body is not giving you any help. According to the Parkinson's Disease Foundation, at least 40 percent of people with PD experience clinical depression at some time during the illness. This depression tends to occur early on and may wax and wane in severity.

 Essential

If you have PD, you experience some of the same difficulties as do people who have survived a stroke. Your brain, instead of being your strong ally, turns out to be the renegade. Dealing with this renegade on your terms can be extremely challenging for both you and those who care about you.

Your Brain Is the Culprit

At first, you deal with the confirmation of the diagnosis, and that takes some processing. This early depression is not the end of the problem, however, for as Parkinson's progresses, it alters the neurochemistry of the brain, and these changes may result in symptoms of depression. The areas of the brain that control mood are affected, and the neurotransmitters serotonin and dopamine are involved. Also, the frontal lobe of the brain is underactive in PD, and this area also controls moods. So, in PD, depression truly isn't anything you have control over.

Treating Depression in PD

First, it's vital that you keep up with your treatments for PD to realize the best possible control for your symptoms. Symptoms that are not under control make you more prone to depression. Poor sleep, constipation, and fatigue are conditions that should also be treated, to help you live better with PD. Exercise is important, and so is making the almost superhuman effort to maintain your social life. Support groups can help you here. Antidepressants are also useful, so check with your physician about the right medications to help you stay on top of things. Stress management and relaxation exercises also can give you a needed lift. It's no joke to tell you to "keep moving." Remain active!

What the Research Reveals

At the annual meeting of the American Academy of Neurology, a study was presented concerning depression and PD. What the researchers found is that depression often precedes PD. In the next section on diabetes and depression, you'll read something quite similar. Is depression an early sign of PD and other conditions? If this is true, it will allow researchers to get a leg up on diagnosis, at some point in the not-too-distant future.

Research is continuing at a good clip for PD. If you have PD and are suffering from depression, consider volunteering for a study conducted under the auspices of the National Institutes of Health (NIH). You might very easily find yourself on the cutting edge of some exciting discoveries.

Diabetes

Type 2 diabetes, also known as adult-onset diabetes, has become an epidemic in the United States. Latest statistics report that 20.8 million Americans, 7 percent of the population, have this form of the disease. What's to blame? Genetics, racial group, and unfortunately, in more and more cases, an increasingly sedentary and obese population overdosed on sugar and fats. Interestingly, what can help stave off type 2 diabetes is also good at warding off depression: exercise and a good diet.

 Alert

The American Diabetes Association (ADA) reports that type 2 diabetes is more common in African Americans, Latinos, Native Americans, and Asian Americans/Pacific Islanders, as well as within the elderly population. If you belong to one of these higher risk groups, watch your weight and exercise!

Not everyone with diabetes, however, fits into the unhealthy demographics. Athletes, children, and the physically fit among the rest of us can also find ourselves confronted with diabetes. But for everyone dealing with this condition, depression can be a unexpected complicating factor.

Implicating Depression

Just as it is an early symptom of Parkinson's disease, depression may be an early symptom of diabetes. A Kaiser Permanente study of some 1,680 subjects found that those with diabetes were more likely to have been treated for depression within six months before their diabetes diagnosis. About 84 percent of diabetics also reported a higher rate of earlier depressive episodes.

A 2004 Johns Hopkins study tracking 11,615 initially nondiabetic adults aged forty-eight to sixty-seven over six years found that "depressive symptoms predicted incident type 2 diabetes." An analysis of twenty studies conducted over the past ten years shows that the prevalence rate of diabetics with major depression is three to four times greater than in the general population (American Diabetes Association). Whether depression comes before diabetes or after the diagnosis is made, treating the depression can help you keep your diabetes under control. Why? Because you'll feel more up to the challenge.

Treating Depression in People with Diabetes

Managing your diabetes means testing your blood sugar when it's required. Probably more so than in other diseases, with diabetes you have a great deal to say about how you're going to feel. If you feel depressed, you may not eat properly. Diabetes that is in poor control can cause symptoms that look like depression. If your blood sugar is high, you'll feel anxiety. If it's low, you'll experience fatigue. Balance is key to managing this disease, but if you don't feel like doing anything, let alone monitoring your blood sugar levels, you're going to be so out of balance that you're likely to crash and burn. But if that blood sugar's too low at night, you'll find sleeping difficult. Antidepressants work for depression in diabetes. So does psychotherapy. You're making significant changes in your life, and for now, diabetes seems to be in charge. With time, however, you'll come out on top.

Thyroid Disease

Thyroid hormone (TH) controls your body's metabolism. Talk about a huge job! Thyroid hormone needs iodine to function properly, and if you don't have enough iodine in your system, you may become hypothyroid. Hypothyroidism refers to any state in which thyroid hormone production is below normal. Over five million Americans have hypothyroidism, and as many as 10 percent of women may have some degree of thyroid hormone deficiency.

 Fact

> The Greeks (of course!) gave us the word hormone. It's derived from hormon, meaning "to urge or excite." This definition probably applies more to sex hormones, but the thyroid hormone definitely urges on the body's internal workings.

How TH Works

TH is a neurotransmitter that exists in two forms: T3 and T4. T3 influences serotonin levels, and low T3 levels can cause depression and, in severe cases, those with low T3 levels can become suicidal. This is serious business and needs to be treated.

Treating Depression in Hypothyroidism

If the thyroid gland has been removed, as in cancer surgery, or if the existing thyroid gland is not producing enough T3, depression is a very real result. Cancer surgery patients may be put on antidepressants, until they can be placed on the correct dosage of thyroid replacement hormone. Adjusting the T3 hormone in others suffering from depression usually relieves the symptoms of depression.

Fact

An autoimmune disease is one in which the body turns on itself, attacking its own tissues, as if they were foreign bodies.

Lupus

Lupus is an autoimmune disease that can involve the skin, heart, lungs, kidneys, joints, and nervous system. It's more common in women than in men—eight times more common, in fact. Medicinenet.com describes it as a chronic inflammatory condition in which Lupus patients have unusual antibodies in the blood that target their own body tissues.

The Lupus Foundation of America notes that people with lupus often ask, "What degree of depression is normal?" and, "When should a patient seek professional help?" What these questions indicate, of course, is that depression is an inconvenient corollary to lupus. Lupus can create symptoms of depression, the medications used to treat lupus (steroids) can cause depressive symptoms, and the stresses of dealing with the disease itself can create depression. It's a triple threat.

The uncertainty of a diagnosis can lead to increased stress levels. It takes time to diagnose lupus, and there are other conditions, such as rheumatoid arthritis, that may mimic lupus's symptoms.

Question

What's a steroid?
Corticosteroid drugs, called steroids for short, are drugs that are used to relieve inflammation and swelling. Many hormones and drugs are steroids. Prednisone, vitamin D, and testosterone are all considered steroids. Corticosteroids are not the same drugs as anabolic steroids, used by athletes to "bulk up."

As with all the other conditions discussed in this chapter, early diagnosis means early intervention. The bright spot, however, in dealing with this chronic condition, is that most episodes of depressive illness in people with lupus are not long-term and will abate on their own within a few months. That makes coping with this condition just a bit easier.

CHAPTER 15

Sexuality and Depression

FEEL AS IF depression is hitting you below the belt—literally? Romance is one of the areas of life that depression makes especially difficult. It's the mind/body connection at work again, and if your brain isn't cooperating, nothing else is going to be all that willing to cooperate, either. In this chapter you'll learn why this is and what you can do about it.

Is the Love Gone?

When depression's symptoms are at their worst, they may cause your partner to think you no longer love him. The problem isn't a lack of love, however, but rather has to do with your neurotransmitters being out of whack. Remember them? They're sex communication central, and if they aren't speaking to each other—if these chemicals are not working properly—desire is dead in the water. So what do you feel? Not much. And this low level of libido is what is causing your partner to think that something is wrong with the relationship. Your partner is right, of course, but the problem, in a nutshell, is depression. You've only to look to the symptoms of depression to see how they're to blame for your loss of libido.

As you read earlier, anhedonia is the loss of interest in things that used to prime your pump. Perhaps you were an avid cyclist, boat enthusiast, motorcycle nut, or armchair football fanatic. Now you just can't seem to work up any interest, let alone enthusiasm, for a whole host of activities that you previously took pleasure in. Unfortunately, for both you and your partner, sex can be one of those activities. Anhedonia is one of the symptoms of depression.

⌐ Essential

Quick quiz! What's your most important sex organ? This is a trick question. Your most important sex organ is your brain. Desire begins there and then travels south.

Body Image

You're not happy with yourself; you don't like the way you look. Maybe you've not been eating well and have either packed on the pounds or shed too many. Either way, your body image—as you see it—doesn't do much for you, and you're sure that it isn't going to be much of a turn-on for the opposite sex. Those feelings of worthlessness and hopelessness have come to the surface, and you're left feeling that you don't measure up—at least, you sure don't look like those models in the magazines. You find yourself obsessing about your flaws, and your depression deepens.

His Fears, Her Fears

You have already read about how the power of advertising can capitalize on your insecurities and perceived body imperfections. Now it's time to take a closer look. You probably have a pet problem area—one part of your body that you're convinced is a serious flaw. If you can, you cover it up with clothing, hairstyle, or makeup. If you can't, you may adopt a grim attitude and poor posture. So what worries the human race? The worries are surprisingly constant:

- Men worry about penis size, going bald, and gaining a pot belly.
- Women worry about breast size, "thunder thighs," and their weight.
- Both sexes worry about being too tall or too short. Remember, if your feet touch the ground, you're tall enough! Then there's having feet that are too big or a nose that's the size of Sicily. If you can think of a body part, you can be sure someone is worrying about it.

What exactly is a perfect body? Or more to the point: Is there such a thing as a perfect body? Actually, perfection is a moving target—or at least the definition of perfection is. Your body is unique, just as you are unique.

Fact

According to the National Institutes of Health (NIH), about 75 percent of people who suffer from depression experience a loss of libido. Antidepressants may clear up the depression but leave sexual dysfunction in their wake.

Culture Shock

Body image is culturally defined. At different times and in different places, the concept of beauty has changed. What's in during one era may be out in another. Take a brief stroll through history, and you'll get a pretty good idea of how this works. Study a few Greek sculptures and you'll see they didn't much care for skinny. Jump ahead to the 17th century and you have Peter Paul Rubens, the Baroque Flemish painter who gave us the term *Rubenesque*. He painted women with some meat on their bones. Not an anorexic in the lot. Why was fat socially acceptable? Simple. Throughout history, only the wealthy could afford enough food to get fat. It was a mark of high social status to be portly. Today, however, thin—or rather, emaciation—is the societal standard for the body beautiful. It's not healthy.

Embracing Your Outer Self

When you're feeling good, you can shrug off the media messages about your "imperfect" body and take them for what they are—fad and fashion hype. When you're dealing with depression, however, each advertisement and each picture is a constant reminder that you're not okay. They cause more stress and then you feel worse. If you could see into the lives of those model-perfect people, you'd find anxiety and worry enough for the super-sized. So, what do you do?

You make yourself focus on one part of your body that you know is good. Do you have good cheekbones? A rugged jaw? Slim, shapely legs? Depression hasn't changed them, you know. When you get your depression under control, you'll begin to feel better about how you look, overall. The interesting aspect of this is that once you begin feeling better, you'll begin taking better care of yourself, as well.

Hormonal Handicapping

Making sure that your hormones are helping instead of hindering can go a long way toward restoring a healthy libido and helping you deal with depression. Good sex is powerful medicine!

If you are male, have your testosterone level checked. Low testosterone can dampen your desire. Same thing applies to low thyroid, and this can affect both men and women. Hypothyroidism can create symptoms of depression.

You read about postpartum depression in Chapter 4. This kind of depression is directly related to hormone fluctuations. Women who are experiencing postpartum depression usually have minimal interest in sex. This tends to be fleeting, and once hormonal equilibrium has been restored, interest in sex usually returns, as well. At the other end of the reproductive years, menopause brings on all manner of hormonal symptoms—once again, it's like going through puberty, although this time, in reverse. Insomnia, hot flashes, mood swings, and the physical discomforts of vaginal dryness and low libido can make sexual intercourse both uncomfortable and unsatisfying. If these symptoms are negatively affecting your quality of life, talk with your doctor. You don't have to suffer through menopause.

Sexual Side Effects of Medications

For men, some antidepressants can cause sexual dysfunction, so if you hadn't experienced problems before you began your course of treatment, talk with your prescribing physician. This is not a topic to be embarrassed about. Healthy sexual functioning is the goal and adjusting your medications may help you achieve it.

How Can a Little Pill Cause Such a Big Problem?

There's a great deal that science still doesn't know, and the inner secrets of sexual functioning are among them. What scientists do know, however, is that hormones are involved—you're probably not surprised about that. After that, it gets complicated. Two neurotransmitters, dopamine and serotonin, are involved. Dopamine increases sexual function, while serotonin inhibits it. Testosterone, another hormone, is also involved. That's the cast. Enter the medicines, stage left.

Names, Please

It may feel as if you're taking two steps forward and three steps backward. You have a decreased sex drive because of depression, but the medications used to treat the depression put their own damper on performance. Not all medications are implicated, however, so talking with your doctor about options is important. Here are some of the most frequently prescribed antidepressants with their indicated uses and possible side effects relative to sexual functioning:

- **MAOIs** (Monoamine oxidase inhibitors):
  - Moclobemide (Manerix or Aurorix) and phenelzine (Nardil)—May result in decreased sex drive, impotence, delayed orgasm, ejaculatory disturbances. Other examples of MAOIs include isocarboxazid (Marplan), selegiline (Eldepryl), and tranylcypromine (Parnate).
- **SSRIs** (Selective serotonin reuptake inhibitors):
  - Prozac (fluoxetine hydrochloride) has been reported to cause a decreased sex drive and impotence (*www.prozac.com*).
  - Other examples of SSRIs include citalopram (Celexa), fluvoxamine (Luvox), paroxetine (Paxil), and sertraline (Zoloft).

- **Tricyclic antidepressants:**
    - Amitryptiline—May cause decreased sex drive, impotence, delayed or absent orgasm, ejaculatory disturbances

SSRIs come in at #1 in causing the highest frequency of sexual dysfunction, followed by MAOIs, and then tricyclics.

 Alert

> Time to be honest. If you indulge in recreational drugs, your physician needs to know. Some of these may also interact with your prescription medications. They may also be the source of your problem!

Okay, So What Do I Do?

First of all, read the labels on your medications. If they tell you not to consume alcohol while you're taking them, or if they caution you not to drive, take those warnings seriously. Talk with the pharmacist or your physician if you've got questions. Ask if these new medications will have any negative interactions with other prescriptions you're taking. Also mention any over-the-counter drugs you consume. Be an informed a consumer of medications.

You Think There's a Problem

If you're experiencing what appear to be side effects of your medications, talk with your doctor. Don't wait. There's no need to be miserable. Also, don't stop taking your prescribed medications on your own. You may find yourself dealing with worse problems if you do. Some medications need to be tapered off rather than stopped abruptly. So find out the best course of action.

Does This Mean I'll Have to Be Depressed?

No! Depression didn't happen overnight and neither will the cure. There are other medications your doctor can prescribe, as well as different dosages to try. Be patient and be persistent. You'll find the right medication and dosage for you.

Sexuality and Different Kinds of Depression

Since there are different kinds of depression, there are different ways the sex drive can be affected. It stands to reason then, that there are different ways of restoring your sexual well-being.

Seasonal Affective Disorder (SAD)

It's dark, dreary, and dismal, and you're feeling down in the dumps and depressed. If you've tried light therapy and found that it helped, bring some of that light into the bedroom. If you can't escape to a sunnier clime, do some creative planning on the home front. Sex doesn't have to happen in the dark. Transform your boudoir and turn night into day. It might be fun to see what you're doing, instead of fumbling in the dark!

Dysthymia

Dysthymia is common in older folks. It's a bit like having a low-grade fever. You're always down, and some days more so than others. Depression is a constant companion. It's not a nice bedfellow, however, so it will take some work to kick dysthymia out of the bedroom. Are you feeling better as the day wears on? Mornings may not be the best time for sex. If you're feeling your best around midnight, that may be the time to pull out all the stops and play your own moonlight sonata.

Major Depressive Disorder

Here's where the double whammy occurs. First of all, the loss of interest in sex—that's part of anhedonia—is one of depression's symptoms. Then, finding the right medication that doesn't offer sexual dysfunction as an unwelcome side effect comes next. The good news here is that once you get your medications sorted out, and they've begun to work on the symptoms of your depression, libido generally returns and you can reclaim this important area of your life.

It's All about Relationships

Human beings are social creatures. We're herd animals, to be accurate, and we need others around us. We join service organizations, fraternal societies, churches, and volunteer groups. We gather with others who share our interests and hobbies. And the family remains the basic unit of society. It's difficult to see how someone could ever be lonely, with all these options. But loneliness is common to us all.

There's a world of difference between being alone and being lonely. You may choose to be alone at times, knowing that when you want companionship, you can to reach out to others. Loneliness, however, is a different kind of feeling. It comes unbidden and stays and goes on its own terms. Loneliness and depression are first cousins.

If you're depressed, you're better off being married than staying single—at least according to a study conducted at the Ohio State University in Columbus, Ohio, and published in the June 2007 issue of *Journal of Health and Social Behavior*. For the study, researchers looked at 3,066 people, aged 55 and younger. They found that, overall, participants who got married scored an average of 3.5 points lower on a twelve-item depression test. Depressed participants scored an average of 7.5 points lower than those who remained single. Even though the quality of their marriages was not optimal, with less happiness and more conflict reported, the psychological improvement was considered to be statistically significant.

Want to Beat Depression? Consider Sex as Therapy!

That's right. You read that correctly. You need to take your medicine, if you want to get better. You've heard this advice all your life, and, if you've got children, you've told them pretty much the same thing. Now it's your turn. Sex is good for you, and what's more, it can help you relieve the symptoms of depression. The best part is that you've already got all the equipment you'll need, and maintenance of that equipment means using it on a regular basis. If you're struggling with low libido, ask your doctor how you can restore your oomph.

Rx for Stress

Sometimes you just have to force yourself to do something, even if, at that particular moment, it's not all that appealing. When you're depressed, the thought of engaging in sex seems like more trouble than it's worth, and your libido isn't operating at maximum strength, either. Does that mean sex is out of the question? Doesn't have to be. Not every act of intimacy needs to end in intercourse. Consider your options—when it comes to romance, there are quite a few.

Cuddle, Snuggle, Neck, and Pet

Human touch is a great healer. Massage is a great stress reducer, and it's something you and your partner can do for each other. Foot rubs, back rubs, neck and shoulder rubs—pick one or all and relax. You may decide to talk or not, but you'll find that the topics that come to mind, while you're getting or giving a massage, are of a pleasant nature. With that comes a sense of increased well-being. And who knows what this might lead to? It's definitely worth the effort.

Doing Your Homework

Researchers have been busy studying the beneficial effects of sex and are glad to report that they've found them. *Forbes* online reported on a longitudinal study of about 1,000 middle-aged men, conducted by Queens University in Belfast. The research findings were published in the *British Medical Journal* in 1997. Other studies continued this research and their results confirm the findings:

- After sex, your sense of smell improves. This is why you get hungry! A good meal will also help you deal with depression—and if you order take-out or delivery, you don't have to leave home.
- The risk of heart attack or stroke for men is cut in half for men who have sex three or more times per week.
- Sex is good exercise. You can burn 200 calories during sex. That equates to fifteen minutes on a treadmill. Researchers found that your pulse rate rises from about 70 beats per minute to 150—that's equivalent to an athlete going full out.

- What those scientists research is nothing short of amazing. Sex can help you control your weight. Getting that body in shape will help you work on improving that self-image. Those dedicated researchers determined that you can work off the equivalent of six Big Macs if you have sex three times a week for a year.
- For women, as they approach orgasm, levels of the hormone oxytocin increase up to five times their normal level. This triggers a release of endorphins, which act as your body's personal pain relievers.
- Getting older can mean less bladder control, and sex can help you with this embarrassing problem. Sex works the same muscles that control urine flow, so the more sex, the more you tone up! Do those Kegels!

 ## Question

What are Kegels?
Kegels, named for Dr. Arnold Kegel, a gynecologist who discovered them, are pelvic floor exercises that work to strengthen the pubococcygeus muscles. To clarify here, we're talking about the pelvic floor, not floor exercises! The exercises involve alternately tightening and then releasing these muscles.

- When you're depressed, so is your immune system. According to a Wilkes University study, participants who engaged in sex once or twice a week had 30 percent higher levels of the antibody immunoglobulin A. That antibody is believed to give your immune system a boost.
- And finally, for the men, how about a healthier prostate? *Forbes* online reports on a study published by the *British Journal of Urology International* that found men in their twenties can reduce their chances of getting prostate cancer by ejaculating more than five times a week.

With no reported drawbacks and several obvious benefits, healthy sex can go a long way toward helping you deal with the symptoms of depression.

Communication

You've already read how walking the walk can help your body confront the more debilitating effects of depression, but there's still more you can do. Silence may be golden in some situations, but resolving difficulties is not one of those situations. Good relationships can weather all manner of storms, but you've both got to know which way the wind is blowing. If you're married, it comes down to the "for better or worse, in sickness and in health" aspects of the ceremony.

It's Your Turn to Carry the Load

In all relationships, the ideal give-and-take on both parts is 50 percent. That's the ideal, and life is never ideal. There are good times and bad times, and often the bad things seem to come in clusters. It's as if the fates were toying with you to see just how much you can take. So, if you've just had a root canal, are feeling boxed in by seasonal affective disorder (SAD), and can't remember the last time your partner said, "I love you," realize that all this is temporary. Your mouth will heal, the sun will come out again, and if your partner still hasn't said those three little words, try saying them yourself. It might be your turn to carry the load.

When I Said, "I Do," I Wasn't Thinking about This

It's easy to be with someone, when everything is fine—when you're feeling great, looking good, and enjoying what life has to offer. During the down times, however, it's not that much fun to be with someone who is trolling the bottom, looking for a place to bed down among the bottom fish. At these times, it helps to repeat the mantra mentioned earlier, "This too, shall pass." And it's highly probable that at some point, you'll be the one needing the care and attention. During this time of high stress, when your partner is suffering from depression, take some time to care for yourself. It can be draining to be the 80 in an 80/20 relationship.

Some Final Thoughts on Sexuality

Humans are all sexual beings, but sexuality is a complex concept. People are genetically programmed, biologically equipped, mentally conditioned, and emotionally engaged to present ourselves to the best advantage for one purpose—to ensure the continuation of the species. It's a heavy responsibility, but the performance of the duty can be among the most pleasurable experiences that life has to offer.

Use It or Lose It

When physical or mental illness impacts the ability to participate in sex, it's no wonder people become irritable. As you've read, however, getting back on track mentally means using your body the way nature intended. While the advice, "use it or lose it" may not have been coined to deal with depression, it certainly works here and has the added benefit of keeping your relationship healthy.

Eye of the Beholder

People do well when they are with others who share their interests and passions. People do even better when they find partners who will accept them as they are and for who they are. Some of the happiest couples will never win any kind of beauty contest. You've got to go back to those old, timeworn and time-tested adages: "Beauty is only skin deep." It's what's inside that matters. And if that inside is compassionate and understanding of a partner who is going through some tough times, that's the relationship that will stand the test of time.

Looking for a 50/50 relationship? You'll look a long time—perhaps forever. Look instead for one in which the two of you can take turns carrying the load. Maybe that will look like 60/40 or 70/30, but how do you measure love? And the truth of it is, if you're really in love, you don't keep score.

When Terminal
Thoughts Arise

CHAPTER 16

THIS IS A SUBTOPIC of depression that no one wants to discuss, but it deserves perhaps the most attention. Suicide is a tragic response to depression, but unfortunately, it does happen. This does not mean that if you're battling depression you will become suicidal or are in danger of becoming so. This chapter is simply meant to be an educational look at the extreme end of the depression spectrum. In this chapter you'll get a view of the big picture of suicide—statistics, risk factors, and myths—as well as specific, prescriptive information to help steer you well clear of this dark place.

Depression and Suicide

We understand a great deal more about the brain than we used to, but there is still so much we don't yet know. At what point does a depressed person make the decision that the pain of living is worse than the finality of death? Each person is an individual, responding to life events and physical and mental illness, including depression, on highly personal terms.

It can be easy to be judgmental if you've never experienced the depths of despair that can lead someone to consider suicide as the only escape. If you *have* experienced this, however, you understand why and how this can be. There are no words that can give voice to this total and ultimate sense of hopelessness.

What's the link between depression and suicide? You can't reason with depression. It takes over and becomes almost a living entity, wearing away at your resolve to see it through, and there can come a time when the struggle seems more than you're capable of. That doesn't mean that everyone who is depressed goes on to commit suicide. But thoughts of suicide are common, especially among the severely depressed. Pain hurts, and the pain of depression goes so deep that it can become too much. That is when suicide and thoughts of suicide can arise.

What Drives Us

The strongest of our human instincts revolve around the preservation of the species. Self-preservation, reproduction, and the maternal instinct can all be considered aspects of that central focus. In that regard, some important characteristics are shared with other members of the animal world. However, humans are different from them in that people tend to think about their drives—analyzing them, denying them on occasion, and reveling in them, when possible. Suicide raises all manner of interesting questions about the fundamental drives of our species.

 Fact

Believe it or not, suicide is illegal. It's a criminal act. So, technically, you can be prosecuted for committing suicide, although the idea is bizarre beyond belief. You may believe that your life is your own, to do with as you please, but society does not share that opinion. Society has a vested interest in you, for its own purposes, and it has set laws and taboos in place to protect that interest.

Was It Accidental?

When someone who is cared for commits suicide, there's always a faint hope that perhaps the death was really accidental. It's so difficult to accept that someone would actually, purposefully end his or her life. Even in the face of overwhelming evidence to the contrary, that slim hope persists. Suicide is a breach of an unwritten and unspoken contract with other members of the human race. It's a premature separation that contributes nothing to the clan. There are other ramifications of suicide, as well. For a family left behind, struggling financially, an official cause of death that reads suicide is an automatic termination of life insurance benefits. Now, in addition to the grief, there's real hardship. That hardship can turn initial grief into anger.

Suicide Statistics

It is difficult to compile accurate statistics on suicide, since many deaths that are actually suicides are ruled to be accidental. Working with available data, however, researchers have been able to put together an incomplete picture. According to the National Institutes of Health (NIH):

- Suicide is the third leading cause of death for adolescents in the United States.
- There were 31,655 documented suicides in the United States in 2002.
- 80 percent of suicides are committed by men.
- Whites are two times as likely to commit suicide as are African Americans and Hispanics.
- More women than men attempt suicide, but four times more men than women complete the act.
- The risk of suicide increases with age. White males age eighty-five and over have a suicide rate six times the national average.
- For every suicide completed, there are an estimated eight to twenty-five attempts.

Statistics give us the numbers but tell us little or nothing about the people who make up the percentages. The following sections look at specific populations, risk factors, and some signs of what to look for if someone you know falls into these groups.

Adolescents

With the hormonal factor of paramount concern here, feelings of loneliness, abandonment, or not fitting in with the in group can lead to depression. Losing a boyfriend or girlfriend can be the trigger for suicidal feelings to surface. Frequently, the desire is not to complete the act, but rather to garner attention and sympathy. For those young people who lack other means of gaining entrée into a desired social setting, a suicide attempt may seem to offer the possibility of attaining that goal.

Copycat or cluster suicides are not uncommon in adolescents. When a teen has committed suicide, the media can be the catalyst that turns one tragic death into a tabloid spectacle and sets a chain reaction of copycat suicide attempts in motion. Through extensive coverage of the suicide, interviews with friends of the young person, and meticulous attention to the grisly details of the death, the media works the romance angle to the max.

Vulnerable teens are paying attention, and those who have been on the fringes of the social scene may see suicide as a way to be noticed. In that strange fantasy, they see themselves finally the center of attention, looking down on grieving friends and family from some celestial viewpoint. Caught up in the delusion, they can't comprehend the finality of the act.

 Alert

Teens, especially teens who are not part of the in-crowd, may exhibit signs that show they're fascinated with death. Talk to them about the finality of suicide and how it doesn't solve problems but creates more of them. If you belong to a religious organization, enlist the help of your pastor, rabbi, or minister. Contact your physician for recommendations as to how to proceed.

If there has been a teen suicide in your community, be especially aware of what this may mean for your own teenager and be aware of any behaviors or talk that may indicate a fascination with the death.

Substance abuse may also play a role, in that it removes inhibitions. Teenagers who are contemplating suicide may get their "courage fix" with alcohol or drugs.

Women

Women attempt suicide more often than men but succeed less frequently, and may choose a means—such as slashing wrists or taking an overdose—that allows for the possibility that they'll be found before death occurs. In this case, the goal may be to rekindle a romantic partner's interest or to mend a relationship that has been on the rocks. The reality, of course, is that such a reconciliation may never happen if the suicide turns out to be successful. Also, this attempt may be the final straw that irrevocably severs the romantic relationship. Women who seriously intend to commit suicide are more likely to use a firearm or other lethal means that do not allow for interception. Always take any mention of suicide seriously. Don't assume someone is merely looking for attention.

Men

Some of the same factors that account for men not seeking help for physical ailments also apply to the mental health sector. When there is a depressive disorder, men may find themselves without the necessary coping tools and may feel impotent to deal with their problems. They may then turn to thoughts of suicide.

While women may attempt suicide four times more frequently than men, men tend to complete the act more often than women do. Men tend to use more lethal means, such as guns or hanging themselves, which don't give a window of time during which they can be found and rescued before death occurs. Men may also remove themselves from locations where they are likely to be intercepted. If someone says that he is thinking about suicide, take this seriously.

You probably won't have the luxury of finding him quickly, in time to help, before he succeeds with the act.

The Elderly

Isolation is a major risk factor for suicide, and the elderly can be the most isolated of all our subpopulations. If isolation is coupled with physical illness and incapacitation, the risk increases exponentially. The tragedy here is that many elderly folks see their physicians on a regular basis but may not let their doctors know about their symptoms of depression. If an older person makes a suicide attempt, his overall physical condition may not permit full recovery. That may lead to a deepening depression and a subsequent and successful attempt. The tragedy here is that the depression could have been treated. Age should not be a death sentence.

Risk Factors

Many of the risk factors for suicide can be found by reading the statistics, but the underlying causes are not always so evident. Loss is the lurker—loss of health, loss of a loved one, loss of a job, or any other significant loss. Any of these can be the precursor to depression. When people turn to drugs and alcohol to help them cope with this loss, the low feelings just get worse. If you, or someone you love, has had a recent loss, be especially aware of how this may impact mental health and take appropriate measures to get help.

Essential

Life and loss are partners. All of us go through life experiencing a series of goodbyes. When the loss is more than you can cope with at the moment, you may feel the symptoms of depression. Professional help is available to help you get through those feelings.

Secondary Medical Conditions

Certain medical conditions, or the medications used to treat them, can result in depression that may lead to thoughts of suicide. The realization of compromised health and possibly long-term diminished physical capacity may initially lead to feelings of despondency. Chronic illness may result in chronic depression, or dysthymia. Without treatment, antidepressants, and/or psychotherapy, these thoughts may progress to the point that the individual begins to consider suicide. If you have a chronic condition, you don't need to wrestle with depression as well. Talk to your primary health care provider about your options. You need all the resources you can muster to help you through.

 ## Question

How can I make my home suicide-proof?
The answer is, you can't. Someone who is determined to take his or her life will find a way. All you can do is secure your home to the best of your ability and realize that you are not at fault, should the worst happen.

Access to Lethal Means

It isn't possible to remove every possible potential harmful device from the home, so it's essential to be vigilant. Weapons or other substances, when abused, may provide a determined person with a means of committing suicide. Weapons may include firearms, rope, poison, and materials able to be used in asphyxiation. Again, gender plays a role. When there is a heightened possibility of a suicide attempt, firearms should be made inaccessible. Particularly for women with severe depression, be concerned if you see signs of hoarding prescription medications until there are enough to commit suicide by overdosing.

A Previous Attempt

Someone who has tried to commit suicide at some point in the past should be considered at risk for making another attempt in the future. People do create patterns, whether for good or bad. So, if you have prior knowledge, you can expect that this behavior may occur again, given a specific set of circumstances. In this case, past attempts may be an indicator of future attempts.

An Impulsive Personality

People who tend to act without regard to the consequences of their actions may be at increased risk for suicide, when depressed. This characteristic appears to have more influence in adolescent suicide attempts than in adult attempts. Spur of the moment decisions, in these cases, may have permanent consequences.

 Alert

Risk behaviors may be associated with impulsive personalities. If your teenager drives recklessly, consumes alcohol, or exhibits other tendencies that worry you, be vigilant.

Increased Alcohol and Drug Use

If you drink socially, and as a means of relaxing after the workday, you may not see alcohol as a problem. However, alcohol is a depressant, and its effects on the body are considerable. For people coping with depression, alcohol can be a double-edged sword. It may interfere and interact with antidepressants, and it may complicate mood patterns—and not for the better. Alcohol can dull the inhibitions, and for someone contemplating suicide, this may result in a loss of perspective.

Myths

There are certain folk sayings or common knowledge surrounding the topic of suicide. Many of them are literally "whistling past the graveyard." Here are some of those myths, along with some explanations of why they need to be debunked.

"People who say they're going to commit suicide never do."

The truth is that, while not all people who say that they're going to kill themselves will make the attempt, some will. How can you be certain which category the person you're talking about falls into? Simply stated, you can't be. Doctors can't predict with certainty, and neither can you. Take every suicide threat seriously. At the very least, the threat is an indication that the person in question needs help with certain issues. Better to be on the safe side than regret your failure to act.

"If you mention suicide to someone who's depressed, you'll put the idea in his head."

If someone is seriously depressed, the idea of suicide has already occurred. By talking about it openly, you initiate a conversation that can help lead to effective treatment. There is a sense of isolation that accompanies suicidal thoughts, and your compassion and concern can be an important step in breaking down those boundaries.

"It's her own business. You should stay out of it."

It's difficult to see how someone could be so cool about the potential loss of life. Suicide may be a personal decision, but it's a personal decision with a ripple effect that spreads far beyond the act itself, reaching across time and space to torment friends and loved ones left behind. By the same measure, if you reach out to help, you're helping not only the suicidal person; you're helping the family and friends of that person, as well.

"He's bound to kill himself anyway, so what's the point in trying to stop him?"

Nobody's got a crystal ball that accurately foretells the future. Perhaps your friend's medication is causing the problem, and a dosage adjustment will fix it. Perhaps he's just waiting for someone to step in and take over, for a bit, to see that he gets help. No one can know for sure what another person will do at any given time.

"She's just looking for attention."

This is quite possible. The problem is real, however. Someone who would consider suicide as the only option for gaining attention needs help. This sort of last resort thinking indicates this person feels she has exhausted all her other options. It's a desperation move.

"He's plain nuts. You've got to be crazy to try to kill yourself."

No. You don't. You just have to hurt so much that death seems to be the only option to release you from the pain. This is not the time for name-calling or shunning. This is the time for an intervention—getting this person to help, before it's too late.

 Alert

> If you suspect a friend or loved one is about to commit suicide, don't wait. Call 911, take the person to the emergency room, call the doctor, do whatever it takes to stop the act, and be right at that person's side. You may not get another chance.

Warning Signs

In a seriously depressed individual, there are certain warning signs that should be heeded, as they may indicate the person has arrived at the decision to commit suicide. If someone who has been depressed suddenly seems cheerful, this may mean he or she has resolved an inner conflict and has made the decision to commit suicide. Other signs include giving away prized possessions—sort of a final housecleaning—putting financial affairs in order, being unwilling to engage in conversations about future plans, and writing a suicide note.

Antidepressants and Suicide

Back in 1990, when selective serotonin reuptake inhibitors (SSRIs) had been on the market only a short time, there were some early reports of people experiencing suicidal thoughts after starting to take the medication. The Federal Drug Administration (FDA) did not feel the reports constituted a red flag, and SSRIs continued to be prescribed.

The Plot Thickens

In 2003, a possible connection between Paxil (paroxetine) and suicidal thoughts and self-destructive behavior in some teenagers and children was noted by British drug authorities, leading to an FDA review of SSRI use in those populations.

 Question

What should I look for if my child is on antidepressants?
Any change in behavior should get you paying close attention. Keep a close watch while your child is on medication and report any concerns to your physician, immediately.

The Black Box

In 2004, the FDA issued its strongest advisory short of mandating a drug's withdrawal from approved use. This warning, called the "black box," required all package inserts to include the warning that use of antidepressants might result in increased risk of suicidal thoughts, hostility, and agitation, in both children and adults.

Fact

Every prescription comes with a package insert. Read it and be an informed consumer. If you are having trouble deciphering the medical jargon, ask your pharmacist to interpret for you.

New Study

A study by the University of Illinois at Chicago and published in the July 2007 issue of the *American Journal of Psychiatry* found that the risk of suicidal behavior was lower in all adults who received treatment with SSRIs. This included the previous age group that had been a concern, eight to twenty-five. Participants in the study were divided into four age groups: eighteen to twenty-five, twenty-six to forty-five, forty-six to sixty-five, and older than sixty-five. All groups who took SSRIs showed a significantly lower risk of suicide attempts when compared with those who did not receive the treatment. More studies will be forthcoming.

Antidepressant Use in Children

It is important to follow your doctor's recommendations when considering use of antidepressant medications in children under the age of eighteen. If your physician does prescribe antidepressants for your child, address any concerns you have immediately. This is not an area where a "wait and see" approach is indicated.

Getting Help

It's been said that suicide is a permanent solution to a temporary problem. If you're struggling with depression and are wrestling with thoughts of suicide, it seems impossible to imagine how anything could possibly be worse than what you're going through. There is something worse, however, and it's the painful legacy suicide leaves to those who love you.

Life Is Worth Living

One of depression's many symptoms is the feeling that nothing is worth the effort that it takes. If you wake in the morning with the thought that this is one more day to struggle through and endure and there won't be a drop of joy in it, it's time to talk to your doctor. Even in the midst of life's greatest struggles, life is still worth living. There is help for this anhedonia, and you owe it to yourself and your loved ones to get it.

The Armchair Counselor

It's great that you're ready to lend an ear and listen to your loved one or friend share concerns. What you want to do next is offer advice, but this can be tricky. Knowing when to listen, when to talk, and especially what to say requires training. You are the family member or the friend. You are not a trained professional. This is where a counselor, psychiatrist, clinical psychologist, psychiatric nurse practitioner, or family physician comes in. And when you're concerned about suicide, this is not the time to agree to an appointment in two months. You need assistance now.

It's an Emergency

The front of your telephone directory contains some important emergency contact information, but if you're convinced someone is in imminent danger of attempting suicide, call 911. There is also the suicide hotline: 1-800-SUICIDE.

Better Safe Than Sorry

"Better safe than sorry" should be the rule to live by when you or a loved one begins to experience thoughts of suicide. So much of what people experience in life is temporary—pain, as well as joy. In those darkest moments, death may seem to be a release. Death, however is permanent. Life is precious. Find help. Live.

Electroconvulsive Therapy

Most people have a respectful fear of electricity. Combine that with general attitudes toward convulsions, and you can see why electroconvulsive therapy (ECT) hasn't been high on anybody's favorite activities list. ECT has been around since the late 1930s, however, and back in its infancy, was administered without anesthetic. Today, however, ECT has gone modern. The procedure is done under general anesthesia, so it's painless. If you are having suicidal thoughts, and these thoughts are progressing to the point you may decide to act on them, ECT is a viable option.

According to the Mayo Clinic, approximately 100,000 Americans receive ECT each year. Making the decision to have ECT is something you should discuss with your psychotherapist, psychiatrist, or primary health care provider. Also, if you aren't able to tolerate antidepressants or have already had a positive experience with ECT, you may decide on this course of treatment.

Essential

ECT is done on either an in-patient or out-patient basis at the hospital. You'll have an anesthesiologist, primary physician (your psychiatrist), and nursing staff as your team.

How It Works

During ECT, you're put under anesthesia and then given the drug succinylcholine to temporarily relax the muscles so that they do not contract during the treatment and cause fractures. Then an electric current is passed through electrodes that are positioned on your head. The current is applied for one second or less. During this time, your heart function is monitored by an electrocardiogram (EKG) and your brain function with an electroencephalogram (EEG).

Risks

No medical treatment is 100 percent safe. There is always the possibility of potential risk, and some risks can be life-threatening. If you've had surgery, you're aware of the forms you're required to fill out—the ones that explain that even the simplest, most benign procedure may result in your death. It's a result of our litigious society. Risks, such as cardiac arrest, associated with anesthesia are not common in otherwise healthy individuals.

 Alert

A rare, potentially fatal condition called malignant hyperthermia (MH) may be triggered by some anesthetics. The anesthetics most commonly associated with malignant hyperthermia include the muscle relaxant succinylcholine.

Side Effects

Side effects of ECT are generally of short duration. Immediately after you awaken, you may feel confused and have some memory loss. This may last from a few minutes to several hours. You may also experience nausea, vomiting, headache, muscle ache, or jaw pain. The length of time that you feel confused may increase with subsequent treatments, but everything usually subsides after the course of treatment is completed.

How Many Treatments Are Necessary?

The course of ECT therapy usually extends over a few weeks, with three sessions being the typical number per week. Nine treatments are about average. When your therapy is completed, your doctor may suggest follow-up sessions to prevent relapse. The National Alliance for the Mentally Ill estimates that ECT is effective in about 80 percent of people who receive the full course.

Why Does It Work?

Scientists don't know with absolute certainty why ECT works, although they have some theories. One theory suggests that the induced seizures cause changes in the brain's neurotransmitters. Another line of thinking is that stress levels are changed at their source—in the brain. What is known, though, is that many chemical aspects of brain function are altered during and after seizure activity. Also, researchers think that these changes may be cumulative, building over the course of treatment. That's the reason for having a series of treatments rather than just one session.

Work Issues

CLOSE YOUR EYES and think of the last social gathering you attended. You were introduced to someone and you exchanged names. What was the next question asked? Most likely it was "What do you do?" More than any other aspect of your life, your work defines you. Whether you're self-employed, a stay-at-home mom or dad, a tele-commuter, or part of the office-bound workforce, work occupies your mind and your time. When your mental or physical health is compromised, such as when you have depression, you struggle to get through the day, and work changes from a source of fulfillment to a source of frustration.

Depression as Disability

Depression and anxiety are closing in on back ailments as the top reasons for people missing work. What's the reason for the increase in emotional and psychological stress? It's not all that difficult to understand if you take a look at what's going on in the world of work these days. Corporate downsizing, outsourcing, and budget tighten-ing all contribute to stress in the workplace, and the situation doesn't show signs of improving anytime soon.

Trying to Cope

You may notice that just getting to work—with all that entails—may have taxed you to the max. Then, you're expected to work, once you've made it to your cubicle, desk, or whatever. Practically speaking, however, you're exhausted. And when you gather your energy to plunge into your day, you may find that:

- You can't concentrate.
- You can't keep track of what you've done or remember important details.
- You're messing up. You're making mistakes that you don't usually make.
- You aren't operating at your usual pace. You're slow.
- You forget to show up at important meetings.
- You're short-tempered. People are starting to give you a wide berth.

Eventually, your co-workers may confront you, or worse, they may talk to your supervisor behind your back. Before this happens, however, you may decide you need to get medical help and talk to your boss or to someone else you trust at work.

 Fact

Having a job can cause depressive symptoms, and losing a job can cause them as well. Work, whether coming or going, is a major source of stress and can lead to depression.

Some Real Concerns

How secure is your job? If you've been recently hired, you may not feel on solid enough ground to tell your employer about your medical condition. If your depression will adversely impact the organization—if there are safety issues involved—you may have a moral and ethical responsibility to divulge it. You worry that you'll be let go, or that the stigma of depression will taint all your work relationships. Or perhaps there's someone who's just waiting for a sign of weakness on your part to make a move to get your job. All of these concerns are valid. There are ways, however, of dealing with all of them.

 Essential

> If you're job hunting and suffer from depression or another disability, the time to disclose your condition is after you've been offered the job and have accepted it. If you can perform the duties required of you, with or without reasonable accommodation, you cannot be fired because of that disability.

Know the Law

The Americans with Disabilities Act (ADA), passed in 1990, went into effect on July 26, 1992. This law prohibits private employers with fifteen or more employees, state and local governments, employment agencies, and labor unions from discriminating against qualified individuals with disabilities in job application procedures, hiring, firing, advancement, compensation, job training, and other terms, conditions, and privileges of employment. Under the ADA, employers are required to make what is called a "reasonable accommodation" to those with a known disability, as long as doing so would not impose an "undue hardship" on the operation of the employer's business.

 Question

> **How does the government define disability?**
> With respect to an individual, the ADA defines disability as a physical or mental impairment that substantially limits one or more of the major life activities of such individual; a record of such an impairment; or being regarded as having such an impairment.

Reasonable Accommodation

If you would be able to perform your duties if your employer moved you to part-time, modified your work schedule, restructured your job, or reassigned you to a vacant position, those actions would qualify as reasonable accommodations. It is your responsibility to inform your employer that you need reasonable accommodation, and it's also your obligation to suggest the types of accommodations that would work for you. Your goal is to keep your job, so it just makes sense that you would do everything you possibly can to ensure this will happen.

Recourse

If you believe you've been discriminated against because of your disability, you should contact the Equal Opportunity Employment Commission (EEOC). The time frame for filing a charge of discrimination is generally within 180 days of the alleged discrimination. The EEOC's telephone number is 1-800-669-4000.

Prepare Your Case

You've thought the whole thing over and discussed it with your family, your psychotherapist or physician, or a good friend, and you've decided that it's in your best interests to tell your employer about your depression. Before you enter the boss's office and have the one on one chat, do your homework. This won't be easy, and it will take energy, but it's essential to your welfare.

Schedule the Doctor's Appointment

This is the first step. Make the appointment and then keep it. Once you have made this commitment to yourself, you'll be in a better frame of mind to make other decisions. Taking the initiative here shows responsibility, along with a sincere desire to regain your health.

Essential

Start keeping the paper trail now. The worst diary is better than the best memory when it comes to recalling important dates and events. Keep all your medical records, receipts, schedule of appointments, and anything else that's pertinent in a file that you can access when you need to.

Use Your Sick Days

You're a stellar employee, and you don't take much sick time. Now is the right time to do this, however. If your doctor prescribes antidepressant medications, these may take a little time— perhaps up to three weeks—to work up to an effective level in your body. If you have accumulated some days, take them. If your workplace has a sick pool where you all donate a day to be used when someone needs extra days, apply for some. Eliminating the stress of working, while you're getting better, will help you get better faster.

Talk to the Boss

There are advantages and disadvantages to disclosing your medical condition to management. You'll be relieved of the burden of pretending you're operating at 100 percent. (It's probably apparent to everyone close to you, anyway, that you're subpar right now, so you'll defuse this as an issue.) You'll also open the door for reasonable accommodation. Then, if your employer uses your disclosure against you and either demotes you or terminates you, you may be protected by the law. If you don't disclose, you won't be protected.

Realize however, that human nature is human nature. Your boss may decide to give a plum assignment to someone else, or you may experience some difficulties in dealing with your associates, as a result of them perceiving you as privileged or mentally ill. Of course, this is foolish, and you'd give just about anything not to need accommodations. Unless others have walked in your shoes, however, it's nearly impossible for them to understand how depression feels. Only you can decide what the right course of action is.

Talk to Your Trusted Colleagues

Go slowly, here. Take your time and decide exactly what you want to say and the best way to say it. It's probably not a great idea to burst into the office tomorrow morning and announce or snarl to everyone who'll listen, "I have depression!!" That will sound more like a challenge than anything else. And what exactly are your co-workers going to do with that tidbit of information, anyway? No, give this some careful thought, before proceeding. Time to back up a bit and do some planning. What do you need from them? A willing hand? A sounding board? Take a trusted friend or two aside and talk. Her support will help you cope when the day gets long.

Essential

Tough to make a decision? Paper and pencil time again. Take a sheet of paper and fold it in half, vertically. Label the left side of the paper: Reasons to Disclose and label the right side of the paper: Reasons Not To. List everything you can think of. Let the paper sit a day or so and add to it, until you've got everything down. If you can discuss this with family, so much the better, as it will undoubtedly bring up some areas you may have overlooked. Read through your reasons for each course of action. Where is the advantage? It's a good tool for getting the big picture out in the open and can help you see what decision will be in your best interest.

Strategies for Holding the Line

If you continue working while in therapy, or if you've just returned after a few weeks leave, you'll need to take care of yourself and reduce stress as much as you can. It's going to take a while to heal, and you're going to need to modify your routines to give yourself every advantage.

Managing Stressors

Tackling one stressor at a time will help you make some inroads into managing your work environment. Here's where you'll want the paper and pencil again. What causes you the most stress at work? Is it an individual? A procedure? Unscheduled meetings? Some things are beyond your control to change, but you can work on ways to modify your responses and lower your stress level in the process. Your goal here is to simplify the situation to the greatest extent possible. You'll probably discover that work isn't the main problem. The culprit might be that new hire that's been eyeing your desk and toadying up to the boss. Or perhaps it's the new competitor down the block or across the Pacific, that's eating into your market share. Narrowing the stressor down to something you can accurately name will be the first step in identifying a strategy to handle it. And when you're done, destroy the paper or, at the very least, leave the paper home! This is for your eyes only. Here's how this might look:

Stressor: There's one co-worker who talks behind your back, spreading rumors about your mental health condition. This person wants your job and is nice to your face, offering support and sympathy, but you know it's a sham.

Strategy: Actually, there are a couple of strategies here. How far you want to go depends upon you.

First of all, document. Document everything. And back up your files. This takes time, extra time that is not always easy to find, but it's essential that you have a written record of your work output and productivity. Think of this as a variation on the ledger system of accounting. The task goes on the left of the ledger, along with the date assigned. Date completed goes to the right, along with any pertinent comments. In addition to providing concrete refutation of whatever the co-worker conjures up, this info will serve you well come time for performance review and raise time.

You know that this person is talking about you. Enlist one of the folks this co-worker has talked to, someone you trust, and confront your co-worker about his actions. If your boss or supervisor is also someone you trust, bring her in on the confrontation, as a witness. It's unlikely you'll have to do this more than once. You'll be seen as someone in charge, someone who's prepared to fight for her honor, and as someone who's definitely not mentally incompetent. Yes, you may be exhausted when it's done, but this exhaustion will be a catharsis.

Exercise

In Chapter 13 you read about the importance of exercise in combating the symptoms of depression. If you followed one of the tips there, you've already got a comfortable pair of walking or running shoes in your car. They're not going to do you a whole lot of good there, so you're going to need to put them on and get moving. Pick the best time for some exercise and make it a priority. If you can walk or bicycle to work, so much the better. If you only have the lunch hour or half hour, make it count. Make it work for you. If after work is the best time, that's fine too. Exercise will raise your endorphin level and work off the negative energy and lower your stress levels.

Priorities

Health is Priority One. If you're not taking care of yourself, you can't take care of the job or your family. You've got to come first. Make health the bottom line for every decision and you'll come out ahead. That may very well mean learning to say, "No thanks," when you have to. Here's how that looks in practice: Your colleagues say, "We're going out for margaritas after work. Join us. We've got a lot to catch up on."

You hesitate. You've used up your daily quota of energy, and you're tired. You had plans to exercise after work, and you've noticed that you feel better, when you do. Besides, alcohol and your antidepressants don't mix, so you've decided to pass on the booze. What do you do?

You smile and say, "Thanks, but I'm going for a run after work. How about joining me?"

That puts the onus back on your co-workers. They're going boozing, and you're going running on the moral high ground. You're in control and you've got a plan. Soon, they're going to wonder who the one battling depression is!

Keep Your Distance

Distance yourself from negative people, whenever possible. Every workplace seems to have at least one person who never has a good word to say about anyone or anything. These people drain your energy and sap your strength. Avoid them when you can. Engage them minimally, when you must. These are not happy people, and they spread their own discontent around the office like a virus. Limit your exposure to them.

L. Essential

Keep something that inspires you on your desk. Choose something with positive associations that makes you feel good when you see it or handle it. When the negative folks try to make some inroads, as they stop by your work station, focus instead on your inspiration and let their words drop like stones on the floor. You can sweep up after they've gone.

Lighten Up

Bring some extra light into your workspace. Whether that means hauling in some natural spectrum lighting for your desk lamp, buying a floor lamp with high intensity light to stick in the corner, or having the fluorescent bulbs replaced with something that will deliver more light, do it! This is not the time for economy. Hang holiday icicles around your doorway if that's what it takes. Your mood will improve as a result.

Breathe

You've been informed another meeting has been scheduled for exactly the time you'd planned on getting the report finished and sent on. You can't control the situation, but you can control your stress reaction. This is the time to do those isometric exercises, practice your relaxation techniques, and control your breathing. The report will still be there when you return and your more relaxed frame of mind will allow you to tackle it.

Knowing When to Call It Quits

You're making progress, but you're still slow. You're not getting things done as quickly as you'd like, so you're thinking maybe some overtime would help clear your desk. But before you decide to stay late, consider the following:

- The reward for a job well done is more work.
- Your desk will fill up tomorrow, no matter how clean it is today.
- Work expands to fill the time allotted for it.
- If you don't say no, you're saying yes.

Nope. Call it quits at the end of the day and call it good. Tomorrow is another day. Leave on time. If you've been accustomed to staying late, going in on weekends, and taking a slew of work home, it's time to get your priorities straight. Nobody, as the old saying goes, has ever decided at the end of his life that he wished he'd spent more time at the office.

When You Work at Home

More and more people are telecommuting and working as freelancers. If you're one of them, you enjoy some special benefits, but you also have some problems specific to your situation. Depression may want to keep you in bed or otherwise occupied, but you can overcome these tendencies with some special strategies.

 Alert

Don't mix your work areas and your play areas. Keep your work where it belongs—in your home office. Likewise, keep the distractions in your office to a minimum. Balance is key to managing your work, your life, and not so coincidentally—getting one up on depression.

Start Simply

Get dressed. Your goal for the day, as you begin to work through the dark clouds, can be as simple as getting out of bed and getting dressed for work. Depression or not, working at home takes a considerable amount of mental discipline. It's easy to do anything but what you're supposed to be doing. If you're feeling good, you may decide to organize a closet instead of sitting down at the computer. If you're not feeling good, you may want to roll over and go back to sleep. Here's where you need a little help. You probably feel better as the day goes on, so get your clothes ready the afternoon before. Put them within eyesight of the bed. In the morning, you won't have to waste energy deciding what to wear or even if to wear. Get out of your pajamas or your nightgown, and climb into your work clothes. You're going to feel a little stupid crawling back to bed when you're dressed for the office. Since you're up and dressed, might as well move on to the next thing. Leave the bedroom.

Reward Yourself

Promise yourself a treat for getting ready for work. Schedule a massage, brew a pot of really good coffee, pencil in a run after work—whatever you'd like that will keep you on track. You're going to need to build in plenty of rewards for yourself, as you accomplish your goals. And you know what? You deserve every one of them!

Avoid Extra Responsibilities

Soon enough, you'll feel like tackling more than what's on your plate. This is not the time to ask for that extra portion. Deal with what's at hand, do the best you can, and let the extra helpings wait until later. There's always time for the extras. Right now, you are what's the main course.

Make a Schedule

Don't rely on your memory right now. Write everything down. You should have a notepad and pencil easily accessible at all times. Carry a little spiral notebook and stubby pencil in your pocket. Each morning, as you sit down at the computer, transfer the important information—dates and times—to your personal calendar. With the schedule in front of you, you'll stay on track and have a visual record of your accomplishments. Success breeds success. Success also helps elevate your mood and allows you to get more done. It's a happy circle, not a vicious one.

Essential

When you're on antidepressant medications, it's important to have your blood levels checked on a regular basis. This will tell your doctor if your dosage is at optimal levels and will also alert her to any potential side effects, especially regarding problems with liver functions. Antidepressants can require some fine tuning before they get you humming along.

Make Time Your Friend

You may not feel that you're making much progress, but you're too close to the situation. Realize that even as you're making steady progress, there will be days when you feel that you're slipping backwards. Acknowledge those feelings, and if they persist for more than a couple of days, contact your psychotherapist or physician.

Whether you're working at home or outside the home, unless the building is on fire, or somebody's leg is caught in the paper shredder, those office "emergencies" probably aren't. You're not at the top of your form right now and snap decisions aren't going to be a snap for you. Learn the following sentence and repeat as often as necessary: "I'll get back to you on that." With those seven words, you've acknowledged the question or situation, accepted your part in coming up with some answer, and made a promise to follow through. What more could anyone want? And when you do follow through, your credibility gets a nice boost.

Reframing Your World

Keep it positive. The best conversations, and quite probably the most intelligent, will be those you have with you. Become your own personal coach and develop a few handy and useful affirmations that will see you through the more difficult times at the old salt mill:

- I know what I'm doing.
- I'm an intelligent and productive person.
- No one can take away my talents, capabilities, and expertise.

- In a thousand years (or less, if I'm lucky) this pain in the butt will be dust.

When Depression Is Severe

If your depression is severe, you may be eligible for Social Security Disability Benefits. There are two Social Security programs that provide these disability benefits: Supplemental Security Income (SSI) and Social Security Disability Insurance (SSDI). The medical requirements for qualifying are the same under both programs and disability is determined by the same process.

Social Security Disability Insurance will pay benefits to you and to certain members of your family if you have worked long enough to be covered under Social Security and have paid into the system. Supplemental Security Income will pay you benefits based upon demonstrated financial need.

Definition of Disability

Social Security's definition of disability is based upon your inability to work. That's it. Period. You will be considered to be disabled if you can't do the work you previously did. Also, they get to determine whether your medical condition means you can or cannot adjust to other work. The burden of proof is on you. Additionally, your disability must be expected to last for at least a year or to result in your death.

If you are feeling stressed because your financial situation is not in the best shape right now, be prepared to accept the fact that Social Security assumes you have other sources of income to see you through your disability—these include workers' comp, insurance, and personal financial investments and savings accounts. Social Security can be a safety net, but remember, nets have holes in them.

Applying for Benefits

First, be sure to have all of your medical records available and in order. You may want to have a supportive family member help you with this. You can begin the process of applying for benefits by choosing one of these methods:

- Go to *www.ssa.gov/d&s1.htm* to complete an online application
- Call Social Security's toll-free number: 1-800-772-1213
- Hearing-impaired individuals can call: TTY 1-800-325-0778
- Call or visit your local Social Security Office (You'll find their number and address in the government pages of your local telephone directory.)

Alert

There are special instructions available for the visually impaired. The government uses the term blind. You'll need to click on the link at the bottom of the page (*www.ssa.gov/d&s1.htm*).

You will need specific records and information in order to complete your application. Social Security provides a Disability Planner that tells you exactly how to go about the process of applying for benefits. You will need the following materials:

1. Your Social Security number and proof of your age.
2. Names, addresses, and phone numbers of doctors, caseworkers, hospitals, and clinics that took care of you and the dates of your visits.
3. Names and dosages of all the medications you are taking.
4. Medical records from your doctors, therapists, hospitals, clinics, and caseworkers, that you already have in your possession.
5. Laboratory and test results.
6. A summary of where you worked and the kind of work you did.
7. Your most recent W-2 form or, if you were self-employed, a copy of your federal tax return (*www.ssa.gov/online/ssa-16.html*).

Essential

Two out of three applications for benefits are initially denied. If your initial application is denied, you may request a review of Social Security's decision. Be patient. Claims for disability benefits take more time to process than other types of Social Security claims. The process may take from three to five months.

Depression and the Workplace—The Bottom Line

With mental health issues accounting for an increasingly large percentage of absenteeism from work, it makes good sense for employers to become knowledgeable about how depression can affect the bottom line. Recent studies have demonstrated the serious impact depression can have on productivity and profits.

The Costs

The July 18, 2003, issue of *Psychiatric News*, published by the American Psychiatric Association (APA), reported on the findings of a *Depressive Disorders Study* completed in 2002. The study found that workers with depression cost employers more than three times the amount associated with lost productivity from all other illnesses. The study estimated that workplace depression cost employers $44 billion a year, with 20 percent of costs due to absenteeism and 80 percent due to "presenteeism,"—their term for reduced productivity on the job.

Being Vigilant

Each employee represents a significant investment in both time and money. Recruiting and training the best people gives companies the corporate edge. Maximizing that investment is what good business is all about. It makes good business sense, then, to be able to recognize the symptoms of depression earlier, rather than later, and be prepared to make those "reasonable accommodations" and keep your best workers on the job. If you are an employer with fifteen or more employees in the public sector, you are bound by the provisions of the Americans with Disabilities Act (ADA).

No Good Time

The annual performance review is your opportunity to discuss everything that relates to an employee's work performance over the past year. If your company has a policy of semi-annual reviews or ties reviews to wage increases or bonuses, you have additional times to check in with your workers. There is no good time to tell an employee that she isn't cutting it and you're going to have to let her go. However, suppose, at that review, your worker discloses that she is suffering from depression and produces a doctor's certificate attesting to that fact. As you have probably guessed, this changes everything. Now, you've got to follow the specifics of the ADA. If that employee's sales quotas have slumped, and this can be attributable to depression, you cannot fire her. You can make what are called "reasonable accommodations" that do not cause you an "undue financial burden or do not disrupt the workplace or the service being provided." Defining those terms is an attorney's bread and butter.

Employee Responsibility

It is the responsibility of the employee to inform the employer about a disability that will affect the ability to perform the duties of the job and to suggest accommodations that will allow you to perform your duties. Employees who do not disclose their disabilities may find they are not protected under the provisions of the ADA.

CHAPTER 18

Helping Yourself

IT'S TIME TO take a look at everything you've accomplished and give yourself a well-deserved pat on the shoulder. You've made positive changes in your life—you're eating better and exercising more. You're taking your prescribed medications and working with your psychotherapist to get to the root of your depression. Now it's time to examine how your thought patterns can help or hinder your recovery. It's time to revisit the mind/body connection.

Naming Your Demons

"If wishes were horses, beggars would ride." It's another old saying but it gets to the point. A more modern version is, "Unless something changes, nothing will change." Either way, the message is clear: If you want to make improvements or changes in your life, you've got to stop thinking about them and start doing something about them. In the initial stages of depression, you may feel a wide range of emotions, and most of them are negative ones. You want to be free of them, but first you need to identify just what they are. As you work through each one, you'll see how to reduce the power it has to influence the way you think and the way you feel.

Anger

Anger is an emotional reaction to a perceived wrong or a hurt. Anger carries negative energy with it, and how you use that energy can determine the effect that anger has on your body and on your psyche. If you lash out in anger, you may not weigh your words before you say them and may later regret what you said. If you strike out in anger, you may miss your intended target and cut a wide swath of unintended damage. Anger and depression are closely related; in fact, depression has been defined as "repressed anger" or "anger directed inward." You can experience anger, if you feel powerless to effect change. Instead of internalizing anger, ask yourself:

1. What am I angry about?
2. How can I express that anger in constructive ways?
3. How can I work off that negative energy?
4. How can I put that anger to good use?

 Alert

> Count to ten before you say something you might regret. Once a word has left your lips, you cannot recall it. It lives forever. Of all the weapons man or woman has ever used, words are the most powerful.

Guilt

You may feel that you deserve to feel depressed—that you're not worthy of a happier life. It's easy enough to bring up a list of errors and omissions that can be used to attest to your shortcomings. Everybody can do this. No one leads a perfect, blameless life. Everyone makes mistakes. If you've made your share, or even what you think is more than your share, this only means you're human. It doesn't mean you deserve less of the good things that life has to offer. Just as with anger, get to the root of those guilt feelings. What exactly makes you think you deserve to be depressed? This is something you and your psychotherapist can explore together. Freeing yourself from guilt will speed your recovery from depression.

Despair

"It's all so hopeless. Nothing will ever change. It's useless to try." You have to admit that, even if you're feeling this way, seeing it in print makes it seem a little over the top. In fact, writing down your negative thoughts is a good tool for gaining power over them.

Essential

Be true to yourself, and don't feel guilty about this. Even when pursued by his "black dog" of depression, Winston Churchill understood the fundamental importance of being his own person:" You have enemies? Good. That means you've stood up for something, some time in your life."

When you're feeling despair, it takes an enormous act of will-power to resist the impulse to give up on your treatment. You've gotten this far, however, because you know in your heart of hearts that depression is not hopeless. You will make the changes you need to make in order to break free. Useless to try? Not by a long shot.

The Power of Negative Thinking

Everything good is powerful, but not everything powerful is good. Negative thoughts fall into the latter category. They can adversely impact your relationships, including the all-important relationship you have with yourself. These thoughts have the potential to reinforce the symptoms of depression and throw up roadblocks on your road to recovery. Recognize this kind of thinking for what it is—damaging and destructive. Here are some common negatives, along with suggestions for effectively managing them.

I Know What I Know

There's a line in *Moonstruck*, the movie starring Cher and Nicolas Cage, when Loretta (Cher) says to her new boyfriend, "I know what I know." He's been trying to convince her to consider another perspective on her life, but she's put on the blinders, shut the shades, locked the door, and closed up the house for the summer. She doesn't want to hear anything that will challenge or contradict her thinking. As far as she's concerned, the subject is closed.

Depression can be like that. Your thinking gets narrow and muddled, and you begin to believe there's no other way of looking at the situation. When you find yourself thinking along these lines, take a deep, cleansing breath and say to yourself, "Maybe, just maybe, there's another way to think about this. What do you suppose that would be?" You might not get an answer immediately, but continue in this direction. You can retrain your mind to open itself to other possibilities.

This Is It. My Life Is Over

Perhaps a little dramatic, but sometimes it's easy to think this way when you're feeling hemmed in and shut off from life. With this form of negative thinking, tomorrow will be no better than today, and quite possibly, will be even worse.

Ĺ. Essential

> "The bend in the road isn't the end of the road, unless you refuse to make the turn" —Anonymous. Life throws some S-curves and some hairpin turns at all of us. You can handle them if you keep both hands on the wheel and go easy on the brakes.

The truth is you don't know what tomorrow will have in store. Nobody does. But one thing is certain: If you expect things to be bad, they will be. You can't control the unfolding of the universe. The only control you have is in the way you react. When you feel yourself in the gloom and doom—"We're all gonna' die!"—mood, give yourself one of those mental head slaps and replace that thought with something a little more realistic. One word can make a difference. Even if the best you can come up with right now is "Maybe we're all gonna' die"—at least you're beginning to get your mind around some different possibilities. And after all, life is all about possibilities.

Perfect is the Only Option

Perfectionists are prone to depression. If you're a perfectionist, you're hard on yourself and on everyone else, as well. There's only one way to do the job—and that's the perfect way. You want to control the situation. But there is no perfect way. There's always one more improvement that could have been made, or one more rough edge that should have been sanded off better. You'll never be satisfied, and even your best work isn't good enough. What you're really feeling is that you aren't good enough. Just how good do you have to be? And by whose standards? Perfectionism lends itself to specific, scripted routines and rituals. In this regard, it shares some characteristics with obsessive-compulsive disorder (OCD)—got to do it right. Got to do it again, to make sure it's right. An effective therapy for OCD is desensitization. You learn to go longer and longer without performing the ritual. You learn to accept that you've done the procedure right the first time. Consider using this technique to manage perfectionism. Set yourself some limits and commit to them. "I'll just fine tune the project two more times and then I'll call it quits." Then do it and accept the thanks or praise that others give you, with a clear conscience.

It's All About Me

Self-consciousness is an interesting aspect of ego. You feel conspicuous. You think that everybody is focused on you, being critical of you, blaming you, talking about you, and generally, making you center stage in their lives. The result is that you're afraid to make a move for fear of messing up and drawing attention to yourself.

When your mind is working optimally, you understand that your self-worth is not determined by what others think of you. When you're dealing with depression, your sense of self-worth and self-consciousness get all mixed up together. Understand that not everyone is going to like you. If you think about this, you'll realize you wouldn't want everyone to like you. After all, you have your standards. Not everyone is worthy of your friendship. The person most worthy of that friendship, however, is you. When you find yourself running scared, stop in your tracks. Ask yourself, "What exactly am I running away from?" The next question is, "Why am I doing this?" You most likely won't come up with a very satisfying answer. And that's good. It's time to stop running.

Everything Is My Fault

This is perfectionism's opposite—sort of its evil twin. It's a lack of self-respect. With this kind of thinking, you become the world's doormat. Whatever goes wrong, you feel that somehow you're to blame for the situation. No matter that circumstances may be so far out of your control to make this impossible, you must have caused the foul-up. You feel that you should have done this, or you could have done that, and then everything would be different, somehow. Pull yourself back to Mother Earth. Nobody has that kind of power. Talk to your psychotherapist to develop strategies that will help you work through these feelings and replace them with more constructive thoughts.

 Alert

> Children can feel the same way adults do, and if your child is coping with depression, this may be an avenue to explore. Psychologists refer to this as "magical thinking." Here's how it works: A child is angry at a parent and wishes that parent dead. The parent then has a heart attack and dies. The child is convinced that he is responsible for the death. This places an incredible burden of incalculable power on the child and the child can't cope. Play therapy is often used for children who are struggling with these issues.

Truth in Labeling

Sometimes the only exercise people get is in skipping logic and jumping to conclusions. This is common, whether you have depression or not. In this case, you confuse the action with the person who's performed the action. Here are a few common expressions to illustrate the point. The labeling has gotten confused.

1. You said, "I can't do anything right." (You broke a glass.)
2. You said, "I'm an idiot."(You couldn't decipher the assembly instructions for that new treadmill.)
3. You said, "I am such a loser." (You made a mistake.)

By upping the ante in each of these examples, you've lost sight of the truth, which is: Everybody drops things. Everyone has had difficulty following assembly directions. Everybody makes mistakes. Instead, you've accepted some self-destructive labels: Loser, idiot, inept. Don't accept future deliveries! Next time something happens, accept the responsibility for the action. If you can prevent it from happening again, great! But don't heap abuse on yourself. It's counterproductive.

Positive Self-Talk

Used to be, if you saw someone talking to herself at the airport, at a restaurant, or while walking down the street, you made an assumption that she might be mentally ill. Not anymore. Technology has revolutionized the way people talk on the phone. Everyone seems to have an earpiece that replaces the old handheld devices. As a result, you don't know who's talking to whom, anymore. Talking to yourself, however, may not be crazy. In fact, it might be one of the sanest and most intelligent conversations you'll have all day.

 Question

How is self-talk different from talking to yourself?
With self-talk, you analyze problems, weigh options, and devise strategies for dealing with various situations. In some cases, you may find yourself talking out loud, as you work through whatever issue is occupying your mind. Negative self-talk can hold you back. Positive self-talk can help you make giant strides in coping with depression. It's a lot different from random mutterings and mumblings!

Changing Your Focus

Positive self-talk is all about changing how you see your role in difficult situations. You want to change that perception from a negative to a positive one. One way to accomplish this is to practice affirmations. Affirmations are short and snappy statements that hone in on your best qualities. They help you remember all the good things about yourself. Here are some practical and applicable affirmations for coping with depression:

1. Every day, I am getting stronger.
2. Every day, I see positive changes in my moods.
3. I have control over how I feel.
4. I eat healthy foods that help my body grow strong.
5. I exercise to increase my energy.
6. I reach out to others, when I need help.

Silly mind games? No, not at all. If anything is silly, it's the negative mind games you can play, when depression has control over your thoughts and feelings.

L. Essential

The Little Engine That Could has become part of American folklore. No matter what anybody else told him, he kept repeating the same positive thought over and over again. He had his own affirmation, and you know exactly what that was: "I think I can, I think I can..." He kept his focus and achieved his goal. You can too!

Changing Your Habits

Want to quit smoking? You're told to make changes in your routines. First, clean house. Get rid of all the cigarettes. Then, examine your habits. If you always sit down and read the morning paper with a cigarette in hand, go for a walk instead. If you smoke to keep your hands busy, try one of those exercise squeeze balls and work your fingers that way. Or, if your friends are smokers and you can't keep from smoking when you're with them, you may need to make new friends who don't smoke. The point is that you're going to need to make some changes, if you're to achieve your goal.

 Fact

> It takes three weeks to change a habit, so don't despair if your new regimen to improve your body and your mind seems to be taking longer than you want. Out with the old and in with the new! Each day you're getting closer to making that new habit a part of your life.

Changing negative thoughts into positive ones works the same way. First, clean house. Sweep all those self-defeating thoughts out the door and into the trash bin. Then, when one of those thoughts tries to slip back in, remind yourself of your goal—a healthy, happy life—and turn that thought around to something more positive, change your activity, or call someone who will support you. Keep your focus.

This Is Taking Too Long!

Do you feel sometimes that your progress seems so slow that a snail is making better time than you are? This is common. Many people feel this way. It will take time to break free of depression. Recognizing and affirming each positive step you make will help you deal with the little setbacks that are a normal part of living. You know all the negatives associated with depression. In fact, you're living with them on a daily basis. It's time to change your focus and look at life from a 180-degree change of perspective. The reassuring news is that there are many ways to do this. None of them hurt. None of them are complicated. There's a partnership that can work wonders in your life: Humor and its sidekick, Responsibility. At first glance, these may not seem to have much in common, but they do.

Humor

When was the last time you laughed? Really, really laughed? Can't remember, can you? Depression is such a thief. It steals all the fun out of life and leaves you trying to cope without the tools you need. Humor is one of those tools, and it's more important than you might think.

There are many kinds of humor: the gentle ribbing that family and good friends enjoy, the silliness of the Three Stooges or the Marx Brothers, the sarcastic, biting humor that some comedians inflict on their audiences, or the helpless kind of laughter that sends tears streaming down your cheeks and leaves you feeling drained, but oddly restored.

Whatever form humor takes, it has the ability to lift you out of the moment and out of yourself. It can lift your mood and your spirits. Humor may be absolutely the last thing on your mind right now. "There's nothing remotely funny about the way I'm feeling," you say—and you're right. The goal is not to laugh at yourself but rather to find the absurd in the situation.

The Whole World Loves a Clown

Actually, the whole world doesn't, and many people are afraid of them. Clowns are paradoxes. The masks painted on their faces show either exaggerated expressions of laughter or pathos. There's no real emotion, and you can't tell what they're feeling inside. You may feel like a clown if you're working to put on your "happy face" and it doesn't feel right. You're not a clown, however, and you're actively working to change your perspective on the world. You're not a sham and your efforts are real.

Making Humor Work for You

"Did you hear the one about the short-tempered psychotherapist?
"Yeah, he lost his patients."

Learning not to take yourself too seriously is important for managing depression. Humor can reduce stress, help you cope with anxiety, and put events into perspective. Humor gets the point across without being tedious, and an occasional joke can help you cope. Making the jokes relevant is the key! Each profession has its inside jokes, and so do most medical conditions. Why? There are a couple of reasons. First, humor is a bond. It's insider knowledge. It builds camaraderie and a shared world view. Second, and of specific relevance here, when you can laugh at something, it loses its power to control you.

Laugh and the World Laughs with You, Cry and You Cry Alone

It's true. People are sympathetic to a point, but after a while, if all you're doing is feeling sorry for yourself, pretty soon you'll be the only attendee at your pity party. Take action, after you've shared what you're feeling. Use that initial outpouring of sympathy and empathy to gear yourself up for some forward progress. The encouragement will continue if you're making a good effort.

Taking Responsibility

Are you responsible for having depression? Of course not. Are you responsible for doing everything you can to work your way through this condition? Yes, you are. And why wouldn't you want to be? Accepting responsibility is not the same thing as taking the blame. Responsibility means you understand your role in managing your health and seeking positive avenues for optimizing your recovery.

L. Essential

When you're feeling confused about what you can and cannot do, remember the Serenity Prayer. Pastor Reinhold Niebuhr is the author of this famous prayer. "God, grant me the serenity to accept the things I cannot change; courage to change the things I can; and wisdom to know the difference." Serenity, courage, and wisdom are powerful, positive attributes to cultivate in your daily life to fight depression.

So, what exactly does accepting responsibility mean? It means that:

- You understand that while you cannot control your medical condition, you do understand that you can choose how you will deal with it.
- You will make good health choices—eat well and exercise—because you know this will help you.
- You let go of the "Life isn't fair" script and realize that all people have something on their plate that they'd rather not have.
- You find positive and appropriate outlets for your frustration and anger.
- You truly believe that while pain and suffering are certainties, misery is optional.

Coping Strategies

There are tricks—shortcuts, actually—for just about anything you want to do in life. Right now, you want to relieve the symptoms of depression and get about the business of living your life on your own terms, once again. Coping strategies can get you to where you want to be.

The Jigsaw Puzzle Approach

A jigsaw puzzle goes together one piece at a time. If you're persistent, eventually the 500 or 1,000 or 1,500 pieces will come to look like the picture on the box. You can apply this analogy to your daily routine, when you're faced with those big jobs at home or at work. These can be overwhelming and discouraging, but if you break those jobs into smaller tasks, you'll find that you can manage more easily and, just like the jigsaw puzzle, eventually the job will get done. You'll also enjoy the satisfaction of being able to put a check by each task, as you accomplish it. You're monitoring your progress and seeing the visual reminder of what you've produced.

Deferring Decisions

During times of stress, it's not advisable to make important decisions. Depression is stressful. If you don't have to sell the house right now, change jobs, or break off a serious relationship, don't. Postpone the big decisions until you're feeling better. You may find that your depression was responsible for creating or at least intensifying the difficult situation in the first place. Even if this turns out not to be the case, time is on your side. Wait, if you can.

 Fact

Once you let worry into your mind, everything takes on equal weight. You can't assign the appropriate value to what's causing you distress. A house fire is just as worrisome as a misplaced set of car keys. Depression keeps you from putting things in a proper perspective.

Scheduling Worries

Often, worries seem to come in torrents, when you're depressed. Nothing seems to be working right, and everything has the potential for reinforcing your down mood. Take charge of your worries and they'll lose their power over you. Before you go to bed, write down everything that is worrying you. Don't leave anything off the list. When you've written it all down, promise yourself that in the morning, or when you start to feel better during the day, you're going to take the first worry on your list and decide upon a strategy for dealing with it. Why the first worry? Because it's probably the one that's most on your mind. The big ones come to mind quickly. It's only toward the end that you're scraping the bottom of the worry barrel. Here's how this might look:

1. **Worry:** I'll be depressed forever. **Strategy:** Nothing lasts forever, and that includes depression. I'll take my antidepressants, eat right, exercise, and keep my appointments with

my psychotherapist. I'll work through this depression, even though it may take longer than I'd like.

2. **Worry:** I'm never going to have the energy to be able to leave the house and enjoy myself again. I'll be trapped inside forever. **Strategy:** Look at what I said—never and forever. This black-and-white thinking isn't getting me anywhere. I'm going to find out why I'm so tired and talk to my psychotherapist about this. Together we'll find ways I can gradually get my life back.

3. **Worry:** I've lost the person I used to be. I never laugh anymore, and I hurt so much. **Strategy:** I can't believe I said never. I'll think of a way to turn that sentence around to make it sound foolish. Okay. I'm going to go looking for myself. I'm probably just misplaced. That's ridiculous, but it made me smile just a little. I can do this, even if I try it just once every day.

4. **Worry:** I am the worst mother in the world. I don't even care about the baby right now. **Strategy:** I understand that I have postpartum depression. This will pass in a couple of weeks. It's just that my hormones aren't back in sync yet. In the meantime, I'll get some help taking care of the baby. I really do love her.

5. **Worry:** I dread the coming winter. Winter is the worst time of year for me. I don't think I'm going to be able to survive another one without going stark, raving mad. **Strategy:** Okay. Forget the stark, raving mad. I have seasonal affective disorder (SAD), and I'm going to discuss light therapy with my physician and make some changes this year.

In each of these examples, you have taken responsibility for your actions. You aren't blaming yourself, because even though you're depressed, you know that finger pointing doesn't accomplish anything. You're on track. You understand that time is now on your side. With good self-care and positive self-talk, you'll beat this depression.

Chapter 19

When a Loved One Has Depression

DEPRESSION MAY MAKE you feel isolated, but you're never the only one affected by your struggle. Your family, friends, and co-workers form the basis of your social network. They love you and care about your welfare. Add in members of your church, community organizations, volunteer groups, and any other individual or group that touches your life, and you will see that depression cuts a wide swath through your personal life. In this chapter, you'll take a look at depression from the outside in—from the perspective of those whose loved ones are wrestling with this condition. You'll find some tips and some cautions to help you navigate these rough waters.

Everyone Is Involved

That's right. A brief word to those of you who are trying to work through depression: You aren't in this alone, and even if you wanted to be, it's just not possible. So, you might as well face up to the truth: you are coping with depression, and everyone else is coping with you! The good news is that, in most cases, people sincerely want to help. Wanting to help and being able to help can be two different animals, however. The former requires compassion, the latter knowledge. Without the necessary information, wanting to help may fall short of the mark. You'll need to tell people how they can help. You'll need to tell them what you need.

▐▌ Essential

> Now is the time to marshal all your resources. You're going to need everyone's help, as you work to help a loved one through these difficult times. There's no additional prize for going this on your own—on the contrary, you'll be shortchanging both yourself and your loved one, if you do.

Is that the sound of eggshells cracking, as you tiptoe around the house? It's a tense atmosphere all around. Nothing you say is the right thing to say. Nothing you do is the right thing to do. When loved ones face dark times, you want to help. It's just that you don't know how, and as a result, you frequently find yourself in an argument with the one person you're trying to understand. It's so frustrating. Is there some way to find out what the right approach is? Everyone is an individual, and what works in one case isn't guaranteed to be foolproof in another. However, there are some guidelines that can help. First, let's take a look at what your loved one is experiencing from his or her particular point of view.

How Your Partner Is Affected

Men who are depressed may lose interest in sex, or they may use sex as an outlet to deal with their depression. Sex doesn't solve the problem, however; it merely helps channel the focus away from the problem by releasing energy. He takes some reassurance in knowing that on one level, at least, he can function and the relationship is still working. Women, on the other hand, may take their partner's interest as a sign he's feeling better—that all is now well. Afterwards, men are still stressed and angry, their depression is still there, and women are more confused than they were before they agreed to bed down. Things aren't any better, after all.

Women who are depressed frequently lose interest in sex, although they may crave touch—as in being held, without the expectation of sex. Her partner then figures, "If she wants to be held, she must want sex." She doesn't, and he's confused. Frustration and anger can now enter into the mix.

 Alert

> Your first attempts to engage your loved one in conversation about what's wrong may not be successful. Don't despair. Be gentle, but persistent. If the first conversation isn't productive, try back a little later. The important thing here is to keep calm and keep your cool.

Love is still there. It's pretty much the same scenario you'd be facing if your partner were diagnosed with cancer, heart disease, or a hernia. It's just that for a certain period of time, this condition, depression, is taking center stage and stealing all the lines. The person you love is still there and will be there when this is over and done. Coping, in the meantime, is the challenge. And to be frank, there are days when you're not up to it. You're human, you have needs of your own, and you may feel that you've been stretched to the max. Take a deep breath, exhale, and repeat the mantra, "This too, shall pass." And it will. Strategies for taking care of yourself come later on in this chapter.

What Not to Say

The Nots are fairly easy to categorize. They have certain things in common: They cast blame, they are reproachful, they're angry, and they don't work. Here's the top four things you should not to say and why:

- **"Snap out of it."** You can no more snap out of depression than you can snap out of a heart attack. It's a medical condition that needs to be treated.

- **"Are you still in your bathrobe?"** Overwhelming fatigue and inability to do simple tasks are symptoms of depression. They're not character flaws.
- **"Get a backbone, for God's sake. There's nothing to be worried about."** Your loved one understands this, on an intellectual plane. The body, however, doesn't, and the fear is still real.
- **"Don't bite my head off, I just asked a question."** Irritability is one of the symptoms of depression. This is the one that may tax your patience severely. Don't take this personally.

You may think "tough love" is the way to go, but most depression sufferers will only have an adverse reaction to this kind of approach. Even softer approaches might not be the best. "I know exactly how you feel" is a common expression, showing empathy. However, you don't know exactly how someone else feels—to do so would mean you'd have experienced life exactly the same way. Everyone is an individual and has different life experiences. Speak what you do know. Try a simple, "I love you."

Hide and Go Seek

If a disability isn't visible, people tend to overlook it. How many times have you parked by the grocery store and seen someone, seemingly healthy, park a car in the handicapped spot? If you didn't notice the sticker, you might think this person was just looking for a quick entrance to the store. You might even have heard someone challenge a person who parked in the handicapped place and perhaps were witness to a polite explanation that the challenged person had a heart condition. Humble pie for the attacker. The truth is that so many of our disabilities are below the surface, invisible to the casual observer. It's only when you go deeper that you see what the problem is. Depression is like that. Since it doesn't come with a rash or a full body cast, it's sometimes easy to forget that your loved one is suffering inside.

Learning Patience

You did not cause your loved one's depression. You also cannot cure it. Understanding and accepting these two truths can be difficult and will require massive amounts of patience on your part. Patience is not easy to come by. There are so many times when you just want to scream, throw something, or hit the wall. You know that's not productive, and you'll probably have some repairs to attend to when your venting is finished, so you pass on venting. There are other outlets that work better, and some of the recommendations for folks suffering from depression work very well for the rest of us. Yoga is one of them. If it's at all possible to sign up for a class with your loved one, there are a lot worse things you could do with your time. Even if you have to go alone, yoga will teach you patience, discipline, and relaxation. All of these will stand you in good stead during this tough time. Physical exercise is another outlet that has benefits for both your body and your mind. Getting out of the house and involved in an activity that burns off calories and negative energy is healthy for you.

What to Say

These are the positives. People like to hear them, and they tend to get much better results than the negative carping. That doesn't mean these words are candy-coated, however. Your objective is not to continue the status quo but to move things forward. Not all of these will apply. Choose the ones that seem appropriate for your situation. Your goal is to get the person you care about talking. Once you've begun the conversation, you can proceed to the next step, which is getting help.

Let's Talk

There is no substitute for face-to-face interaction. Telephones and computers are wonderful, but when you're trying to get to the bottom of a problem, you need to be there physically. Once you've put yourself in the vicinity of the person you care about, there's nothing threatening about walking up, cup of coffee or tea in hand, and saying, "You seem down. What's wrong?" This is an invitation, not an accusation. If you get a response, then sit down and continue the dialogue. Don't rush the discussion. Anything at all, for right now, is good progress.

Do Your Homework

It's very possible you are recognizing the symptoms of depression in your loved one before he or she is even aware of the nature of the problem. In this case, you'll need to proceed carefully. The first thing to do is to become informed about depression. Do your homework and read up on the symptoms, the kinds of depression, possible causes, and treatments. This will give you a solid base for the conversations you will be having with your loved one. It will also prepare you to suggest a visit to the doctor. You'll be able to proceed with some confidence, instead of finding yourself in a position of reacting or arguing. You may find it easier to discuss changes in sleep patterns or weight gain or loss as logical reasons to see the doctor. You can mention your concerns to the doctor before the visit, so that depression finds itself on the checklist of conditions to evaluate.

 # Question

> **Why should I skirt the issue, talking about sleep problems and weight issues?**
> You do this because these are concerns that may not be as threatening as depression. There's no stigma here, and so your loved one may be more willing to make that trip to the doctor.

Gather the Troops

You're going to need some help and support. You can't manage everything else you have to do in your life and take on the added responsibility of managing your loved one's depression as well. Something's bound to give, and it will probably be your peace of mind. Close friends and family can be of tremendous assistance, whether in lending a compassionate ear or lending their time to drive your loved one to the doctor's office or to therapy. It's a false pride that insists it doesn't need anyone else's help. Everyone needs this, from time to time—it's part of what makes us human. Accept the offers and don't be ashamed to ask when you need something. It's a certainty carved in stone that your friends and relatives will need your help at some point as well.

What to Do

So much of what you're called upon to do in life sure isn't what you had planned. Sometimes it seems as if your own plans are the very last things to be considered, and that can create internal discontent and anger. When you feel this way, sometimes reflecting upon your place in the grand scheme of things can help. When you think of the billions and billions of people who have walked this earth before you, it can be a humbling experience. It also can help to put life in perspective. So much of what people think is urgent, isn't. In a hundred years, no one will care whether you washed the car on Friday or not. Focusing on what's important is necessary. Planning to leave this planet a better place is important. And caring for another person who needs your help is not only important, it's noble. It would certainly be nice if someone were standing over you, keeping track of all your good deeds and entering them into the Permanent Record. And who knows? Maybe someone is.

Essential, Important, and Can Wait

If you were to take an honest look at what you have planned for the day, you'd probably find the following list:

- Get up.
- Go to work.
- Go home.
- Relax.
- Go to bed.

We're creatures of habit. Of course the weekends would look a bit different, with added chores and maybe something fun thrown into the mix. The point of this is that people protect their free time, plan their leisure, and get set in their routines, and when something interrupts that, they're taken off guard. An honest look at the routine, however, should let us know that routine is just that—routine. Some of the items that seem so pressing probably can wait a while. Hold on to hope. As soon as your loved one's depression is under control, you can fall right back into your pattern. In the meantime, there are higher goals to meet and someone needs your time.

⌐. Essential

Make a new to-do list that doesn't include chores. Make it a list of things that will help you cope and take this list as seriously as you would one that contained taking out the garbage and doing the laundry.

Opportunity in a Strange Package

It's easy to take good health for granted; especially if you've been one of the fortunate ones who've managed to avoid major illness or accident. However, when these unwelcome visitors show up on your doorstep, you may find they are actually cleverly disguised opportunities for personal growth. They can lead you to adopt some healthy behaviors. After all, it's an ill wind that doesn't blow some good, as the saying goes.

Healthy Behaviors

We're a sedentary society and becoming more so every year. Many people work sitting down, and they recreate in the same position—watching television or playing games or corresponding on the computer. Depression takes away your motivation to exercise and be active, so if you're feeling hemmed in and constrained by your loved one's lack of energy, it's time to lace up the walking shoes and venture outdoors. If you can encourage your loved one to join you, so much the better. It needn't be a five-mile trek with fully loaded backpack, either. Even a stroll around the block will get the blood moving and be a helpful adjunct to therapy.

 # Fact

> Exercise is an essential part of therapy for depression. Getting the body moving can greatly enhance the recovery process. And since one good thing usually follows another, exercise can help in getting some good health habits started or re-established.

Finding the Good and Praising It

You're probably hearing a litany from your loved one about all her faults, but even a broken clock is right twice a day. This is the right time to mention all the good things about her—not all at once, of course. Spread out the compliments throughout the course of the day. And especially mention how important she is in your life. Unless you've walked in depression's ill-fitting shoes, you can't know how much they hurt. All you can do is be compassionate and understanding of your loved one's efforts to shake free of depression's grip. This isn't going to go away quickly, but with proper therapy, it will go away in time.

A Sense of Humor

You may think that there's not a whole lot to laugh about, and you would be right. Sometimes it takes a bit of digging to see the brighter side. What a sense of humor can do for you, however, is to put life in perspective, and there are elements of humor in even the most dire of circumstances. It's actually considered a sign of healing when you can find some vestige of the absurd or silly in any situation. And that car that needed washing? You realize, don't you, that as soon as you got it done, it was going to rain? That's the irony of humor. It helps you take things not quite so intensely. It helps you back off a bit from the moment.

⌷⌷⌷ Essential

Remember *M*A*S*H*, the television series about medical staff working in impossible conditions during the Korean War? Humor, even in the face of death, helped them cope. Everyone needs to laugh—it's our way of staring down the enemy and coming out on the other end of the problem with our psyches bruised but still intact.

Knowing Your Limitations

You cannot make your loved one well. Only he can do that, given support, therapy, and time. Trying to remain objective is going to be difficult. Sometimes you might just want to scream with the frustration of it all. You want to solve the problem. It all seems so simple. Just do this and do that, and everything will be fine. It's not that easy, however. You have no control over how another person acts, and this goes doubly for someone with depression. If you can coax a smile here and there, that's a good sign. Don't be discouraged, however, if that small smile doesn't become a big grin. It's going to take some time for your loved one to break free. Remember, no one wants to be depressed. Being depressed is—depressing!

Dealing with a Loved One's Postpartum Depression

Postpartum depression is not uncommon in new mothers. When you're depressed, even simple chores can seem like monumental tasks. All new moms feel overwhelmed. No one hands out a set of instructions for baby care when you leave the hospital with your new son or daughter. Especially if this is the first child, the sense of responsibility can be daunting. There's so much you can do to help mom through the postpartum depression phase, when those hormones are re-establishing themselves back to pre-pregnancy levels. The Dos:

- Encourage the new mom to sleep when the baby sleeps.
- Wash the dishes.
- Do the laundry.
- Help with the general housework and cleanup.
- Do the grocery shopping.
- Spend some time with the other children, so they don't feel pushed out of the picture.
- Schedule a massage for mom.
- Spend some time just talking about non-stressful topics.
- Say "I love you."
- Spend time with the baby. It's definitely time well spent.

If you're the new father, you may feel as if you've been set aside. It can be frustrating, and you may even feel some anger, as you want your family life to return to a normal pattern. This will happen, but it may take a little time to get everything running smoothly. Postpartum depression usually passes within a few weeks, and your patience and understanding will be much appreciated.

The Don'ts:

- Don't let your own routine suffer. You need time to yourself, as much as your partner does.
- Don't let your own health regimen slide. Keep yourself healthy. Work out, eat right, and get enough sleep.
- Don't let a sense of needing to do it all keep you from asking for help from friends and family.
- Don't pressure your partner into resuming sexual relations before she's ready.
- Don't get drawn into an argument, but be willing to talk through the problems.
- Don't forget that your partner is still the same woman you fell in love with. She'll be back shortly!

Dealing with a Child's Depression

Childhood is full of bumps, bruises, scrapes, and cuts. You treat these minor problems with a hug and a bandage, but the bigger hurts may leave you scared. Two emotions may be competing with scared: guilt and denial. Here's what these may mean for you.

⌷ Essential

Find a support group for parents with children with depression. Talking to others who are in your situation can help relieve stress and give you good information on strategies for daily living. You'll be able to share what you've learned as well, and the feeling that you've helped another parent will lift your spirits. Your local hospital may be able to put you in touch with just the right group for your needs.

It's All My Fault

If your child has bipolar disorder, you understand the role genetics plays in it, and you may feel some guilt about having passed on that gene. Telling you that feeling that guilt is nonsense, doesn't help one bit. Understanding that this was not a conscious decision may help. You didn't sit down one evening and decide, "Let's have a child. Oh, and by the way, let's be sure he inherits your bipolar disorder." Genetics happen. Just as brown hair, blue eyes, left-handedness, or a tendency toward high blood pressure happen, so can depression. As a parent, you learn to roll with the punches, taking the bad along with the good. Bipolar disorder can be managed, and you'll see to it that your child learns the best self-care possible.

Denial

You want your child to be perfect, and when you get handed that baby for the very first time, you truly believe in perfection. When that bubble is burst by a diagnosis that frightens you, your first reaction may be rejection. "No," you say. "It's got to be something else." (Something simpler is what you're hoping, inside.) Actually, this initial denial gives your mind and body time to adjust. You're just buying a little time. Get all the information you can and become educated about your child's form of depression. You will work through this together, and your child will need your love, guidance, and support during the recovery process. Your initial response is born out of love. Your commitment to follow through with whatever you can do is also born out of that love and can be powerful medicine.

Every Parent's Nightmare

If your child has been the victim of a trauma, and this may include a serious accident or even sexual abuse, the pain you feel is indescribable. And as you watch your child coping with therapy sessions, you sometimes feel your heart will break. As much as you would like to be everywhere, watching over your child all the time, you know that's not possible. Tragedies happen. The most difficult task for you during this time is to show strength and love. Play therapy and counseling can work wonders for your child, and family counseling can help all of you process the feelings and move forward.

 Alert

> If at any time your child mentions suicide, take this very seriously. Even children have been known to commit suicide, so call your therapist or physician immediately to get help and keep your child within sight, until that help arrives.

Getting Help

Now you're ready to begin doing something to tackle that depression. You've already spoken with your family doctor, and your loved one has agreed to have a checkup. If at all possible, accompany your loved one to that first appointment. Once the appointment has been kept, it's important to follow through with medications and/or therapy. Ultimately, however, the burden is on your loved one. You can be there to give support and offer a willing ear to listen, but the person suffering from depression needs to want to get better for that to happen. Here are some agencies that can help steer you in the right direction, if you're looking for help close to home:

- National Alliance for the Mentally Ill (NAMI) (1-800-950-6264)
- National Depressive and Manic Depressive Association (1-800-82-NDMDA)
- National Mental Health Association (NMHA) (1-800-969-6642)
- National Foundation for Depressive Illness, Inc. (1-800-248-4344)

When Concerns Surface

Check with the doctor at any time during the course of therapy if you have concerns. Getting through depression is a partnership that involves your loved one, you, and your therapist. This partnership requires careful attention to the daily details. One big concern with certain types of depression is thoughts of suicide. Suicidal thoughts need to be taken seriously and dealt with immediately. Call the therapist or physician and explain what's going on. Then be prepared to follow through on the directions you're given.

Online Support

There are many support groups for people dealing with depression, and also for the people dealing with the people dealing with depression. Many of these groups are online chats and can offer good feedback and encouragement. Call your local hospital and ask for sites they recommend.

Chapter 20

What Does the Future Hold?

PROGRESS IS SO OFTEN MEASURED in such small increments that it can be sometimes difficult to see how far we've come. Sometimes it's difficult to look back at the historical record and see even if we've made any progress. With all the problems people face, it's instructive and downright essential to think about how much you've accomplished in dealing with your own depression or with the depression of a loved one.

The Human Genome Project

Wasn't too long ago that scientists thought the atom was the smallest unit of creation. Today, the atom almost seems to be a mega-structure in the total picture—a portrait made up of countless smaller subdivisions of matter that play pivotal roles in the order of the universe. As the atom gives up its secrets, scientists go deeper and deeper into the structure of life itself, seeking to understand the mysteries of the human body.

Once Upon a Gene

Were you paying attention during your high school science classes? Even if you weren't, you couldn't have missed the part about DNA and RNA. At the very least, these terms were tongue twisters, and the models that showed how they looked were really awesome. These were the foundations of genetics, a science that owes its existence to Gregor Mendel. Genetics is a branch of biology that concerns itself with heredity—that is, how different traits are inherited and how this inheritance varies among individuals of the same or related species. Genetics has gotten a real boost in recent years, as the tantalizing lure of a cure for some troublesome diseases, including depression, motivates researchers to find answers.

 Fact

> DNA is the shorthand for deoxyribonucleic acid, a molecule that holds the genetic instructions for every living organism. RNA, or ribonucleic acid, translates the DNA into protein products. Together, DNA and RNA are often called the "building blocks of life."

Lucky Thirteen

True science knows no borders, and for the Human Genome Project (GNP) scientists from around the world worked together in this thirteen-year effort that began in October 1990. Its purpose was to map every gene in the human body—all the estimated 20,000 to 25,000 of them. Once this was done, researchers would have laid the groundwork for all future genetic research. This was a very big deal. The project was funded by the U.S. Department of Energy through its Office of Biological and Environmental Research. During this project, scientists asked their questions: Why? When? How? To these, they added, What if? Their goal was to begin to understand the genetics of disease. They would do this by determining the DNA sequence for all twenty-three pairs of chromosomes in the human body.

 Question

> **What's a genome?**
> A genome is all of the genetic information possessed by an organism. It's the complete package of genetic material for each living creature, organized by chromosomes.

Can You Patent a Gene?

Here's where problems, questions, and a sizzling controversy have arisen. Since the research of the Genome Project was funded by both public and private sector money, who owns the information the research produced? The ramifications of this question are immense. If private companies are permitted to patent their work—in essence, patent a gene—this means they own the rights to that gene and that allows them exclusive rights to work with that gene. If that particular gene turns out to be a blockbuster gene—perhaps holding the keys to understanding cancer—then they've cornered the market. The moral and ethical implications of this are staggering.

L. Essential

A researcher who wishes to study gene segments that have been patented by another research institution or pharmaceutical company would need permission for that study. In addition, whoever owns that patent can charge the researcher a fee for providing access to the gene. This could effectively curtail freedom of research and hold back significant advances in the development of critical drugs.

Privacy Concerns

As genetics reveals more and more information about us, questions about who gets to see this information become paramount. If you suffer from depression, and your test results reveal that you carry the gene for depression, will you be denied employment? Will you be unable to get insurance coverage? These questions remain at the forefront of this new research frontier. It may be a tradeoff. By finding the genes responsible for specific medical conditions, the door is opened to find a cure. However, the economic costs of carrying employees with identifiable genetic markers for certain diseases are significant. As an employee, you want to protect your privacy. As an employer, your primary responsibility is to the economic health of your company. It remains to be seen, just how this will all play out.

Stem Cell Research

Just as there are innovator (brand name) drugs and generics, there are also human cells that are specific and some that are generic. A stem cell is one of those "generic" cells. It can make copies of itself indefinitely. In addition, a stem cell has the ability to produce specialized cells for various tissues in the body, including heart muscle, brain, and liver. There are two basic types of stem cells: embryonic and adult. The National Institute of Health (*www.nih.gov*) provides a solid primer on understanding stem cells. Adult stem cells are found throughout the body. They are undifferentiated cells whose function is to maintain and repair the tissues in the area where they're located. Embryonic stem cells derive from the fetus.

Why Are Stem Cells Such a Big Deal?

With all the billions of cells in your body, it's difficult to understand how you might benefit from adding some more to the mix. It's not the same as whipping up a batch of brownies and deciding to toss in a handful of walnuts at the end. Stem cells do some pretty amazing things:

1. They can be used to replace diseased or destroyed tissue.
2. They can be test agents for experimental drugs.
3. They can help geneticists learn how cells are affected in the early stages of specific diseases.

 Fact

Gregor Mendel is known as the father of modern genetics. He was an Austrian physicist and also a monk. Mendel used pea plants as his research medium, and he went though a whole lot of pea plants before he proved that the inheritance of certain traits follows particular laws of heredity. He also discovered the laws of dominant and recessive genes.

Give Me a "For Instance"

Okay. Here's one. Suppose you've been in an accident in which you suffered severe burns. Stem cells could be grown as skin tissue and then transferred to your burns. You would grow new skin without having to undergo painful skin grafts. In cases where someone is burned over massive portions of the body, grafting may not even be possible. Infection, disfigurement, and the real possibility of death become concerns. Stem cells, in this case, could save a life.

That's Good, But Is That All?

No. Spinal cord injury patients could walk again. That's the hope of researchers, who look to the day when stem cells could be used to re-grow spinal cord tissue, restore nerve function, and reverse paralysis. The possibilities go on and on. Parkinson's disease, diabetes, cancer, stroke—all of these conditions and more, may one day be cured by stem cells. Then, there's the genetic aspect of stem cell research. Here's where scientists can learn about the genetic basis of numerous medical conditions, including depression. This is where the cure might arise. Finally, drug trials could be speeded up, if researchers can use stem cells as the first-wave guinea pigs. By testing the drug on the actual tissue the drug is targeting, much time will be saved—and that means more lives saved, as well.

So, What's the Fuss All About?

It's more than a fuss. This is a religious, philosophical, and scientific discussion of significant proportions. Some people believe that human life begins at conception—that from the moment sperm and egg join up, a baby has come into being. Some people believe that the fertilized egg is a potential human life. Those who hold the latter view share two different perspectives on it. One perspective holds that since this is a potential human being, everything should be done to insure its well-being and afford it all the protections of a human. The other viewpoint is that many factors and conditions must come together before the fertilized egg realizes its potential. Therefore, potentiality doesn't equal actuality.

Why This Matters

Traditionally, stem cells have been harvested from aborted human fetuses. This is where the controversy arises. For those who hold that life begins at conception, abortion is murder. For those who believe that the fertilized egg is a potential human being, with all the rights of a human, using an aborted fetus for cloning stem cells is abhorrent. For those who believe in the conditional potentiality of the fetus, harvesting the stem cells is logical, since the fetus would not develop to maturity, in any regard. Those are the positions, and they're as firm as if they'd been carved into granite. This can be frustrating for those who are looking to stem cells to provide the keys to unlocking the secrets of depression.

The Politics of It All

Stem cell research is a political hot potato. In September 2006, President George W. Bush vetoed a bill to authorize stem cell research and instead encouraged researchers to study stem cells gathered from umbilical cords and adult stem cells rather than pursue research with aborted fetuses. There are twelve currently existing sources of embryonic stem cells in the United States, and access to these has not been prohibited by the government. In Europe, however, research is moving ahead, unfettered by the constraints imposed by the government in the United States. In 2003, the European Parliament approved the use of stem cell research on aborted human embryos. Indeed, this may be where the breakthrough in curing depression originates.

The Consequences of the Politics

At the moment, stem cell research in the United States is continuing as it has—limited, but exploring sources other than aborted fetuses for stem cells, while scientists wait to see if a change in political administration in the forthcoming election will change the current law. In Europe, however, the research is steaming full speed ahead. Currently, EuroStemCell and ESTOOLs are the two major European-funded stem cell research groups and this consortium is calling for uniform regulations throughout Europe (*www.eurostemcell.org*).

⨆⸴ Essential

The United States isn't the only country putting on the brakes for embryonic stem cell research. Germany and Italy currently have restrictions on stem cell research. Germany's horrific experiments on human subjects during World War II still haunts Germany today. As a result, the government is reluctant to allow unrestricted research freedom to the scientific community. Italy, home to the Roman Catholic Church, is also reluctant to ease restrictions on stem cell research—research that the Church condemns.

Current Research into Depression

Behind the major news stories, researchers continue to go about the business of finding the answers that will lead to a cure for depression. Regardless of the political climate, and in spite of inconsistent funding, scientists keep plugging away. Piece by piece, the puzzle is coming together.

A Model for Depression

No, this isn't a chance to try out your "runway strut." This kind of model is like a roadmap, but it's a three-dimensional one. Before the invention of the microchip, if a scientist wanted to construct a 3-D model of something, there was a lot of stuff involved—wire, plastic, tape—all the things that you remember from that science class. Now, there's software. With the click of the mouse, wonderful images appear on the computer screen, and these images can be rotated, superimposed, turned inside out. As scientists study those neurotransmitters and the role they play in depression, those computer models come in really handy.

A Study of Note

At the Centre for Addiction and Mental Health (CAMH), a team of researchers, led by Dr. Jeffrey Meyer, wanted to understand how the chemical imbalance that occurs in major depression worked.

Scientists already believed that monoamine levels of serotonin, norepinephrine, and dopamine in the brain decreased during episodes of major depression; but they didn't know why. Meyer and his team discovered that elevated enzyme levels of monoamine oxidase A (MAO-A) was responsible. This explained why different people who suffered from depression lost brain chemicals such as serotonin and dopamine at different rates. This led to a new monoamine model of depression. Now that they know what's involved, the next step is to find out why. (If you'd like to see what the model looks like, go to *www.camh.net/Research/Areas_of_research/new_depression_model%20.html*.)

Adult Neurogenesis

Neurogenesis is a process by which adult brain stem cells self-renew and maintain themselves. Researchers are now studying the complex relationship between specific diseases, such as depression and neurogenesis. Remember the hippocampus? That's the area of your brain that's involved here. Since chronic and acute stress decrease neurogenesis, it makes sense that in people suffering from depression, these cells aren't developing as much, according to Fred Gage of the Salk Institute for Biological Studies. Decreasing your stress, exercising, having a complex physical environment, and continuing to learn, can help increase neurogenesis. That's good for you!

Protein Power

Paul Greengard, working at the Laboratory of Molecular and Cellular Neuroscience at the Rockefeller University, has discovered a protein called P11. He believes P11 may be a key determinant in whether or not people become depressed. He and his team of researchers determined that if they lowered levels of P11 in animals, the animals became depressed. If they raised P11 levels, the depression eased. There are many areas they'll be exploring, and one of them is to see whether P11 levels in the blood can be used as a biomarker for depression. They'll be working with P11 at the genetic level in future studies (see *www.dana.org*).

Fact

> A biomarker is used to indicate or measure a biological process. Biomarkers can be levels of certain proteins in the blood. Finding the biomarker may be an indication that an individual either has a specific disease or is at risk of developing that disease with which the marker is associated.

Faster-Acting Antidepressants May Be Coming Soon

Antidepressants are generally quite effective in treating the symptoms of depression, but they can take weeks to reach optimal levels in your system. In severe cases, where an individual is suicidal, this can result in life-threatening situations. In chronic cases, it results in added misery. A new study has found that ketamine can relieve the symptoms of depression within hours. Ketamine has side effects—such as hallucinations—that will keep it from being used as an antidepressant, but its success will send researchers off in a specific direction now, striving to repeat ketamine's successes without having to deal with its side effects. The study, funded by the National Institute of Mental Health (NIMH), appeared online in *Biological Psychiatry* on July 23, 2007.

Want to Be Part of the Future?

Nothing happens slowly anymore, and it seems especially true in science. When one question is answered, it raises hundreds more, and our knowledge is now increasing exponentially. With breakthroughs now coming along on an almost regular basis, there is an increased opportunity to get in on the clinical trials for some important new drugs.

First Things First

The first thing to do, of course, if you're considering volunteering for a clinical trial, is to discuss this with your physician. This is a serious commitment and may have important health consequences for you. If you both determine that this is a good option for you, your next step is to check out what's available. A good place to start is the Web site provided by the National Institutes of Health: *www.clinical trials.gov.*

How the Process Works

Researchers look for two kinds of people for their trials: people with the condition they're researching and people who are healthy. The first group is called the treatment group, because this group receives a treatment or a drug. The second group is called the control group. This group doesn't receive the treatment or the drug, but receives a placebo instead. This provides a method of comparison, or control, so the researcher can measure the effectiveness of the treatment or drug. You won't be told what group you'll be in. Doing so would defeat the purpose!

Narrowing the Candidates

Once you've found a study that you'd like to join, you'll have to qualify for it. Depending upon the nature of the study, researchers will be interested in working with specific age groups, specific gender groups, and people with specific stages of the disease or condition. If you have a comorbid condition, you may or may not be eligible for the study. Also, your previous treatment history may be a determining factor in whether or not you are accepted into the study.

 Alert

It is vitally important that you disclose all of your physical information to the review team for the study. You don't know how your own medical condition may be affected by the treatment or drug given during the study. Full disclosure is necessary to protect your health as well as maintain the integrity of the research!

The Good Parts

Time for a cost/benefit analysis! Participating in a clinical trial can get you access to important, new medications before they come on the market. Especially with depression, the sense of personal control that you'll experience can help relieve your symptoms. Also, you'll have access to experts in the health care field every step of the way and you'll be contributing to the pool of knowledge. These are the good things.

The Possibly Not-So-Good Parts

Somewhere around the neutral line separating good from bad is the possibility that the drug or treatment won't do anything—that it's ineffective. If you are in the control group, you will not receive any immediate benefit from the drug if it's proven to be successful, but you will benefit when it becomes available. Across that line, there are some real risks that you'll need to consider. If you are in the treatment group, perhaps the treatment will be uncomfortable. It may take more of your time than you are willing to commit to. And, there may be serious side effects. Some side effects can be life-threatening. Think carefully and get all the information you can before you commit.

 Alert

The researchers won't be able to inform you of the possible side effects of the drug you'll be taking. That's the purpose of the study—to determine if there are any side effects and how severe they will be.

Who Is Monitoring the Study?

An Institutional Review Board (IRB), made up of physicians, members of the community, and other professionals, will ensure that your rights are protected and that the study complies with federal rules and regulations. The law requires that personal risk be kept to an acceptable minimum and that any risks are outweighed by the potential benefits of the study.

What If I Change My Mind?

You can leave a study at any time you wish. Don't just stop the study, however. Tell the researchers why you are leaving the study, as this can help them possibly revise procedures to make the experience easier.

Clinical Studies in Depression

Clinical trials in depression are ongoing at major research universities, teaching hospitals, and other institutions. Be patient if you are interested in joining one or more of these studies, as it may take time to find the study that will be of most benefit to you. In addition to the following suggested organizations, check with your physician and local or regional hospital, to see what is available close to home. Many studies require that you be able to travel to their site. This can be difficult if you have job and family responsibilities that keep you close to home. You will receive compensation for your participation, but these amounts vary from organization to organization. Whatever compensation you receive won't match the income from your regular job, that's for sure!

The Mayo Clinic

The Mayo Clinic has locations in Arizona, Florida, and Minnesota. It is actively involved in researching depression, particularly depression that relates to other medical problems, psychiatric disorders, or addictions. The results of one study at the Mayo Clinic was a blood test that shows at what rate a person metabolizes a specific drug, including antidepressants. A person who metabolizes the antidepressant slowly may experience side effects or toxicity, while a person who metabolizes the drug quickly may not receive any benefit from it, before it's eliminated from the system. The test is called the cytochrome P450 test. Clinical studies are ongoing at the Mayo

Clinic, and volunteers are always being recruited. Go to *www.mayo clinic.com* to learn more about participating in a Mayo Clinic study.

Depression and Bipolar Support Alliance

The Depression and Bipolar Support Alliance (DBSA) supports the efforts of scientists and clinicians to develop new and more effective treatments for mood disorders. DBSA has a sixty-seven member advisory board that recommends and advises on specific research activities. This is an extensive site that provides a variety of opportunities to participate in clinical trials for depression. Go to *www .dbsalliance.org*.

Depression and ClinicalTrials.gov

ClinicalTrials.gov is the clearinghouse for the NIH. It provides an exhaustive list of ongoing clinical trials and studies that are actively recruiting volunteers. You will type in your condition (depression) and a city (somewhere close to where you live) and you will pull up literally hundreds of opportunities for participating. Go to *www .clinicaltrials.gov*.

The Future of Depression

The first question a child learns to ask is, "Why?" You answer the question. What happens next? The next word from your child is, "Why?" This will go on and on until you utter the words that signal the end of this discussion: "Because I said so." This statement was the position and the world view of the early authorities in civilization, but the children kept asking their questions. Scientists, in a way, are the children whose questions have no end. And for the rest of us, that's good.

Medicine and Depression

Depression has been a disagreeable companion for humankind for as long as there have been humans. Melancholia, as it was called early on, is now recognized to be an umbrella of different conditions, as explained in Chapter 4. Science has come very far very quickly, and it only moves forward. The future looks promising and chances of a cure aren't out of the question. With the human genome project completed, science has the roadmap it wanted. Further research into the workings of the human brain will result in greater understanding of the role of neurotransmitters and depression, and with each new fact learned, prospects of a cure grow closer.

Ethics and Depression

This is the one area that needs some serious attention. Science has bypassed traditional ethical and moral structures, and people need time to catch up. Just because you can do something may not mean that you should. What is for the greater good? When is it acceptable to sacrifice one for the benefit of the whole? Is it ever acceptable? There's always been an allowance for an individual to sacrifice self for others. It's time-honored in the military. When a parent gives up his life to save that of his child, society mourns but approves. It's a conscious decision, however, on the part of the person making the sacrifice. Opponents of fetal stem cell research will say that the donor had no say in the matter. It's an area that requires great sensitivity and respect on both sides of the issue.

Society and Depression

This is a more troubling area to consider. Society is increasingly mobile, and personal connections tend to be more temporary and even virtual in nature. As technology expands our world, it also has the capacity to isolate. Human contact and the healing power of human touch are essential to your mental and physical well-being. For a society always on the move, building strong and permanent personal relationships will be a challenge. Science can and does work miracles, but it can do only so much. The rest is up to each of us. Always has been. Always will be.

APPENDIX A
Glossary

acupuncture

A form of traditional Chinese medicine which works to restore the body's natural flow of energy through the use of needles inserted at specific points in the human body.

aerobic exercise

Intense physical activity, such as running or swimming, that works to primarily improve the cardiovascular system.

anaerobics

Exercise, such as weight-training or strength-training, that improves muscular strength and flexibility.

agoraphobia

Literally, "fear of the marketplace." Anxiety arising from fear of panic attacks occurring in public places which causes the individual to avoid places or situations in which these attacks might be likely to occur.

alternative therapy

Treatment options other than prescription drugs and psychotherapy.

Americans with Disabilities Act (ADA)

A law that prohibits private employers with fifteen or more employees, state and local governments, employment agencies, and labor unions from discriminating against qualified individuals with disabilities in job application procedures, hiring, firing, advancement, compensation, job training, and other terms, conditions, and privileges of employment.

amino acid

One of the twenty building blocks of protein. The function of amino acids are determined by the genetic code in your DNA.

autoimmune disease

A disease in which the body turns on itself, attacking its own tissues as if they were foreign bodies.

anhedonia

Loss of the ability to take pleasure in normally pleasurable activities.

anorexia
An eating disorder in which the individual ingests minimal amounts of food. Emaciation, serious medical complications, and potentially, death can result.

antidepressant
A class of medications that relieve the symptoms of depression.

anxiety
A state of heightened worry, uneasiness, or apprehension.

aromatherapy
A practice that uses the essential oils of certain plants, either as lotions or inhalants, to calm the mind.

behavior modification
A form of psychotherapy in which new, appropriate behaviors are substituted for undesirable ones.

beta blockers
A class of drugs that act upon the autonomic nervous system, blocking substances such as adrenaline (epinephrine) to relieve stress on the heart, lessen the force with which the heart muscle contracts, and reduce blood vessel contraction in the heart, brain, and throughout the body.

biofeedback
A process that harnesses the mind's power to control what previously had been thought to be involuntary body functions, such as blood pressure and brain wave activity.

biomarker
Something used to indicate or measure a biological process. Biomarkers can be levels of certain proteins in the blood. Finding the biomarker may be an indication that an individual either has a specific disease or is at risk of developing that disease with which the marker is associated.

bipolar disorder
A depressive disorder involving periods of extreme elation and extreme sadness, usually with periods of normal feelings in between. Formerly referred to as manic depression.

black box warning
The highest level of warning issued by the Food and Drug Administration. Added to the drug's label, it warns of potentially dangerous side effects.

botanical
A term used to refer to any plant. May be used interchangeably with herb or herbal.

bulimia
An eating disorder in which the individual eats normally, then induces vomiting to purge the stomach contents.

chiropractic
A form of therapy involving manipulation of the spinal column and other body structures.

cholesterol

A white crystalline substance found in animal tissues and various foods that is normally synthesized by the liver and is important as a constituent of cell membranes and a precursor to steroid hormones.

cognitive behavioral therapy (CBT)

A form of psychotherapy that helps patients take control of their illness through insight, behavioral changes, and personal responsibility.

comorbidity

Two conditions or diseases occurring at the same time in the same individual.

complementary therapies

Treatments used in conjunction with conventional medicine.

CPAP

Continuous Positive Airway Pressure. A device that forces a stream of air through the nasal passages to counteract the effects of sleep apnea.

decoction

A tea made by simmering an herb part in water.

depression

A medical condition involving the body and the mind that affects the way a person feels, thinks, and reacts. Symptoms of depression include feelings of hopelessness, worthlessness, and despair; sleep disturbances; extreme fatigue; loss of appetite or overeating with corresponding weight loss or gain; difficulty with concentration; irritability; and anhedonia.

desensitization

A form of psychotherapy that increases a person's tolerance to the object causing stress.

dopamine

A neurotransmitter that is the precursor to norepinephrine and adrenaline.

dual diagnosis

A diagnosis of a mental health condition and a substance abuse problem that occur together.

dysthymia

Also known as neurotic depression, dysthymic disorder, and chronic depression, dysthymia is characterized by moods that are consistently low.

electroconvulsive therapy (ECT)

A form of therapy for depression that uses electric shock to induce a brief and controlled seizure.

endorphins

Neurotransmitters and the body's "feel good" hormones. During hard exercise, endorphins are released, blocking pain and producing what's been called the "runner's high."

extended-release formula
Drug that releases its properties more slowly than standard drugs.

FDA
The U.S. Food and Drug Administration. An agency of the U.S. government.

flashback
A mental state in which an individual is taken back in time to relive the stressing event. Flashbacks may consist of images, sounds, smells, or feelings and seem to be happening in real time.

generalized anxiety disorder (GAD)
An anxiety condition characterized by excessive worry not related to a specific event. Responses to situations are unrealistic, out of proportion to the situation, and ongoing.

generic drugs
Drugs with the chemical equivalent of a brand name drug whose patent has expired.

genetics
Scientific study of heredity

herb
A plant or plant part valued for its medicinal, savory, or aromatic qualities.

hypnosis
An artificially induced altered state of consciousness, characterized by heightened suggestibility and receptivity to direction.

insomnia
A medical condition characterized by lack of sleep or poor quality sleep.

interpersonal therapy (IT)
A form of psychotherapy that works on communication skills, appropriate expression of feelings, and diffusing conflict.

intervention
A meeting in which family and friends of an individual confront that person about issues of substance abuse, emotional, or mental illness, with the purpose of getting that person to treatment.

isometrics
A form of exercise that uses resistance to strengthen muscles.

Kegel exercises
Pelvic floor exercises that work to strengthen the pubococcygeus muscles. The exercises involve alternately tightening and then releasing these muscles.

libido
One's interest in matters of a sexual nature.

lithium
Drug used to treat bipolar disorder.

longitudinal studies
Investigations that follow specific individuals or groups over a period of years.

major depression
Also known as major depressive disorder or unipolar depression. Major depression is a mood disorder, with ongoing symptoms of at least two weeks duration that include feelings of intense sadness, irritability, changes in appetite and sleep habits, and feelings of helplessness or hopelessness, among others.

MAOI
Drug that interferes with the action of monoamine oxidase, slowing the breakdown of certain neurotransmitters. Used in the treatment of depression.

meditation
A self-directed practice involving concentrated focus and specific postures to calm the mind and relax the body.

melancholia
The earlier, historical term used to describe depression. A condition of extreme sadness.

melatonin
A sleep-related hormone.

neurogenesis
The rebirth of nerve cells in the brain

neurotransmitter
A chemical that sends impulses across nerve endings to other nerves or muscles or organs.

norepinephrine
A neurotransmitter, also known as noradrenaline.

psychiatric nurse practitioner (PNP)
A registered nurse with advanced training in the practice of psychiatric and mental health nursing.

obsessive-compulsive disorder (OCD)
An anxiety disorder in which the individual feels compelled to follow certain routines and repeat specific rituals.

panic disorder
An anxiety disorder in which the individual fears loss of control over emotions and therefore becomes increasingly fearful of venturing out in public where that loss of control may occur.

perimenopause
The time before menopause during which hormone production (estrogen and progesterone) begins to slack off. Perimenopause can last a few months or several years.

postpartum depression
A depressive disorder affecting new mothers, who may lose interest in mothering and harbor fears they may hurt their baby. Triggered by

hormonal imbalances after child-birth, the condition usually resolves within two to three weeks. In severe cases, immediate help is necessary to protect both mother and child.

post-traumatic stress disorder (PTSD)

An anxiety disorder in which the individual suffers extreme anxiety as the result of exposure to a terrify-ing event or ordeal in which grave physical harm occurred or was threatened.

psychiatrist

A medical doctor with special train-ing in the diagnosis and treatment of mental and emotional illnesses.

psychodynamic therapy

A type of psychotherapy that draws on psychoanalytic theory to help people understand the roots of emotional distress, often by explor-ing unconscious motives, needs, and defenses.

psychologist

A therapist with an advanced degree from an accredited gradu-ate program in psychology and two or more years of supervised post-graduate work experience.

psychotherapy

A form of treatment in which a licensed psychiatrist, clinical psy-chologist, or counselor works with a patient to help resolve mental issues that interfere with daily living.

psychotropic drugs

A class of medications that effect changes in behaviors, moods, and perceptions. Antidepressants, anti-psychotics, mood stabilizers, and anti-anxiety drugs are included in this category.

regression therapy

Hypnosis that seeks to find the source of trauma. Past lives are treated as metaphors for current problems.

reparative therapy

Immerses an individual in a treat-ment program designed to reverse a specific course of behavior.

role-play

A form of play therapy in which children dress up, pretend to be someone else, create their own dramas, and live out their fantasies. In role-play, children can take on a fictional persona and work through emotional problems in a world they know is make-believe and therefore, safe.

SAM-e

A naturally occurring substance in the body made from an amino acid. Synthetic versions are used as dietary supplements.

seasonal affective disorder (SAD)

A depressive disorder usually asso-ciated with winter but occasionally occurring in summer. Associated with lack of daylight in the more northern latitudes. Treated with light therapy.

self-medicate

To use alcohol or other non-prescribed substances to cope with a medical condition.

serotonin

A key neurotransmitter for maintaining mental and emotional health

sleep apnea

A medical condition in which a sleeping individual stops breathing for an extended period of time, then resumes breathing with loud snorts or gasps. Untreated, sleep apnea can have serious medical consequences.

sleep hygiene

A phrase used by doctors to describe healthy practices and pre-bedtime routines that can help one achieve a good night's rest

social anxiety disorder

Also known as social phobia. An anxiety disorder in which people believe that others are constantly judging them, and judging them negatively.

SSRIs (selective serotonin reuptake inhibitors)

A class of antidepressant drugs. SSRIs work by increasing the amount of the neurotransmitter serotonin in the brain.

stem cells

Cells which have the capacity to grow into any of the body's more than 200 cell types.

steroids

Corticosteroid drugs that are used to relieve inflammation and swelling. Many hormones and drugs are steroids. Prednisone, vitamin D, and testosterone are all considered steroids.

Trauma

Injury or stress caused by some outside force.

tricyclic

An older form of medications used to treat depression. Also used to treat anxiety and to control chronic pain.

unipolar depression

Depression characterized by consistently low moods.

yoga

A form of non-aerobic exercise that teaches precise postures, breathing, and meditation.

APPENDIX B

Resources

Web Sites

American Psychiatric Association (APA)
Based in Washington, DC, the American Psychological Association (APA) is a scientific and professional organization that represents psychology in the United States. With 148,000 members, APA is the largest association of psychologists worldwide. Its mission is to advance psychology as a science and profession and as a means of promoting health, education, and human welfare.
www.HealthyMinds.org

Depression and Bipolar Support Alliance (DBSA)
Resources for families coping with bipolar disorder. Provides education, promotes advocacy, and information about current clinical trials.
www.dbsalliance.org

Food and Drug Administration (FDA)
Regulatory body of the U.S. government providing oversight and licensing of drugs.
www.fda.gov

Johns Hopkins Quarterly Health Alerts
Free public service from Johns Hopkins Medicine provides up-to-date information on a variety of medical conditions and the status of current research.
www.johnshopkinshealthalerts.com

MacArthur Foundation Initiative on Depression and Primary Care
A foundation whose mission is to enhance the ability of primary care physicians to recognize and manage depression. Disseminates research and provides resources.
www.depression-primarycare.org

Mayo Clinic
The Mayo Clinic provides information and tools for coping with chronic diseases and conditions. The clinic's Web site offers a symptom checker as well as service by which patients may ask specific questions about their conditions.
www.mayoclinic.com

Mental Health America (MHA)
A nonprofit organization providing information and answers to FAQs regarding mental health issues.
www.mha.org

National Alliance on Mental Illness (NAMI)
The nation's largest grassroots organization dedicated to education about mental illness. Provides advocacy assistance and resources for families and individuals suffering from mental illness.
www.nami.org

National Institutes of Health (NIH)
One of the world's foremost medical research centers, the NIH is an agency of the U.S. Department of Health and Human Services.
www.nih.gov

National Institute of Mental Health (NIMH)
Part of the National Institutes of Health (NIH), NIMH is the largest scientific organization in the world dedicated to research focused on the understanding, treatment, and prevention of mental disorders and the promotion of mental health.
www.nimh.nih.gov

National Library of Medicine—MedlinePlus
A service of the U.S. National Library of Medicine. Provides assistance in researching over 740 health topics with drug descriptions and well-researched encyclopedic entries.
www.nlm.nih.gov/medlineplus

National Mental Health Information Center
The National Mental Health Information Center was developed for users of mental health services and their families, the general public, policy makers, providers, and the media. The Information Center also has information on federal grants, conferences, and other events.
www.mentalhealth.org

Postpartum Support International
An organization providing resources and support for families experiencing postpartum depression.
www.postpartum.net

Social Security Administration
Government agency responsible for providing disability benefits for individuals suffering from depression and who meet the qualifications of the SSA.
www.ssa.gov

Books

Against Depression by Peter D. Kramer

Cognitive Therapy for Challenging Problems: What to Do When the Basics Don't Work by Judith S. Beck. Ph.D.

The Freedom From Depression Workbook by Les Carter, M.D. and Frank B. Minirth, Ph.D.

Hand-Me-Down Blues: How to Stop Depression from Spreading in Families by Michael D. Yapko, Ph.D.

Living Well with Depression and Bipolar Disorder: What Your Doctor Doesn't Tell You That You Need to Know by John McManamy

Mayo Clinic On Depression: Answers to Help You Understand, Recognize and Manage Depression by Keith Kramlinger, M.D.

Undoing Depression: What Therapy Doesn't Teach You and Medication Can't Give You by Richard O'Connor

An Unquiet Mind by Kay Jamison

What to Do When Someone You Love Is Depressed by Mitch Golant and Susan K. Golant

Yoga for Depression: A Compassionate Guide to Relieve Suffering Through Yoga by Amy Weintraub

Electronic Articles

"Anorexia Symptoms Are Reduced by Massage Therapy." *Eating Disorders,* 9, 289–299.

"Depression and Heart Disease," synthesis of several studies online at *www .mcmanweb.com/article-41.htm*. (July 11, 2003)

"Depression and the Psychological Benefits of Entering Marriage," *Journal of Health and Social Behavior*, 48:2 (June 2007), 149–163.

"Depression Before Parkinson's Disease?" WebMD Medical News, online at *www.medicinenet.com/script/main/art.asp?articlekey=80761*.

"Depressive Symptoms and the Risk of Type 2 Diabetes," *http://care .diabetesjournals.org/cgi/content/abstract/27/2/429*.

"Development and Evaluation of a Yoga Exercise Programme for Older Adults," *Journal of Advanced Nursing* 57:4, 432–441. (February 2007)

"The Effect of Childhood Trauma on Brain Development," *www.leader shipcouncil.org/1/res/brain.html*.

"The Effect of Sexual Behavior on Immune System Function," presented at the Eastern Psychological Association Convention in April 1999 by Carl J. Charnetski, professor of psychology, and Francis X. Brennan, Jr., assistant professor of psychology, at Wilkes University.

"An Evaluation of Echinacea angustifolia in Experimental Rhinovirus Infections," *New England Journal of Medicine*, 353 (July 28, 2005), 341.

"Evidence of Brain Chemistry Abnormalities in Bipolar Disorder," University of Michigan study, October 2000.

"Exercise May be Just as Effective as Medication for Treating Major Depression," Duke University School of Medicine study, reported online at *www .dukemednews.org/news/article.php?id=300*.

"Faster-Acting Antidepressants Closer to Becoming a Reality," reported online at *www.nimh.nih.gov/press/ketamine_2.cfm*. (July 2007)

"Functional Magnetic Resonance Imaging of Cocaine Craving," *American Journal of Psychiatry* 158 (January 2001), 86–95.

"Gene Controls Pain Threshold," University of Michigan study reported online at *http://news.bbc.co.uk/1/hi/health/2784869.stm*. (February 2003)

"The impact of religious practice and religious coping on geriatric depression," *International Journal of Geriatric Psychiatry*, 18:10, 905–914. (September 2003)

"Is Sex Necessary?" *British Medical Journal*, 1997. Reported online at *www .forbes.com/2003/10/08/cz_af_1008health.html*.

"The Link Between Dreaming and Depression," Human Givens Institute, associated with MindFields College in the UK. Reported online at *www .mindfields.org.* (December 2006)

Mental Health, A Report of the Surgeon General, 1999, retrieved online at *www.surgeongeneral.gov/library/mentalhealth/home.html.*

"New Depression Model Advances Disease Frontiers," reported online at *www.camh.net.* (November 2006)

"Omega-3 Fatty Acids Affect Risk Of Depression, Inflammation," reported online at *www.sciencedaily.com/releases/2005/05/050525161319.htm.* (March 2007)

"Omega 3 Fatty Acids in Bipolar Disorder," reported online at *http://arch psyc.ama-assn.org/cgi/reprint/56/5/407.pdf.* (November 2006)

"Optimism, Pessimism and Depression in School Aged Students: A Longitudinal Study, " reported online at *www.aare.edu.au/98pap/yat98152.htm* (citing C. Peterson and L.M. Bossio, *Health and Optimism.* New York: Free Press, 1991).

"Personality styles may predict susceptibility to depression," University of Washington study, reported online at *www.apa.org/monitor/feb00/ depression.html.* (February 2000)

"Primary Care Treatment of Post-traumatic Stress Disorder," *American Family Physician,* September 1, 2000, online at *www.aafp.org/afp/20000901/1035.html.*

"Pituitary-Adrenal and Autonomic Responses to Stress in Women After Sexual and Physical Abuse in Childhood," J*ournal of the American Medical Association,* 284:5, 592–597. (August 2000)

"Sleep Apnea, Depression Linked in Stanford Study," reported online at *www.eurekalert.org/pub_releases/2003-11/sumc-sad110603.php.* (November 2003)

"Stanford-led Study Closes in on Genes That May Predispose Some People to Severe Depression," reported online at *www.eurekalert.org/pub _releases/2007-02/sumc-ssc013007.php.* (February 2003)

"Study Posits Presidents had Mental Illness," Duke University study, *Journal of Nervous and Mental Disease,* January 2007, vol. 194, reported online at *www.dukechronicle.com/media/paper884/news/2006/02/22/News/Study .Posits.Presidents.Had.Mental.Illness-1623561.shtml?norewrite&sourcedomain =www.dukechronicle.com.*

"Suicide Attempts Among Patients Starting Depression Treatment With Medications or Psychotherapy," *American Journal of Psychiatry,* 164 (July 2007), 1029–1034.

"Symptoms of Anxiety and Depression in Childhood and Use of MDMA: Prospective, Population Based Study," *www.pubmedcentral.nih.gov/article render.fcgi?artid=1432198.* (February 2006)

Trends in the Use of Psychotropic Medications Among Adolescents," 1999–2004, *Journal of Psychiatric Services,* 57, 63–69. (January 2006)

"Toward a New Approach to Depression," *Biological Psychiatry,* July 23, 2007. Online at *www.dana.org.*

Antidepressant Medications

The following medications are currently prescribed as antidepressants. All carry the FDA black box warning for restricted use in children and adolescents.

Anafranil (clomipramine)

A chemical cousin of tricyclic antidepressant medications, such as Tofranil and Elavil. Used to treat people who suffer from obsessions and compulsions.

Asendin (amoxapine); Aventyl (nortriptyline)

A tricyclic antidepressant sometimes prescribed in the treatment of bipolar disorder and in patients who have not responded well to other antidepressants.

Celexa (citalopram hydrobromide)

An SSRI used in treating depression and generalized anxiety disorder (GAD). Lexapro is the next generation of Celexa.

Cymbalta (duloxetine)

A selective serotonin-norepinephrine reuptake inhibitor (SNRI) used in treating major depressive disorder, generalized anxiety disorder (GAD), and for the management of diabetic peripheral neuropathic pain (DPNP).

Desyrel (trazodone HCl)

An antidepressant used in the treatment of depression and occasionally prescribed as a sedative.

Effexor (venlafaxine HCl)

An SNRI or serotonin-norepinephrine reuptake inhibitor used to treat clinical depression and anxiety disorders.

Elavil (amitriptyline)

A tricyclic antidepressant used to treat depression and chronic pain.

Emsam (selegiline)

A monoamine oxidase inhibitor used in treating major depressive disorder. Used as a skin patch (transdermal).

Etrafon (perphenazine/amitriptyline)
An antipsychotic used in treating bipolar disorder.

Lexapro (escitalopram oxalate)
An SSRI (selective serotonin reuptake inhibitor) used to treat major depressive disorder and generalized anxiety disorder. The next generation of Celexa.

Limbitrol (chlordiazepoxide/amitriptyline)
Combines an antidepressant with an anti-anxiety medication. Used in treating moderate to severe depression associated with moderate to severe anxiety.

Ludiomil (maprotiline)
A tricyclic used in treating bipolar depression.

Luvox (fluvoxamine maleate)
An SSRI (selective serotonin reuptake inhibitor) used to treat depression and OCD (obsessive-compulsive disorder).

Marplan (isocarboxazid)
A monoamine oxidase inhibitor (MAO) prescribed for patients with depression. Used after patients have failed to respond to other drugs.

Nardil (phenelzine sulfate)
A monoamine oxidase inhibitor (MAO) prescribed for patients with mixed anxiety and depression. Used after patients have failed to respond to other drugs.

Nefazodone HCl
A tricyclic used in treating depression and attention deficit disorders.

Norpramin (desipramine HCl)
A tricyclic used in treating depression.

Pamelor (nortriptyline)
A second-generation tricyclic used to lift mood in patients with depression. Also used to treat chronic pain.

Parnate (tranylcypromine sulfate)
A monoamine oxidase (MAO) inhibitor. Works by increasing levels of the neurotransmitters serotonin, epinephrine, and norepinephrine. Used to treat moderate to severe depression and the depressive phases of bipolar disorder.

Paxil (paroxetine HCl)
An SSRI used in treatment of major depressive disorder and anxiety disorders.

Pexeva (paroxetine mesylate)
An SSRI used in treating depression and panic disorders.

Prozac (fluoxetine HCl)
The first SSRI and the most widely prescribed antidepressant in the world. Blocks reuptake of serotonin.

Remeron (mirtazapine)
A tetracyclic antidepressant used in treating moderate to severe depression.

Sarafem (fluoxetine HCl)
An SSRI used in treating premenstrual dysphoric disorder (PMDD).

Seroquel (quetiapine)
An antidepressant used in treating bipolar disorder.

Sinequan (doxepin)
A tricyclic used to treat depression. Effective in people whose depression is associated with alcoholism, or a result of another disease, such as cancer.

Surmontil (trimipramine)
A tricyclic used to treat depression.

Symbyax (olanzapine/fluoxetine)
Combination of olanzapine, the active ingredient in Zyprexa, and fluoxetine, the active ingredient in Prozac. Used in treating bipolar disorder.

Tofranil (imipramine hydrochloride)
A tricyclic used to treat depression.

Tofranil-PM (imipramine pamoate)
A tricyclic. Usually taken once daily, at bedtime, to treat major depressive disorder.

Triavil (perphenazine/amitriptyline)
A combination of an antidepressant and a tranquilizer. A tricyclic. Contains the same ingredients as Elavil and Trilafon and should not be used with these drugs.

Vivactil (protriptyline)
Member of the tricyclic class of antidepressants. Has been prescribed for use in withdrawn and inactive patients and close monitoring is required, due to possibility of severe side effects.

Wellbutrin (bupropion HCl)
Antidepressant often prescribed for treatment of seasonal affective disorder (SAD).

Zoloft (sertraline HCl)
SSRI class of antidepressants. Acts as a serotonin reuptake inhibitor.

Zyban (bupropion HCl)
SSRI class of antidepressants. Acts as a norepinephrine and dopamine reuptake inhibitor.

Index